GRASSES
for Gardens and Landscapes

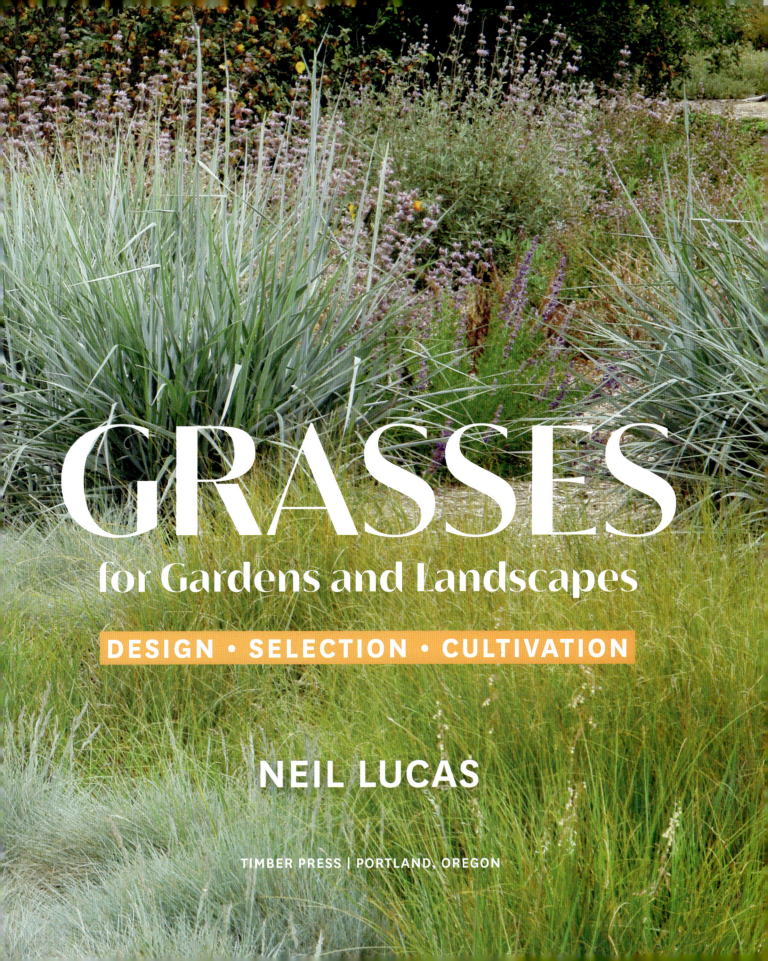

GRASSES
for Gardens and Landscapes

DESIGN · SELECTION · CULTIVATION

NEIL LUCAS

TIMBER PRESS | PORTLAND, OREGON

Frontispiece: A subtle, beautiful, and regionally appropriate planting of native grasses in the Californian garden of Dave and Rainie Fross. This page: *Achnatherum calamagrostis* 'Lemperg' growing in a private area at Knoll Gardens, Dorset, England.

Copyright © 2023 by Neil Lucas. All rights reserved.
Photography credits appear on page 314.

Published in 2023 by Timber Press, Inc.,
a subsidiary of Workman Publishing Co., Inc.,
a subsidiary of Hachette Book Group, Inc.
1290 Avenue of the Americas
New York, New York 10104
timberpress.com

Printed in China on paper from responsible sources
Text design by Mary Winkelman Velgos
Cover design by Hillary Caudle

The publisher is not responsible for websites
(or their content) that are not owned by the publisher.

The Hachette Speakers Bureau provides a wide range
of authors for speaking events. To find out more,
go to hachettespeakersbureau.com or email
HachetteSpeakers@hbgusa.com.

ISBN 978-1-64326-115-7
Catalog records for this book
are available from the
Library of Congress and
the British Library.

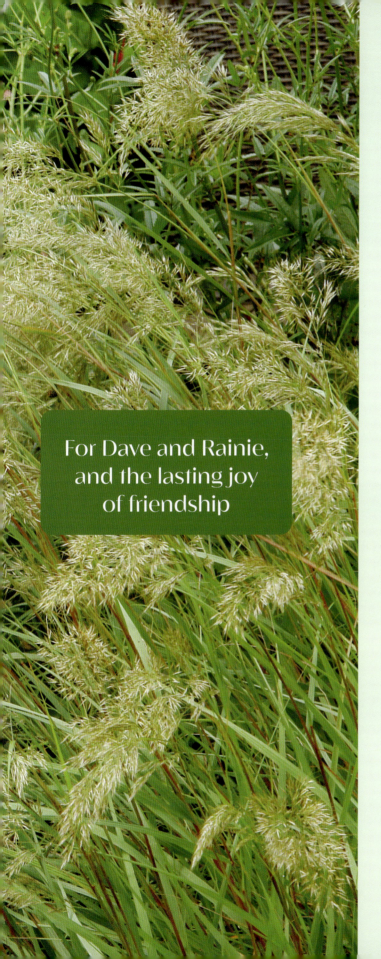

Contents

- 6 Acknowledgements
- 9 Discovering Grasses
- 17 Natural Rhythm
- 37 Designing with Grasses
- 59 Grasses and the Naturalistic Approach
- 75 Right Grass, Right Place
- 113 Grasses for a Greener World
- 135 Looking After Grasses
- 149 Directory of Grasses and Grass-Like Plants
- 306 Where to See Grasses
- 308 Where to Buy Grasses
- 310 Resources
- 312 References
- 314 Photography Credits
- 316 Index

For Dave and Rainie, and the lasting joy of friendship

Acknowledgements

A distinct pleasure associated with writing this book has been that I have necessarily come into contact with so many like-minded, plant loving people who have been willing to share their knowledge and passion for plants; and especially for grasses. Not only have their kind contributions helped to considerably enrich my book, the generosity shown to me throughout this process has served to remind me of the unselfish nature and willingness to share of so many people who are connected with the growing of plants.

My lasting gratitude to the team at Knoll Gardens, without whom I would have achieved nothing. To Ross Humphrey with whom I share the running of the nursery and garden, and to Luke Al'Thor, Rob Bascombe, Jan Coombs, Sharon Coombs, Steve Coombs, Mike Humphrey, Pat Humphrey, Robert Goodlife, Sally Wilkins, Pam Lel, Sarah Meyer, Karen Miles, and Val Weston.

And equally to the Trustees of our associated charity, the Knoll Gardens Foundation, especially the current chair, Rowena Jecock, and also to the charity volunteers to whom, while now too many to name individually, I shall always be truly grateful.

For their expert knowledge, patience, and much valued help I would particularly like to thank; Fred Ballerini, Carol Bornstein, Robert Bett, Steve Castorani, Shannon Currey, Dave Fross, Tim Fuller, Fergus Garrett, Graham Gough, John Greenlee, Wayne Hanna, Brent Horvath, David Jewell, Nigel Judd, David Kerr, Henry Macauley, Klaus Menzel, Mary Meyer, Keith Powrie, Tom Ranney, Becky Rochester, Kim and Stephen Rogers, and David Ward.

Image Acknowledgements

My continued thanks to Rick Darke whose initial patience had such a profound effect on my limited photographic abilities.

I am indebted to those individuals including Alexandre Bailhache, Elizabeth Collins, Rick Darke, Dave Fross, Wayne Hanna, Saxon Holt, Ross Humphrey, John and Jenny Makepeace, Klaus Menzel, Ed Snodgrass, and Amanda Walker for generously supplying or otherwise helping with images.

Thanks also to the multiple gardens, nurseries, reserves, institutions, and organizations who have so generously assisted me in various ways with images. Sincere thanks to: Arizona Native Plant Society; California Academy of Sciences; California Botanic Garden; Beth Chatto Gardens; Cambridge University Botanic Garden; Chicago Botanic Garden; Devon Pond Plants; Desert Botanical Garden; Genesis Plant Marketing; Gothenburg Botanical Garden; Great Dixter House and Gardens; Greenlee and Associates; Hauser and Wirth; Hoffman Nurseries; Huntington Library, Art Museum, and Botanical Gardens; Intrinsic Perennial Gardens; Longwood Gardens; Marchants Garden and Nursery; Millennium Park Foundation and Lurie Garden; Native Sons; Natural History Museum of Los Angeles County; North Carolina State University; North Creek Nurseries; Pensthorpe Natural Park; PlantHaven; Plantipp; Royal Botanic Gardens, Kew; Royal Horticultural Society gardens at Hyde Hall, and Wisley; Scampston Hall; Santa Barbara Botanic Garden; Sir Harold Hillier Gardens; Springs Preserve; University of Georgia; and University of Minnesota.

Naturally occurring plant communities such as this meadow in Zion National Park, Utah, are balanced, self-renewing systems that have much to commend them to gardeners and designers. Grasses form a significant part of many of these natural systems, being found in virtually every area from high mountains to sea shore, and consequently have an important part to play in the modern, low-maintenance, nature-tolerant gardens of the future.

Discovering Grasses

WHEN I WAS A CHILD, my grandfather was very keen on delphiniums, and during my summer visits to his expansive garden I came to love them too. Uninspiring mounds of green foliage would gradually form tall, graceful, towering spikes of colour that, at least in the earlier years, towered over the top of my head. Some of my earliest memories involve being captivated by the sheer beauty of the flowers, their colours, and the way they were arranged on the stems. In time, I started my own plant collections, expanding to dahlias, and would spend hours observing their mind-boggling variety of shape, form, and colour. I became transfixed by my plants' growing cycles—the complex processes they underwent in the course of a single season—and the way they would react differently to the various conditions that could exist in the same garden. Grass, on the other hand, was merely for walking on.

While clearly within a garden setting, and composed of largely exotic species, the design intention of this meadow-style planting attempts to mirror a natural community of woody plants and open, grassy spaces.

Growing up and beginning to explore in earnest, I visited as many gardens as I could, increasingly enchanted by these magical places where lots of different plants grew together. While most of my friends aspired to become train drivers and secret agents, I dreamt of becoming a gardener and eventually having my own garden. I spent every possible moment around plants and people who knew about them.

Developing My Approach

By the time I came to Knoll Gardens in Dorset, my love affair with plants as individuals had been supplanted by a fascination with gardens as living systems or communities of plants, and the processes that make them work. Having spent years looking after gardens professionally for others, I had witnessed the most attractive of plants become ugly and disappointing under conditions they did not like. I came to understand that seeing the garden as a whole, with its various moods and conditions, was just as important as understanding the plants that go in it.

'Right plant, right place' is a simple, practical maxim encouraging us to choose plants that will best suit the conditions available. So many gardens fail because this simple piece of common sense is ignored or forgotten. Certainly soil can be improved, water added, and climatic factors softened to some extent, but essentially for a garden to be successful its plants must be happy with, or at least able to tolerate, the prevailing cultural conditions.

Knoll, for instance, was originally a private botanical collection, principally containing woody plants drawn from around the world. Many, like *Eucalyptus* and *Euonymus*, took to the garden's generally dry, sandy conditions; others, such as the collection of rhododendrons, needed copious amounts of water and feeding to survive and prosper. Once this level of care was stopped, it became obvious that these rhododendrons would not thrive in the garden's conditions if left on their own, so they have since been largely removed.

Why Grasses?

At first woody plants were my main focus, but I later found that grasses were effective in the garden for as long as the woody plants were—and that grasses provided not only structure and form but also movement and a range of talents to perfectly complement most other plants. Grasses were also versatile and adaptable, capable of growing on sandy soils or heavy clay, in sun or shade, in pools or other wet areas, and even among root systems under trees. And when used together in large informal drifts, they created a feeling of relaxed naturalness that, to me, hinted strongly at childhood days spent on coasts and other exciting, invigorating, and untamed grassy places.

If this were not enough, I soon found that a 'naturalistic' approach to gardening spearheaded by the use of grasses (see fourth chapter) led to noticeably less work than I had been accustomed to. Not having to constantly deadhead, stake, tidy, and spray slowly encouraged a subtly different sort of environment—one perhaps just beginning to mimic the flavour of an established natural system, which a greater variety of wildlife seemed to find attractive. As I drew upon an ever-widening palette of grasses, their usefulness and adaptability became clear.

Tough and adaptable grasses, such as ***Panicum virgatum*** seen here by the riverside in New York, will happily tolerate comparatively inhospitable urban situations to bring a natural touch to what might otherwise be an unpromising hardscape—for humans as well as all other forms of life.

TOP AND ABOVE While much of the countryside is regarded as green open space, farmland and gardens with large expanses of tightly cut turfgrass, including golf courses, can effectively become monocultures that are comparatively austere places for most other forms of life.

LEFT This tolerant golf links has allowed low-maintenance native sedges and grasses to grow close to the traditionally maintained links without compromising the integrity of the playing surface.

Grasses and the Bigger Picture

Grasses are a worldwide success story—a huge group of plants with more than ten thousand different species in their own family—and with the grass allies such as sedges and rushes contributing at least half that number again. They are arguably the most successful group of plants on the planet, covering more ground and feeding more wildlife than any other group. In our natural systems, grasses and their allies can be found on virtually every landmass, in every region, in every locality, and on every soil type. Wherever there is plant life, grasses are almost certain to have a local representative.

Like many other gardeners, designers, and conservationists working today, I have come to realize that gardens can be more than just decoration. To be sure, they are pleasant havens to be relaxed in and admired, but as our understanding of the world increases, so do our attitudes towards gardening.

We are learning about biodiversity, the all-embracing term for all forms of life including mammals, birds, insects, and plants. And we are learning about our collective effect on all of these living things; as sensitive and environmentally savvy gardeners, we are trying not to waste valuable long-term resources on short-term horticultural effects. We are learning that continually taking over natural areas for our own use puts increased pressure on the remaining natural systems—and that the intricacy and interrelatedness of these systems can be all too easily interrupted, yet not so easily mended.

Above all, we are learning that our gardens and designed spaces increasingly constitute a significant part of the Earth's remaining green space, and that our gardens are therefore gaining a value that could never have been imagined by previous generations of gardeners. As we rely on our natural systems to support us for food, shelter, and the air we breathe, we are inextricably bound up with the plants and animals that make up our world's biodiversity. As natural habitats are destroyed and the landscape is built up, the value of our gardens increases—if we design these outdoor spaces conscientiously. Although they cannot be a replacement for native ecosystems, our gardens, and what is now frequently termed the built environment, can serve as a substitute, providing a place for the other species on which we ourselves depend.

Understanding grasses' origins and their contributions to the wider ecosystem inspires us see our gardens differently. Grasses can offer us insight into a way of working—an attitude and an approach to gardening that combines a focus on adaptability, ease of use, and sheer simplicity with the most strikingly beautiful of spaces.

Blurring and Merging

If asked to sum up what I have learned through gardening with grasses so far, I think I would have to invent a new phrase: 'blur and merge'.

It is in our interests to blur the lines between our natural systems and our designed spaces, and grasses are perhaps the perfect group of plants to help us do this. We have much to learn from natural systems that offer well-adjusted, self-renewing, evolving communities, while our gardens are all too often the very opposite. The principles we see operating so successfully in nature can be mirrored in our designed spaces with real benefits.

And we can merge our love of short-term interest with longer-term satisfaction. Blowsy summertime flowers are wonderful, but not at the price of boring nothingness for the rest of the year. Gardens can and should be of interest at all times.

We can blur the often-sacrosanct lines between border and lawn, between trimmed hedge and natural shelter. Narrow borders and tightly cut lawns are static and unchanging, and moreover they are usually hard work. Blending borders, lawns, and pathways creates a feeling of space and dynamism. And it allows plants to do more of the work.

We can merge our focus on plants as individuals with the cultivation of the garden as a whole. Far greater success can be achieved, and for less effort, by cultivating the garden as a community rather than a series of unrelated individual plants.

A traditional approach to the design and layout of public and private garden areas may have subdivided even modest spaces into disjointed features such as lawn, border, clipped shrubs, and paving. However, a modern, inclusive 'meadow style' approach offers an informal aesthetic that can also be environmentally prudent.

We can blur our search for horticultural perfection with the acceptance of practicality. Plants that need constant attention by way of spraying, staking, deadheading, watering, and general cosseting in order to give anything in return are for the most part just hard work—and often unnecessary, when so many plants will exist happily on almost no attention.

We can also merge our conception of indoor rooms with outdoor spaces. While we lavish much care and attention on our indoor rooms, our outdoor spaces are sometimes ignored. Basic garden design is not a fashion accessory—it is merely a thought process intended to make the best use of finite space and resources, and it is a valuable tool for any gardener.

How to Use this Book

Simply using grasses in the garden is no panacea in itself. But grasses are made incredibly valuable by their inclination towards success under so many different and sometimes challenging conditions, and the feelings they evoke through a happy combination of individual beauty and mass effect.

The world is a very big place, and I live and work in one small corner of it. Grasses have had millions of years to develop and refine their worldwide strategies, whereas I have been gardening in the south of England for just a few decades. This book is about the grasses that I have encountered and how I have seen them used, or indeed used them myself. It is also about why we might want to use grasses, and it looks to our natural systems for that answer.

This book is not just for established gardeners; it is for anyone who takes an interest in outdoor spaces, whether surrounding a small, private home, or a larger and more public space. With an eye towards naturalistic gardening and environmental awareness, I hope to explore how such a worldwide success story as the family of grasses can be used so effectively and easily in our gardens.

Grasses and their potential in planting design is a huge subject which no single book can claim to cover comprehensively. But it is my hope that the following pages will provide you with a real flavour—a taste of the amazing opportunities that this versatile and beautiful group of plants has to offer.

A crisp, well-maintained lawn is a thing of some beauty, however many are now questioning the validity of this long-established tradition, especially where such features are expensive in terms of time and precious resources to maintain them.

On a clear December morning following a cold night, the frost on the dried flower stems of tufted hair grass, *Deschampsia cespitosa* (background), creates a magical, transient, almost ethereal effect in this riverside meadow in Exeter, Devon, England. The hard rush, *Juncus inflexus* (foreground), also thrives in even wetter parts of the meadow and provides solidity of form in successful contrast to the airiness of the hair grass.

Natural Rhythm

WHILE 'COMMUNITY', 'seasonality', and 'rhythm' may not be the very first terms that come to mind when we think of gardening, they evoke important concepts that can shape our gardens into more satisfying places. Understanding a garden's cultural conditions—sun or shade, warm or cold, windy or sheltered, soils that are acid or alkaline, wet or dry—and choosing plants best suited to these conditions is essential for creating long-term and successful plantings. But a garden is also subject to other, less tangible influences which may not be so obvious or clear cut. Some of the most inspirational gardens—those that have the 'wow' factor, imparting a special sense of place or even magic—are the ones that are cultivated as whole communities of plants rather than as a collection of sometimes-disconnected individual specimens.

These gardens encourage natural rhythms within their plantings; they are in tune with their surroundings, and in this sense, they work with nature rather than battling against it. With their amazing versatility and adaptability, grasses can be important tools for achieving this kind of balanced, satisfying garden—where the gardener's role is more akin to that of an editor than an enforcer.

Seasonality and Rhythm

When plants are thoughtfully chosen for year-round interest, we reap the benefits of seasonality in the garden.

'Seasonality' refers to the processes that plants and therefore gardens undergo in response to the changing conditions of the local climate over the course of a year. It is also responsible for the essence of a garden's 'rhythm'—a series of naturally induced changes that happen over the course of a year as the garden and its plants react to seasonal changes in light, temperature, and weather patterns. Through recognizing and celebrating the seasonal variations in a garden, we open up a whole new series of possibilities for our designed landscapes. In a garden, seasonal change is inevitable, strongly desirable, and arguably the single most important component of the garden's natural rhythm.

For instance, the Mill End borders at Knoll in Dorset, England, were designed specifically with a narrow, snaking bark path so visitors can enjoy the plants at relatively close quarters, watching and admiring the sometimes-rapid, sometimes-subtle changes as

OPPOSITE By early summer, foxgloves, poppies, and geraniums join the first of the grasses such as *Pennisetum* 'Red Buttons' and *Molinia* 'Edith Dudszus' in flower.

BELOW Having been cut back in late March, by May, the borders are already a creative tapestry of colours and leaf shapes.

the seasons progressed. In spring, after the area has been cut to the ground, quickly recovering clumps of *Arundo*, *Miscanthus*, *Pennisetum*, *Calamagrostis*, and *Panicum* along with other perennials such as *Eupatorium*, *Geranium*, and *Persicaria* rapidly clothe the bare earth. As poppies and foxgloves flower, so does what must be the earliest of fountain grasses—the admirable *Pennisetum* 'Red Buttons'. Well known for this quality, its initially bright red flowers held on long slender stalks are quite distinctive, and will continue to flower right through into autumn, at least in good soils. As high summer approaches, the border's *Arundo donax* specimens reach their full, majestic height in concert with their associated perennials, while *Miscanthus*, *Panicum*, and *Pennisetum* are in full, fabulous flower before gradually descending into their more subtle garb of beige with the onset of autumn's first frosts. With the coming of winter, the skeletal remains of the plants take on yet another form with a covering of snow or even heavy frosts. Almost every day of the year, this border has something interesting to offer.

Grasses, especially the wide-ranging deciduous group, are excellent seasonal indicators as they perform their annual miracle of fast green growth, magnificent flower, and autumnal tints, followed by their winter brown coats standing tall and resolute until the following spring. Then the whole process is repeated, revealing a time-honoured, dynamic equilibrium where, in the midst of constant change, the annual rhythm remains constant.

In gardens that are severely formal in layout, where hardscape and design considerations outweigh plant content, there is far less opportunity to celebrate seasonal change. Where there is intentionally a much tighter control of seasonal change—and therefore of nature itself—through features like formal parterres

Moving into August, the pathways are now well defined by the plant groups which have reached their mature height. Perennials such as *Eupatorium*, *Echinacea*, and *Persicaria* join *Panicum*, *Pennisetum*, and *Miscanthus* in a high summer extravaganza of flower and form.

The following February, several inches of snow freshen the pathways, highlighting the winter-brown skeletal outlines of the giant reed, *Arundo donax*, together with *Eupatorium*, *Panicum*, *Sedum*, and *Pennisetum*.

and terraces, tightly clipped evergreen hedges, and bedding schemes limited to perhaps two changes a year, it is more difficult to introduce seasonality without a major revision of the original design concept. On a larger, public scale, such comparatively austere layouts may have a place as historical museum pieces, but in my view, they are increasingly less relevant to the needs of the modern-day gardener.

Similarly, gardens that consist largely of purposeless, resource-hungry lawn grass, perhaps framed by narrow and mostly empty borders, have been responsible for the coining of the term 'green desert'. Not a term of endearment, it takes issue with the repetitive and unchanging nature of this design. Even when decorated with the occasional evergreen to provide 'year-round interest', the effect is often the reverse of our intentions.

A garden that honours seasonality and conveys a sense of rhythm is easy to achieve, especially with informal designs, if we follow a few simple guidelines:

- Think big. A few well-chosen features covering a larger area are more effective and easier to look after long term than many separate smaller features, which can look fussy and ill considered. For instance, a meadow that merges into a taller border that doubles as a screen is a better choice as opposed to a hodgepodge of separate lawns, borders, and plantings. Thinking big is especially important in more diminutive gardens, where small lawns, small borders, and small plants add up to a small effect.
- If possible, hardscape such as paving and concrete should comprise a smaller portion of your garden than plants and soft surfaces.

- Remove or downsize the tightly cut lawn, or at least relax your maintenance regime and allow it to grow longer.
- Lose any tightly clipped shrubs and hedges that serve no purpose.
- Choose plants for a purpose and let them do most of the work, such as *Hakonechloa* to cover tree bases in shade, *Carex* to form the base of a meadow, or *Pennisetum* to provide summer flower in dry sun.

Deciduous grasses in particular can exhibit marked differences in their appearance as the seasons alter. Introduced by John Greenlee, the fountain grass hybrid *Pennisetum* 'Fairy Tails' has generously produced, exquisitely delicate pinkish blooms when in fresh flower. As the season progresses, pink flowers fade to white and frequently take on a gently arching outline. Later still, the whole plant dries to its winter outfit that can be lit up to spectacular effect by low seasonal sunshine.

Natural Rhythm

EDITING IN THE GARDEN

So often in our attempts to create the perfect garden (or even the perfect low-maintenance garden), we exercise too much control and ignore the natural processes that can help us achieve our goals more satisfactorily, and with less effort and heartache.

It has been said before that gardeners achieve best results when acting more as 'editors' than as 'enforcers'. If we find we are constantly battling with nature through supervising every action in the garden, then we are simply attempting to exert too much control. Working with rather than against nature; understanding and taking advantage of natural processes; and regarding the garden as a whole rather than a number of disparate areas and features more likely to produce the most satisfying garden—for the gardener who cares for it, as well as those who visit.

The Year-Round Garden

For many gardeners in temperate climates, spring and summer is the period to enjoy the garden. This is when popular flowers are at their peak. But in focusing on roses and annual bedding plants that are showy and colourful yet transient, we sometimes neglect to include valuable plants of interest at other times of the year. After the blowsy summertime period ends, our gardens can seem to languish, virtually forgotten and even unloved, until the following growing season.

Adding grasses to the garden's mix keeps the interest flowing over a much longer period. Take, for example, the prairie switch grass, *Panicum virgatum*. The species (or any of its gardenworthy cultivars) provides green mounds in the early part of the year which act as a foil and background for spring-flowering plants. By midsummer, though still playing a background role, its tall, upright foliage begins to show buds. These later blossom

The ability of many grasses to remain standing through winter is a major factor in their long season of interest and consequent value. *Miscanthus* and *Panicum* are especially valuable throughout most of the winter months, as seen here in December at Knoll Gardens, Dorset, England. Low winter sunshine provides the opportunity for them to display their delicate yet resilient beauty.

into myriad tiny flowers that are again set off by the foliage, which can turn to amazing, warm fall colours. Finally, the whole plant—stems, leaves, and flowers—dries to a strawy beige. It retains this colour through most of the winter, along with its outline, lending a warm hue as well as structure to the garden, amounting to interest for at least nine months out of the year.

Grasses contribute such long-term effects to gardens in Mediterranean climates too, although as the seasons are markedly different, winter dormancy is effectively replaced by summer dormancy. For example, the delicate-looking mosquito grass, *Bouteloua gracilis*, goes strawy and dormant in cooler temperate areas during the winter period, whereas if left to its own devices in warmer climates, it becomes strawy and closes down during the hottest summer period.

Some of the major grasses used in gardens, including *Miscanthus*, *Panicum*, and *Pennisetum*, are all deciduous and contribute fresh flower, mature size, and shape around high summer to early autumn—just when so many other garden plants are quietening down. Combined with later-flowering perennials and then autumn-colouring woody plants, this period could be considered the absolute peak of performance for this group of grasses. However, rather like a good malt whisky, the aftertaste can be long and warming: from the peak of perfection, there is a long and dignified descent through subtle and spectacular autumnal colourings to the final garb of winter brown and beige tones of dried skeletal stems and flowers. All the while these grasses contribute shape, movement, and subtle colouration to garden scenes often bereft of such pleasures otherwise.

Through the use of grasses, gardens can be as pleasurable in autumn and winter as they are during the hectic and heady days of spring and early summer. Grasses' resilience, movement, and quiet beauty bring serenity and grace to our gardens' autumn and winter performance that is virtually unique to these versatile plants. Backed by low winter sunshine or outlined with heavy frost, this background role becomes a commanding presence with a display of delicate beauty rivalling spring or summer displays any other group of garden plants can muster. Grasses allow us to enjoy our gardens when most, more traditional garden plants are least interesting.

Community Living

Grasses are very sociable plants. Rather like heathers or geraniums, they happily accept close planting in groups, and are often most striking and effective in the garden or wider landscape viewed en masse. In close up, a grass may be beautiful, but grown in a bold mass, it can be simply breathtaking. Used well, grasses' sociability can help us to see the garden as a living entity—that it is the community as a whole that matters more than individual plants.

In our natural landscapes, we recognize and admire communities of plants that have adapted to the conditions of a specific environment, whether a cliff face, a prairie, or a redwood forest. In our designed spaces, the hand of nature is necessarily replaced by the hand of the gardener, but the gardener's hand can be guided by the principles we see operating so successfully in nature.

Much like people, plants mostly prefer living in communities; they need a suitable place and a worthwhile function in order to give their best. Where plants are grown solely for their individual qualities, rather than an eye to the part they play in a larger scheme, this association is more accurately termed a collection rather than a garden or a community.

For many, a garden really is something more than just a physical space. It is a combination of different elements brought together, not always intentionally, to create something truly greater than the sum of its parts. At least to some degree, such gardens are created to celebrate the joy, the delight, and the fascination we find not just in the individual plants but in the natural systems, the checks and balances, the annual rhythms that make up both our designed spaces and the natural world with which so many of us feel a deep connection. In this sense, a garden is an outdoor place where aesthetics and practicality, diversity and restraint converge in a harmonious whole: a functioning community.

Drawing Inspiration from Prairies, Steppes, and Meadows

The savannah of central Africa, the veldt of South Africa, the pampas of South America, the prairies of North America, the steppes of Asia, and the meadows of Europe—all of these great grasslands exist (or used to) on a vast scale, covering mile after mile. Yet even when planning the smallest of domestic gardens, we can learn much from these great grasslands. Understanding how they are naturally composed and tuning in to the spirit they evoke can help imbue our own gardens with a pleasing sense of informality and longevity through the use of grasses.

To the casual eye, from a distance, these fabulous natural grasslands may look like monotonous, virtually uninterrupted expanses of 'just grass'. In reality, this is far from the truth; like all successful communities, they are extremely diverse. The great grasslands evolved, sometimes in tandem with human civilization, to become distinctive ecosystems with their own specially adapted flora and fauna. Many so-called traditional garden plants have their roots in wild grasslands. Poppy, that most beloved of garden flowers, hails from European meadows, while goldenrod and coneflower, which we have come to grow and love more recently, are denizens of the American prairie.

The expansive Meadow, or Prairie, at Longwood Gardens, Pennsylvania is in fact a relatively recent creation (1969), on what was previously farmland. It captures perfectly the feeling of abundant growth and wide-open space, creating a home for a rich diversity of animal, insect, and plant life.

As part of Millennium Park in Chicago, Illinois, Piet Oudolf's planting in the Lurie Garden uses repeated sweeps and drifts of native grasses that echo the grassy expanses once so widespread in the U.S., such as *Panicum virgatum* 'Shenandoah'.

The eminent Brazilian landscape designer Roberto Burle Marx is credited with coining the phrase 'less is more'. Perhaps a natural grassland provides the perfect example of what this might mean for our designed spaces: a restrained palette of plants used in bold but sensitive ways can give an arresting feeling of place and space, of nature, and of control. In the wild, grasses' striking ability to define a mood and bring fluidity, movement, and harmoniousness to a space explains why they work so well, albeit on a smaller scale, in our designed gardens. It is precisely these qualities that our gardens so often sorely need.

Grassland actually comes in all shapes and sizes and can be found in many regions. The tallgrass prairie is aptly named, with much of its constituent plants growing to above head height. The grasses making up the European meadows and much of the steppes, on the other hand, are somewhat shorter. Thick, rough *Cortaderia* can make travel through South America's pampas anything but comfortable, and the savannah and many Mediterranean grasslands close down during the heat of summer, going into dormancy until essential life-giving rain arrives in autumn.

Acid, alkaline, or serpentine; pure sand to solid clay; freezing cold or baking hot; dust-dry to distinctly wet—anywhere that has sufficient sunlight will mostly have its associated grassland community. And in no small measure, it is this ability to survive and prosper under such a broad spectrum of conditions that makes grasses so desirable in our gardens.

The term 'meadow' has been applied to an area of predominantly grass (or grass-like plants) which, without intervention, human or otherwise, would eventually end up becoming woodland. This is known as being 'in transition', the natural process of moving from open ground to mature woodland, while contrastingly a true grassland is one where trees cannot grow due to one or more climatological factors such as lack of water, leading to more or less permanently open grassland.

A prairie is an example of a permanent grassland community (although apparently the word 'prairie', bestowed by early French travellers, actually means 'meadow' according to Christopher Lloyd's *Meadows*). The word prairie has become evocative of wide-open spaces; more recently it has come to connote a style of planting which, in much of its detail, can bear little resemblance to the original. Being good for farming, huge tracts of prairie land in the United States have been converted to the extent that the term 'prairie remnant', used to describe what is left of these once-mighty grasslands, is now all too apt. These permanent grasslands have clearly not benefited from human intervention.

By contrast, Ferndown Common in Dorset, England is an example of an impermanent grassland that has benefited directly from human intervention. Although trees could thrive there, the area was cleared by early human activity of much of its tree cover sufficiently long ago for a specialized community of plants, including grasses, to have evolved, taking advantage of the open ground. Purple moor grass, *Molinia caerulea*, is now abundant, but still relies on periodic human intervention to clear trees and scrub for its continued success.

Grassy Inspiration

From a gardener's viewpoint, while such name tags as prairie or meadow have some practical value for describing planting styles, these labels can be counterproductive if taken too literally or out of context. A true North American prairie is no more likely to feel at home in a European urban garden than an authentic English meadow will be happy in a Mediterranean Californian backyard. Both types of grassland have evolved in response to a specific place and a given set of conditions; changing the place or the conditions inevitably affects the outcome. While an accurate recreation of a natural grassland, sometimes known as a 'restoration', can have great merit (see sixth chapter), it is really only practical in places that those individual communities once called home—so try not to have unrealistic expectations for your own grassy garden. Rather than trying to emulate every detail of natural grasslands, gardeners and designers should draw inspiration from their overall effect, feel, and style.

Despite wildly varying local environments and prevailing conditions, all grassland communities owe

RIGHT Grass-only plantings, while lacking more traditional flower, can achieve a spectacular level of interest from high summer onwards as seen in the grass garden at the Royal Botanic Gardens, Kew, London.

BELOW Locally native purple moor grass, *Molinia caerulea*, creates a meadow of warm winter brown in association with darker-coloured heathers and a background of pine, birch, and oak on Ferndown Common, Dorset, England. Demand for timber in ancient times led to the felling of the forest, allowing *Molinia* to colonize newly open spaces. Even today, such grasslands still rely on human intervention to prevent woody plants from reclaiming lost territory.

their characteristic air (and indeed, perhaps their charisma) to their shared feature: a preponderance of grasses, with their characteristic linearity, in a generally open space. To evoke the spirit of natural grasslands in our own gardens, then, we should make grasses a key element of our planting design. But this is not to suggest that only grasses should be used in natural grassland-inspired designs; while there is certainly enough shape, form, colour, and contrast within the group to make a grasses-only planting very effective, in practice this style is more often seen in botanical establishments. One example is the impressive Grass Garden at London's Royal Botanic Gardens, Kew, where the comprehensive collection has both an educational and design ethic. In most gardens, however, blending grasses with other plants offers a more satisfying aesthetic. A grass-inspired approach to planting design might suggest that grasses should comprise between twenty to eighty percent of the overall planting palette.

Look in detail and you will see that grassland composition is a mix of not only different grasses but also bulbs, annuals, perennials, and woody plants. Grasses provide the basic layer (or 'matrix'), but the other plants also have vital roles to play.

Woody plants provide structure, screening, and colour from flowers, leaves, and stems. Interest at a lower level comes from all manner of bulbous plants in the spring, followed by a plethora of different perennials, many originating from grasslands, such as *Rudbeckia*, *Echinacea*, *Helenium*, *Monarda*, and *Aster*, which provide a seasonally varying succession of colour and interest. All of this is framed and supported by the grass layer.

As Ferndown Common and its fabulous man-maintained grassland of *Molinia caerulea* is in fact only a few hundred yards from the garden at Knoll, we have drawn inspiration from it for our own plantings within the garden. Being native to the area, *Molinia* grows well in the sandy soils of the garden, where we have used it as a base and a foil for other more brightly coloured companions such as *Patrinia*, *Succisia*, and *Sanguisorba*. Woody plants are represented by dark green conifers and *Viburnum*, which provide a backing and a screen from another part of the garden, while early-season bulbs such as daffodils and *Camassia* provide colour before the grass has regrown. The whole area measures only about 25 square metres (30 square yards) excluding the backing woody plants, and while *Molinia* in this case makes up something like sixty percent of the actual area, its effects are counterbalanced by the various perennials and woody plants so that the border is far from 'just grass'. Nonetheless, this grassland-inspired area, designed to work in harmony with the garden's conditions, has the effects of grassland: a distinctive linearity, a preponderance of grasses, the feeling of open space.

On a different scale, at Scampston Hall in Yorkshire, master designer Piet Oudolf has again used *Molinia caerulea*—this time a selected form, *Molinia caerulea* subsp. *caerulea* 'Poul Petersen'—in a design that blends a grassland approach with the formality often encountered in larger and more traditional gardens. While the individual beds are one hundred percent *Molinia*, this is balanced by other more formal elements such as lawn grass and hedging, bringing the percentage of actual ground covered by *Molinia* down to about fifty percent. Although very formal in layout, much of the design's 'wow factor' comes from the simple use of a native grass planted in large quantities.

It is easy to understand how a grassland approach works by looking at large areas like Scampston Hall and Evening Island at Chicago Botanic Gardens, where grasses are used in bold swathes to cover significant areas of ground, but a grass-inspired style will also work in much smaller spaces.

Our gardens are typically composed of a varying mixture of borders, hedging, pathways, and lawns. On a

An excellent form of purple moor grass, *Molinia* 'Poul Petersen', is used to breathtaking effect at Scampston Hall, Yorkshire, England in a distinctive interpretation of the grassland effect by master designer Piet Oudolf.

ABOVE Set within the warm climate of the Huntington Library, Art Museum, and Botanical Gardens in California, well-spaced clumps of *Festuca mairei* make up a major part of this most beautiful and drought-adapted meadow style planting.

LEFT Meadow-style planting can create the feel of a grassy open space in even relatively small areas such as this private Californian garden.

large scale, each of these different areas is big enough to work well on its own. But on a smaller scale, borders often lack the proportions to contain any depth of planting; lawns simply cumbersome to cut and not large enough to be useable; and shrubs and hedges sometimes clipped into formless and deeply uninteresting

Natural Rhythm   33

shapes. In other words, dividing a small outdoor space into separate sections often means the whole area risks becoming virtually worthless. We expend time, energy, and precious resources on something that gives little pleasure, or even basic satisfaction. Something new is needed: an approach that takes inspiration from the aesthetic simplicity of our natural grasslands.

Rather than focusing on its subdivisions—borders, hedging, pathways, lawn—think of the small garden as a single area that has several different jobs to do. Merge the lawn space with the border area using a basic ground layer of grasses and a mulch layer for all sorts of plants, from early spring bulbs to floriferous perennials, and woody shrubs to provide permanent shape and screening. We readily carpet or otherwise cover the floors of our interior living spaces, mostly in a similar single material, from wall to wall—there is little reason not to do the same outdoors. Pathways can simply be spaces left between plants, and sitting areas can be almost anywhere, moving as the garden changes. Not only will the same area be much easier to maintain, it will also be of significantly greater value to wildlife and infinitely more pleasing to the gardener.

At Hauser and Wirth, Somerset, U.K., this superb meadow style planting designed by Piet Oudolf blends a limited mix of different grasses with a range of perennials to create a generally even-heighted planting, beautifully effective for the greatest part of the year.

Creating a Garden Grassland

- Grasses should comprise 20–80% of the total number of plants used in the garden mix. If selected carefully, a higher percentage (50% or more) can provide the greatest 'wow factor', strongly evoking the spirit of grassy meadows or prairies. A lower percentage of grasses is useful as a theme or as a support to other plantings, such as perennials.

- When using a higher percentage of grasses, choose a restrained palette of 1–5 different grasses as a basic mix or ground covering. A larger number of different grasses can subsequently be used to accent the remaining planting.

- Avoid using too few specimens of the same plant in one place. Grasses almost always work best when planted in larger numbers, whether as a drift meandering through a space or en masse as part of a larger planting.

- Go large. Make the planting area as big as possible; the larger the area, the greater the grasses' effect. Small borders are always more work and less effective. Merge these with lawns to make more planting space.

- Pathways and sitting areas should be an integral part of the planting, rather than separate from it. For low-use pathways, simply leave sufficient space between the plants for people to walk through. Using a similar material for walkways and as surface mulch for planting areas gives a great sense of space, and is easier to install.

- Woody plants and perennials are essential to most successful plantings. Choose woody plants for year-round effect, bark, and leaf colour, and for permanent screening. Choose perennials that provide flower colour and form, and ideally those that maintain their shape after flowering to provide long-term contrast with grasses. Such perennials include *Echinacea*, *Eupatorium*, *Persicaria*, *Rudbeckia*, and *Sedum*.

- All manner of bulbous plants can be used to provide early-season colour, especially with deciduous grasses, which are at their least interesting in the spring. Bulbs are usually added in autumn wherever a space is suitable.

- Grasses are no different from other garden plants in that favourable soil conditions will ensure best growth and establishment. However, unlike many garden plants, grasses do not need much fertilizer or even water once established. Preparing the ground before planting is the time-honoured approach, although the 'no dig' option can be equally successful. Ensuring the ground is not seriously compacted and laying a surface mulch after planting are two key elements to ensure successful establishment.

Although sharing a common linearity, the amazing variety in shape, colour, texture, and habit of grasses offers an impressive set of design qualities that can be used to great advantage in our gardens and designed spaces.

Designing with Grasses

ALL GARDENS ARE MADE UP of a combination of different elements, of building blocks that need to be put together in the right mix to make a successfully designed whole. By designing with an eye towards screening, structural planting, open spaces (whether grassy or hard surface), pathways, and viewpoint as well as planted areas and borders, we can really make the most of our gardens. And when it comes to garden design, ornamental grasses are endlessly versatile building blocks that can be used in many situations, and for a range of different purposes.

Grasses as Building Blocks

Backbone, foundation, or structural planting generally refers to the practice of using plants to create a permanent framework in the garden—for instance, dividing up the space through internal boundaries or using plantings to separating one's garden from the neighbours'. Woody plants such as trees, shrubs, and hedges are ideal for creating structure as they remain present and contribute to the landscape year-round.

The perfect companions to this essential group of structural plants, grasses offer a range of talents that immeasurably improve a garden's year-round performance. For example, much foundation or backbone planting can consist of relatively solid evergreens to the point of becoming uninteresting and even boring. Much as these evergreens perform an essential function of shelter and screening, using grasses along with them is an easy and effective way of bringing some life and interest, some colour and change, to what can otherwise be static or dull layouts. Larger specimen trees, while hardly boring or uninteresting, can have bare empty spaces below that can be enriched and enlivened by shade-loving grasses. Even well-designed areas of woody plants can benefit from the addition of grasses, simply because their sinuous shape and form, their distinct line, and almost-continuous movement work so well with woody companions.

Ornamental grasses are the ultimate mood setters and stage managers. Gardens have been likened to a theatre set where scenes are changed as the production moves through the different acts. Grasses signal season change most dramatically, as they move from new spring growth to lush summer flowering before their statuesque winter finale. Grasses are great at setting scenes and establishing an atmosphere in which other plants can also thrive.

The ability to remain standing well into the winter, absorbing and reflecting the slightest sunshine, makes grasses such as these *Panicum virgatum* ideal companions to evergreens and other woody backbone shrubs. Lightening and enlivening what might otherwise be a dull winter corner at Knoll Gardens, Dorset, England.

As relatively understated as they can be, grasses also display a variety of talents that make them useful to the gardener and designer. Identified and understood, these qualities can make a huge difference to our gardens, and are so very easy to use successfully. The key characteristics that follow include some that can be enjoyed for their own sake, as well as with others that make grasses particularly useful for certain purposes or situations.

SUNLIT AND BACKLIT

Very few groups of plants are transformed as dramatically as grasses by the effects of different kinds of light. Many light conditions react with grasses to create entrancing performances using sunlight and shadow, evoking mystery and intrigue. Shafts of afternoon sunlight striking even a single blade of grass can imbue the plant with a magical quality. An expansive planting, when backlit by low sunshine in either morning or afternoon, quite literally glows and radiates with light reflected from translucent stems, flowers, and leaves. The effect is further intensified by even the slightest breeze.

Grasses that make the most of the light are those whose flowers are held clear above their foliage, allowing them to take full advantage of reflected sunlight. A real favourite in this respect is *Calamagrostis brachytricha*, whose large, arrow-like heads of flowers point skyward, and almost glow in low sunlight. The fountain grasses such as *Pennisetum* 'Fairy Tails' and 'Dark Desire', with their masses of fluffy, caterpillar-like flowers, also excel. In warm and dry climates, *Aristida purpurea* and *Bouteloua*

TOP The soft purple-tinged flowers of *Aristida purpurea* combining with the intriguing flowers of *Bouteloua gracilis* to catch and reflect the sunshine in the Californian garden of Dave and Rainie Fross.

MIDDLE The billowing massed flowers of *Deschampsia* 'Goldtau' providing their very own light display.

RIGHT Heavily dew-laden flowers of *Calamagrostis brachytricha* making exquisite use of the early morning light at Knoll Gardens, Dorset, England.

Designing with Grasses

TOP An eclectic mix of grasses, including the white flowers of *Bothriochloa barbinodis*, alive with afternoon sunlight by a roadside parking lot in Utah.

ABOVE Few plants have the ability to transform their appearance so magnificently as grasses when backlit, particularly by low sunlight, as seen here early in the morning at the Royal Botanic Gardens, Kew in October. Tall, cylindrical flowerheads of *Pennisetum macrourum* seemingly burst up and outwards.

gracilis reflect the light for many months. *Panicum*, *Eragrostis*, and *Molinia* are all equally responsive, and the combination of all these different flower shapes seen together, such as in the growing field at Knoll Gardens on a sunny winter's morning, is a sight not soon forgotten.

Such sunlight-fuelled performances are easy to achieve simply by placing grasses so they will be viewed with sunlight behind them at some point in the day. These brief but regular presentations can then be enjoyed through a significant part of the year.

COLOUR AND CONTINUITY

Colour is an essential element in a successful garden, but it should not be sought at the expense of other equally desirable elements, such as shape and year-round interest. All grasses produce flowers, but it is the deciduous grasses like *Miscanthus*, *Panicum*, and *Pennisetum* that provide the 'wow factor' so often associated with our garden displays.

Flower colour can range from the purples common to *Panicum* through the many shades of red found in *Bothriochloa*, *Miscanthus*, and *Pennisetum*, to an almost infinite number of pink, cream, and white shades present in most major groups of grasses. Yellows can be found among the fresh flowers of the sedges such as *Carex elata* 'Aurea', and even shades of blue in the foliage of *Helictotrichon*, *Leymus*, *Festuca*, and *Poa labillardierei*, which boasts both foliage and flowers of matching blue.

Unlike the colour of flowering plants, which generally lasts for a relatively short (if spectacular) period, the colour of grasses can last many seasons. Many go through subtle colour changes to provide a succession of interest that makes them excellent indicators of seasonal change as well as long-term garden performers.

For example, *Miscanthus sinensis* 'Ferner Osten' starts its growing cycle with green mounds of foliage that increase in bulk and height almost daily for the first half of the year. During the high summer, flower buds appear, eventually opening to one of the darkest red flowers available, set off beautifully by lush green

In August and in full flower (top) at Knoll Gardens, Dorset, England, *Miscanthus* 'Ferner Osten' is among the darkest of cultivars, contrasting with the purple topped angular stems of *Verbena bonariensis*. Two months later (above), while the verbena remains virtually the same, the grass has changed in both flower and foliage, a dynamic procession of colour, texture, and contrast that lasts for many months.

foliage. As weeks pass, the red fades to burnished silver while the leaves turn a warm burnt orange to provide a second combination of colours no less effective than the first. Finally, in late autumn, the different colours fade, leaving flowers, stems, and leaves in many shades of straw and beige—yet another tasteful ensemble that lasts right through winter.

The term 'successional planting' is used to describe a long-established technique of using a series of different plants, often annuals, to flower one after another for a succession of interest. Although effective when done well, successional planting can also be very labour intensive. The same effect can be achieved with much less effort by planting a grass like *Miscanthus sinensis* 'Ferner Osten', which will provide an entire growing season's worth of interest from just one permanent plant.

TEXTURE AND SHAPE

Often overlooked, the textural qualities of most flowering grasses can contribute much to the garden scene. Bear in mind that the flowers of most grasses will remain intact for many months after the initial flush of colour has faded, so if they have a textural quality or fine shape, they will provide interest in that area for longer. For example, *Miscanthus sinensis* 'Flamingo', a first-class garden plant, has the most elegant, delicately pendulous flowers that are coloured a superb deep pink when first open. Although this fresh colour soon fades, the shapely qualities of the flower remain and arguably transcend that first flush of colour in their effect.

Grasses stand out among perennials for their particular quality of shape and form—their linear distinctiveness. Whether in association with other broadleaved plants, against solid inanimate objects, or in large, grasses-only plantings, their characteristic linear outline brings cohesion to design while

In a public park in Sweden, the elongated, elegant, refined leaves of *Hakonechloa macra* are set in a most effective and long-lasting partnership with architectural woody plants and more solid elements of stone and pathway.

allowing for light and easy movement. Though most grasses tend to 'flow' in this regard, there are some that are valuable for their more upright posture in the landscape. The almost fastigiate nature of *Panicum virgatum* 'Northwind', for example, creates a strong vertical accent in any planting, and while retaining this habit all season, it still offers some lithe movement and fall leaf colour. Such grasses can be used as single specimens, but as grasses are sociable plants that happily accept close grouping without losing impact, nearly all will be even more effective planted in groups.

Muhlenbergia is among the most elegant of grasses, especially for warmer climates and drier soils, where it can produce fountains of narrow stems that spill outward in a never-ending cascade. Although superb as mature individual plants, their effect is magnified and even more stunning en masse. With such generous performers as *Muhlenbergia dubia*, for example, it is important not to plant individuals too close together within groups for fear of cramping their style. Contrastingly, the purple moor grass, *Molinia caerulea*, while retaining an upright habit, has a less expansive nature, and remains happy with closer spacing.

As a rule, the flowers of evergreen grasses and grass-like plants are less than striking, but this is more than compensated by the sculptural qualities of their foliage, which is generally present the whole year. Many of the sedges, including *Carex divulsa*, *Carex*

TOP *Miscanthus* 'Flamingo' is one of the very best of the genus for garden use, known primarily for its freely produced, gently pendulous flowers in soft pink. Once the first flush of fresh colour has faded, however, the amazing textural qualities of the flowers are scarcely less demanding of attention.

MIDDLE The arching habit and careful placing of *Muhlenbergia rigens* set against a plain background creates a simple and satisfying effect at the Huntington Library, Art Museum, and Botanical Gardens, California.

LEFT Planted close, the evergreen *Carex testacea* provides a textural surface reminiscent of waves, combining superbly with woody structural plants in the entry borders of the new glasshouse at RHS Garden Wisley, Surrey, England.

testacea, and the amazing variety of what are generally regarded as cultivars of *Carex oshimensis* excel in this respect; their flowers are sometimes considered insignificant (though close up they are actually fascinating), but their foliage has a remarkable form that is invaluable in the garden.

MATRIX AND MASS

While many grasses are valuable in their ability to bring tactile, mobile qualities to our plantings, when used in certain ways, some combine their innate lightness with a more commanding presence. For example, at the entrance of the RHS Garden Wisley, visitor volume necessitated an area of paving and hardscape adjacent to the welcome building. A bold, simple mass planting of *Calamagrostis* 'Karl Foerster' is a hugely effective choice here, acting as a horticultural feature, a screen, a partial division of open space, and in combination with other structural plantings, a highly effective balance and counterpoint to buildings and hard surfaces.

Less formal but no less effective is a simple mass planting of *Sporobolus airoides* used to superb effect as part of the parking lot landscape at Springs Preserve, Las Vegas, Nevada. This drought-adapted grass is appropriate to the region, and planted en masse over a substantial area, conveys an airy meadow-like feel to the arrival area. It perhaps serves as reference

Often planted en masse in dry soils, this planting of *Anemanthele lessoniana* at the University Botanic Garden, Cambridge, England has been given an elegant twist as a low-level maze though which visitors are encouraged to walk.

Designing with Grasses

As part of an elegantly simple public planting in Sweden, *Sesleria autumnalis* provides a base through which spring-flowering bulbs and later *Sedum* emerge.

to the natural springs found on this site and the reason for the original settlement in this desert landscape.

Grasses that can be used as a base over the entire planting area, and from which other plants are seen to emerge, are frequently referred to as 'matrix' grasses. Often limited to a single species, this approach is becoming increasingly popular as gardeners and designers alike enjoy the simplicity of effect and the comparatively low level of aftercare required to maintain such plantings. Matrix planting is perhaps inspired by the meadow principle of a generally grassy open space from which other plants emerge. For example, in a public park in Sweden, master designer Piet Oudolf has used a single base planting of *Sesleria autumnalis* as a matrix from which spring bulbs and later-season *Sedum* 'Matrona' emerge in turn. With well-chosen partners, this essentially simple design approach creates a long season of interest and display with very little aftercare.

At Tongva Park, Santa Monica, California, designer John Greenlee has created a meadow-like base from which other, more solid companion plants such as trees and architectural succulents emerge. An eclectic mix of grasses and sedges are woven together in a successful matrix which, in spite of its intricate design, creates a peaceful and calming aesthetic.

TOP Planted by John Greenlee, this meadow mix of grasses at Tongva Park, Santa Monica, California provides both an ever-present green oasis and a base from which other plants emerge seamlessly, such as trees, succulents, and bulbs.

MIDDLE Within the parking lot landscape surrounding the entrance to the Springs Preserve, Las Vegas, Nevada, a simple, elegant planting of drought-tolerant *Sporobolus airoides* provides a soft and airy balance to the surrounding hard surfaces.

RIGHT At the entrance of the RHS Garden Wisley in England, a simple, generous planting of *Calamagrostis* 'Karl Foerster' acts as a feature, a partial screen, and effectively balances the numerous hard surfaces of paving and building.

Designing with Grasses

MOVEMENT AND SOUND

Whether it's the graceful movement provoked by a delicate summer breeze or a battering by severe winter gales, the lithe, flexing, almost-continuous motion and rustling sounds of stems, leaves, and flowers are a prime attribute of the grass family. The sound and movement of grasses in our designed spaces breathes life into landscapes that can otherwise appear static and stationary, qualities highly evocative of fabulous natural landscapes. One of the common names for *Briza media* is quaking grass, which is particularly apt as the flowers not only move but rustle seductively in the slightest breeze. *Nassella tenuissima* (*Stipa tenuissima*) is another quick-growing tactile grass that moves in the slightest wind, and can bring life and energy into relatively barren urban landscapes.

Grasses are seldom if ever heavy; their almost constantly moving stems are produced in great profusion which, even at height and when topped with flower, manage to convey an airy lightness almost unequalled in the plant world. *Panicum virgatum* and its many cultivars are expert at creating this light and airy, mobile effect as they produce quite literally masses of tiny flowers that appear to hang, cloud-like, above the stems and leaves, and are the perfect foil for more solid, inanimate partners.

ABOVE Moving in the slightest breeze, a bank of *Nassella tenuissima* works beautifully in association with more solid city buildings, as seen here in San Francisco, California.

LEFT Grasses' unique ability to move in the slightest breeze, providing both movement and sound to otherwise static landscapes, is especially valuable in urban areas, where their softness and pliability act as an antidote to the solidity of city blocks.

Designing with Grasses

TRANSPARENCY

Their quick-growing nature and lightness of stem equips certain grasses such as tall *Molinia*, *Stipa*, and *Muhlenbergia* to act as transparent or semi-transparent dividers of garden space. Excellent at providing height without weight in larger plantings—or in small gardens that are often short of space—these plants provide temporary division and something of an air of mystery as the view beyond can still be glimpsed through the screen. The tall purple moor grass, *Molinia caerulea* subsp. *arundinacea*, is a great choice for cooler areas with its quite unique autumn display that sees the foliage, stems, and flowerheads slowly turn the most amazing, warm butter yellow—an ensemble that makes these plants the absolute stars at this time of year wherever they are used.

Stipa gigantea, with its tall, airy stems is another good choice because although it can exceed 2 m (6 ft.), it can easily be used in front of much smaller plants at the front or middle areas of a border thanks to the 'see-through' nature of its flower stems.

TOP Grasses with airy, light stems create a hazy, transparent division through which other more solid objects can be glimpsed. One is the aptly named *Molinia* 'Transparent', seen here in the garden of John and Jenny Makepeace, Dorset, England,

MIDDLE Deer grass, *Muhlenbergia rigens*, provides an elegant transparency in the landscape, as seen here in the private garden of Dave and Rainie Fross in Arroyo Grande, California.

LEFT Height without undue weight is brought to this planting at Knoll Gardens, Dorset, England, by the use of *Molinia caerulea* ssp. *arundinacea*. Grasses such as *Molinia* and *Stipa gigantea* with basal mounds of foliage and much taller stems and flowers can be used to create a 'see-through' or transparent effect that gives a feeling of division and mystery without the need for heavyweight walling or hedging.

Produced during spring, the giant oat-like flowers of *Stipa gigantea* make an excellent semi-transparent screen in hot, sunny, and open areas.

CLOCKWISE FROM TOP LEFT Partial division of space, while retaining a hint of what lies beyond, can be achieved easily by the use of grasses such as *Calamagrostis* 'Karl Foerster' as used at Knoll Gardens, Dorset, England. • *Aristida purpurea* creates a practical and beautiful low-level division of space between pedestrian and traffic in the parking lot of the Huntington Library, Art Museum, and Botanical Garden, California. • The upright nature of *Pennisetum* 'Fairy Tails' make this grass an almost perfect choice for a floriferous informal hedge or screen as used at the RHS Garden, Wisley, England. • At the Huntington Library, Art Museum, and Botanical Gardens, California, the enthusiastically produced flower stems of *Muhlenbergia dubia* create a delicate, airy screen between pathways. • The bright green foliage of the shy-flowering *Miscanthus* 'Gracillimus' making a beautiful and practical screen surrounding a pool in a public park in Sweden.

Miscanthus ×*giganteus* used as tall screen to disguise an old fence by the garden entrance at Knoll Gardens, Dorset, England.

SCREENING AND DIVISION

The combination of regular outline, flower, movement, and longevity allows a number of grasses to be used successfully as informal screens or hedging. They are just as easy to maintain in this manner as they are elsewhere in the garden. Effectively self-levelling, the grasses grow to the same height each season without needing to be trimmed during the busy summer period.

A significant number of grasses can be used in this way, and are superb in many situations where either a green or floriferous division of space might be desirable. Unlike more permanent screening and common hedging plants, grasses as lightweight 'hedging' have few of the drawbacks of more traditional hedges, are long lived, and seldom become too bulky as the stems are renewed from the base each year. Although most grasses produce a very even outline when grown together in this way, the effect is generally informal, rather in contrast to the strictly formal effect created by tightly clipped woody evergreens such as box and yew. Added to this, the constant movement of stems, flowers, and leaves brings the hedge or screen to life.

Suitable candidates for low, informal hedging include *Aristida purpurea* and *Nassella tenuissima*, while *Muhlenbergia dubia* and *Molinia caerulea* provide a more transparent screening effect. The unique upright habit of *Pennisetum* 'Fairy Tails' is almost perfect for mid-height use in drier sunny soils, and *Miscanthus* 'Gracillimus', selected for its non-flowering tendency, makes for one of the most beautiful green screens. Then there is the rather narrower feather reed grass *Calamagrostis* 'Karl Foerster', whose distinctive vertical stems are produced in such huge quantities on mature plants as to make this an almost perfect choice for taller hedges. Taller still is the architectural *Miscanthus* ×*giganteus*, whose strong green stems support gently cascading wide green leaves that shimmer and float all season. These grass hedges need trimming to ground level each spring, and so work best where temporary loss of the hedge is not an issue.

REPETITION

Repeated use of a single plant, or several similar ones, is an effective way of giving a garden a theme or recognizable pattern. Repeated plants in groups or used as individuals sometimes become known as signature plants because they help give a planting its particular identity. Quick-growing and amenable to close grouping, and with their distinctive linear outline, grasses are well placed to excel in this role. As repeated individual specimens, any grasses that have a distinctive outline—such as *Miscanthus*, *Molinia*, *Muhlenbergia*, *Panicum*, *Poa*, and *Calamagrostis*—are all excellent for this purpose. Those that work well as groups include *Nassella*, *Aristida*, *Molinia*, *Helictotrichon*, *Pennisetum*, and *Hakonechloa*.

ABOVE Using repeated groups of the same type of plant can bring a high degree of unity to a planting. A free-flowering *Miscanthus* is used along a city street in New York City with telling effect.

LEFT A simple and impressive repeated use of *Muhlenbergia capillaris* brings a high degree of unity to the disparate elements of buildings and various hard surfaces of this Californian shopping mall.

OPPOSITE The repeated use of *Molinia caerulea* spp. *arundinacea* helps unify a mixed planting of other plants at Knoll Gardens, Dorset, England.

The Spaces Between: Natural Ground Cover

Almost as important as the plants we use in our gardens are the spaces that we leave between them, and yet so often this essential element is neglected or overlooked.

In nature, bare patches of ground seldom stay bare for long, yet many gardeners assiduously clear the surface of a border or other planting area, leaving expanses of bare ground. Removing all debris, leaf litter, and organic matter requires considerable maintenance, and fails to conserve rainwater or other important and freely available resources. As Doug Tallamy writes in *Bringing Nature Home*: "We lose much when we remove leaf litter because it provides so many free services for us; free mulch, free fertilizer, free weed control, and free soil amendments".

The space in between plants is such an important part of our garden landscape, and a sympathetic surface covering acts as a practical foil, a frame, and a setting for the chosen plants. The right ground cover should be not only visually attractive but also easy to maintain and effective in bringing cohesion to a border or planting. The right ground cover gives plantings a sense of place, and plants a feeling of belonging.

A variety of materials can be used effectively as a surface mulch that not only keeps weeds down and retains water, but allows for a decorative surface between plants to form part of the garden scene.

Even a coating of freshly fallen leaves can provide a decorative and seasonal display.

Any kind of organic material such as chipped bark, stable manure, straw, bracken, garden compost, or simple fallen leaves can be used, and all contribute to the fertility and general health of the soil. The layer need not be thick; a few centimetres (1 to 2 in.) would suffice, though it can be a bit thicker among larger plants. Inorganic materials such as gravel, slate, or chippings do not really improve the soil directly, but still conserve essential moisture, and when used well are very effective aesthetically.

The manner in which a surface material is used also has a major influence on a garden. Clear divisions between lawns, paths, and planted areas can be effective and satisfying in some situations, but in others, a looser approach is more fitting. At Knoll Gardens, we allow 'soft' paths to meander through larger plantings, blurring the edges between walkways and planted areas by using a similar material such as chipped bark on both areas. It brings an air of relaxed naturalness and is so easy to maintain. The simplest way to achieve this effect is often to regard the area as a single planting, threading the pathway through by leaving more space between the plants where pathway is desired.

Using a similar material as a practical and decorative finish for both planting and non-planting areas allows for a softening of the traditional clear division between paths, lawns, and borders. This in itself can lead to a softer, more relaxed garden aesthetic.

Seen through the airy, pendulous flowers of *Molinia caerulea* subsp. *arundinacea*, the massed flowers of *Miscanthus* 'Cindy' (front right), and *Miscanthus* 'Flamingo' (centre) are supported by the tall, feathery white flowers of the pampas, *Cortaderia* 'Sunningdale Silver', which is actually growing in the adjacent border.

Grasses and the Naturalistic Approach

GARDENING, AS WITH MANY other aspects of human endeavour, offers a multiplicity of style names with which to help or confuse the uninitiated. Prairie style, meadow style, the New Perennial Movement, steppe style, New American, and New Wave are just some that are more frequently encountered. What they all have in common, however, is their openness to the use of grasses as an integral part of the design.

The Naturalistic Approach at Knoll

Useful as these individual names are in detail, I have come to prefer 'naturalistic' as an overarching term to describe this distinctive approach to garden-making, and for what I personally feel most closely defines my own approach and ethos. It reflects a desire to garden with an informal aesthetic and to take great pleasure in the garden as an ever-changing, ongoing community that benefits both ourselves and our wider environment. 'Biodiversity', 'low impact', 'sustainability', and 'resource consciousness' are as important as terms for modern gardeners as any horticultural term has ever been. In describing an approach as 'naturalistic', there is no intention to suggest that such gardens are somehow 'natural'—by definition, gardens are designed spaces that are positioned largely within our built environment. They can never replace our natural systems, but by following a more nature-friendly and open-minded approach, they can provide an essential adjunct at the same time as offering an aesthetic I have come to find so much more fulfilling than many a more traditional approach. In the same way that writer Raymond Williams described 'nature' as a singular term for the multiplicity of living things and processes, it could be argued that 'naturalistic' is a singular term for a multiplicity of broadly similar styles and approaches.

THE DECENNIUM BORDER

In my first book, I spent some time detailing the ethos and design process that led to the creation of the Decennium border at Knoll. I described it as a naturalistic experiment that was inspired at least in part by the modern 'New Wave' approach to planting, as might be defined, for example, by the various worldwide projects of Piet Oudolf, or the Hermannshoff Gardens in Weinheim, Germany. Seventeen or so years later, the Decennium has matured and prospered, and like

Early season bulbs such as daffodils offer a hint of the season to come, while the main border retains last year's grass structures virtually intact.

any good planting, has gradually evolved over that time. While the concept—a series of seasonal peaks of interest precipitated by the thoughtful selection of permanent plants—remains as valid today as when the border was first planted, the community of plants that make up the border has subtly altered. The aesthetic effect is similar, but the border's plant community has adapted and evolved in response to challenges and changes that climate and cultural conditions have presented over time. Some plants have grown well and matured, while a few others, such as the short-lived daisy *Leucanthemum vulgare*, gradually found conditions not to their liking and have required replacement. Allowing a planting to evolve in this way is perhaps a good example of the gardener acting as 'editor' and not 'enforcer', and is an important aspect of the naturalistic approach. Our natural systems are not static, and we should allow for a similar fluidity in our gardens.

Each spring, and only a matter of weeks after last season's growth was cut down, *Euphorbia palustris* delights with its bright yellow flowers that are in perfect harmony with the border's spring green foliage.

The tall purple flowers of *Calamagrostis* 'Karl Foerster', the whorled yellow spikes of *Phlomis russeliana*, and the distinctive upright, tapered flowers of *Veronicastrum virginicum* arise from a background of green foliage supplied by *Miscanthus*, *Molinia*, *Euphorbia*, *Rudbeckia*, and *Eupatorium*.

Miscanthus 'Malepartus', *Persicaria* 'Rosea', *Molinia caerulea* 'Dauerstrahl', *Cortaderia* 'Sunningdale Silver', and *Verbena bonariensis* combine in a bonanza of high summer colour, shape, and form.

The onset of autumn sees the arrival of fall colour from woody plants such as *Euonymus*, while the fresh flower colour of the grasses starts to fade.

As late autumn approaches, the border offers a symphony of subtle textures, shapes, colour, and form. *Euphorbia palustris* now offers shrimp pink stems and golden yellow leaves as its second contribution to the seasons' display.

As brighter colours ebb away from the border, winter brown stems, leaves, and flowers of *Veronicastrum virginicum* continue to make an impressive display that will last for some months to come.

In full fall colour, *Molinia caerulea* 'Dauerstrahl' is scarcely less effective than when first in fresh dark flower.

Current Planting Palette for the Decennium Border

GRASSES

- *Calamagrostis* ×*acutiflora* 'Karl Foerster'
- *Calamagrostis* ×*acutiflora* 'Waldenbuch'
- *Miscanthus sinensis* 'Cindy'
- *Miscanthus sinensis* 'Flamingo'
- *Miscanthus sinensis* 'Ferner Osten'
- *Miscanthus sinensis* 'Malepartus'
- *Molinia caerulea* subsp. *arundinacea*
- *Molinia caerulea* subsp. *caerulea* 'Dauerstrahl'
- *Panicum virgatum* 'Heavy Metal'
- *Panicum virgatum* 'Straight Cloud'
- *Pennisetum alopecuroides* 'Hameln'
- *Pennisetum* 'Fairy Tails'

PERENNIALS

- *Eupatorium maculatum* 'Atropurpureum'
- *Euphorbia palustris*
- *Papaver orientale* 'Beauty of Livermere'
- *Persicaria amplexicaulis* 'Rosea'
- *Phlomis russeliana*
- *Rudbeckia laciniata*
- *Sanguisorba* 'Janet's Jewel'
- *Sanguisorba tenuifolia* 'Purpurea'
- *Verbena bonariensis*
- *Veronicastrum virginicum*

Enveloped in the calmness of a late autumnal morning mist, the grasses and perennials in the Decennium merge seamlessly with the surrounding woody plants to create a sensory and reflective mood.

THE DRY MEADOW

Since the original planting of the Decennium border at Knoll all those years ago, the garden has continued to evolve, and in so doing has created the opportunity for the naturalistic ethos to be absorbed more completely into our revised layouts and plantings. As new projects have been imagined, or existing areas come to need rejuvenation, the opportunity has been taken to extend and refine the naturalistic approach as it applies to the specifics of the garden and its conditions. This includes new projects, refining existing plantings, altering maintenance regimes, or indeed, simply adapting what has worked well in other environments.

The planting in the Decennium border consists primarily of informal and often repeated groups or drifts of a limited range of plants, with grasses and perennials each covering about 50 percent of the total border area. A large project in 2020 was the creation of the Dry Meadow, which (as its name might suggest) is based on fairly dry soil, with grasses covering perhaps 80 percent of the area and chosen specifically to create a meadow-style feel throughout. While

Morning light after a cold night in early winter accentuates the frosty blueness of *Poa labillardierei*, even masking the foliage of *Libertia*, *Muhlenbergia*, and *Nepeta* in a similar shade.

the meadow planting takes up the majority of the new space, a series of four lower-lying linked swales were sculpted around two sides of the perimeter and connected to each other to form a new Rain Garden

Grasses and the Naturalistic Approach

(see sixth chapter). Not only does the Rain Garden deal effectively with localized stormwater flooding, it creates another habitat with a different range of plants for both ourselves and the garden's wildlife to enjoy, in close proximity to the dry-loving plants of the meadow.

Whereas the Decennium planting relies on widely varying heights and shapes of the constituent grasses and perennials as part of its appeal, contrastingly the Dry Meadow planting relies on a comparatively even-heighted mix of plants to create the desired look and feel of a stylized meadow. To achieve this garden meadow look, one grass, *Poa labillardierei*, was chosen as the overall matrix plant and used throughout at a varying density of about one plant to every 3 to 4 square metres (4 square yards). This *Poa* was chosen partly for its individual beauty, partly as it would enjoy the sunny, open, and frequently very dry soils, but also partly for its ability to provide a light and delicate grassy effect over a long period. Regarded as semi-evergreen

RIGHT As spring gets underway, the soft mounds of *Poa labillardierei* create a framework for the whole meadow, as well as a foil for early season flowers such as daffodils, the emerging foliage of *Knautia* and *Nepeta*, and the daintily fresh white flowers of *Sesleria nitida*.

BELOW As temperatures rise in late spring, the dark blue of Dutch iris and the starry white flowers of the evergreen *Libertia grandiflora* are highlighted against the soft leaves of *Poa*.

Silvery blue-grey mounds of *Poa labillardierei* are set off by the massed flowers of *Nepeta racemosa* 'Walker's Low', which can repeat flower with some timely deadheading.

The varied flower shapes and colours of Dutch iris, *Nepeta*, and *Libertia* framed almost perfectly by the soft but ever-present mass of foliage and flower from *Poa*.

Where the Dry Meadow meets the lower-lying swale of the Rain Garden, drought-loving *Poa labillardierei* gives way to the white flowers of *Luzula nivea* and the evergreen foliage of *Juncus* and *Carex*.

As the massed flowers of blue *Nepeta* start to fade, the varied pinks of the coneflower *Echinacea pallida* seem to explode into prominence.

As summer peaks and fall beckons, soft lavender flowers of *Aster* 'Lutetia' and bright red of *Hesperantha* 'Major' are highlighted against drying flowers and still-blue foliage of *Poa*. Frothy effervescence (left) is supplied by the drying flowers of *Deschampsia* 'Goldtau' planted within part of the immediately adjacent Rain Garden.

During misty autumnal days, the gradually drying flowers of *Poa* and coneflower are now joined by the distinctive upright flowers of *Molinia* 'Overdam', while *Aster* and *Hesperantha* continue to provide pinpoints of fresh flower colour.

Deep into autumn, as fresh flower diminishes, the shaggy mounds of *Poa labillardierei* and the upright green leaves of *Libertia grandiflora* together make an effective association through which the dried, pin-like flowerheads of *Echinacea pallida* continue to entertain.

in most parts of the United Kingdom, it is usually cut back in early spring, when it will react with a sheaf of fresh foliage and flower that is distinctly blue toned. In using it as the main base grass, the intention was to not cut the *Poa*, and so avoid a significant down time during the early spring period. Thus far it has retained the bluish appearance of its foliage, and has rewarded us with a long succession of variously coloured flowerheads that have maintained the desired airy haze though which other plants can be showcased. Even in early spring, therefore, the daffodils have been able to take advantage of the soft mounds of greenish *Poa* foliage as a foil for their cheerful and most welcome flowers.

Like any grassland, this garden meadow relies on a mix of grasses for its overall effect, though none are perhaps as initially obvious as *Poa*. Three selections of the native *Molinia caerulea* are planted sporadically throughout the meadow, and as they will also cope with wettish soils, some can be seen straying into the wetter areas of the Rain Garden. Their generally upright habit and the comparatively solid outline of their flower spikes contrast with the airiness of the *Poa*. *Sesleria nitida* has been included for

Grasses and the Naturalistic Approach

Planting Palette for the Dry Meadow

GRASSES

- *Poa labillardierei*
- *Molinia caerulea* subsp. caerulea 'Dauerstrahl'
- *Molinia caerulea* subsp. caerulea 'Edith Dudszus'
- *Molinia caerulea* subsp. caerulea 'Overdam'
- *Muhlenbergia rigens*
- *Sporobolus heterolepis*
- *Sesleria nitida*
- *Sesleria caerulea*

PERENNIALS

- *Achillea* 'Terracotta'
- *Agapanthus* 'Northern Star'
- *Allium* 'Millenium'
- *Amsonia* 'Blue Ice'
- *Aster pyrenaeus* 'Lutetia'
- *Echinacea pallida*
- *Francoa sonchifolia* 'Pink Bouquet'
- *Hesperantha coccinea* 'Major' (syn. *Schizostylis coccinea* 'Major')
- *Knautia macedonica*
- *Kniphofia caulescens* 'John May'
- *Libertia grandiflora*
- *Nepeta grandiflora* 'Dawn to Dusk'
- *Nepeta racemosa* 'Walker's Low'
- *Rudbeckia maxima*
- *Sanguisorba* 'Ruby Red'
- *Tritonia disticha* subsp. rubrolucens

BULBS

- *Amaryllis belladonna*
- *Iris* 'Lion King'
- *Iris* 'Rosario'
- *Iris* 'Sapphire Beauty'
- *Ixia* hybrids
- *Narcissus* 'Blushing Lady'
- *Watsonia* species

its year-round blue-grey foliage and welcoming white spring flowers, while *Sporobolus heterolepis* offers frothy masses of tiny flowers arising from autumnally colouring foliage. All have their individual part to play in the wider scheme. While not generally happy in the damp maritime climate of the United Kingdom, *Muhlenbergia rigens* can be convinced to grow successfully in well-drained and sunny spots, and has been included as an occasional accent for its amazing, narrowly cylindrical flowers that ascend clear of the other meadow grasses as summer peaks.

With the grasses occupying the majority of the ground space, and thus creating the grassy meadow effect, the aesthetic function of perennials is primarily to provide a succession of seasonal points of flower colour. While a huge number of perennials can work easily in association with grasses, those that perhaps work best for this kind of garden meadow tend to have minimal supporting foliage, or a generally delicate appearance with flowers that are held clear of the foliage, and so associate with the airy lightness of the grasses most effectively. After daffodils come Dutch iris, offering their impressively complex flowers at the top of thin stems, and these are followed in turn by a virtual parade of *Nepeta*, *Achillea*, *Knautia*, *Amsonia*, *Echinacea*, *Apaganthus*, *Sanguisorba*, and *Tritonia* as the growing season passes by. One notable exception to this foliage rule is the clump-forming *Libertia grandiflora*, whose evergreen, elegantly upright iris-like foliage contrasts so well with the lighter, more mobile grasses. It provides essential background foliage in the early part of the year, should *Poa* need an occasional levelling to refresh its growth. Not content to contribute foliage alone, this *Libertia* also produces many heads of delightful white flowers in late spring.

Finally, as fall becomes winter, the grasses and perennials alike creep into dormancy, though they retain a significant element of their structure and elegance, and the meadow seems almost to be waiting; poised to celebrate the arrival of another spring.

THE SHADY MEADOW

Situated in the oldest part of the garden, and within the canopy and root zone of some of its largest trees, the Shady Meadow has to contend with almost year-round dry soil, the ever-thirsty root systems of woody plants, and very little sunlight. Frequently described as 'dry shade', this can be among the most problematic of garden conditions to plant successfully. Even with the ability to apply copious amounts of water, it is difficult to retain enough soil moisture for many plants to grow successfully in these situations,

The Shady Meadow at Knoll Gardens is blessed with dry soil almost year-round, the pervasive root systems of trees and other woody plants, and little sunlight.

CLOCKWISE FROM TOP LEFT Growing happily in dry shade conditions nearby, seedlings of *Melica uniflora* f. *albida* can now be found moving into the Shady Meadow, just across the path from their original home. • As the days begin to lengthen, and with some moisture in the soil, the meadow lights up with a delicate display from spring-flowering *Primula* and *Anemone*. • Though initially planted, short-lived *Aquilegia vulgaris* survives now through self-seeding, and periodically creates a haze of purplish mauve once early spring flowers of *Primula* and *Anemone* have finished. • Present all year, mound-forming *Carex remota* and mat-forming *Carex* 'Silver Sceptre' create the base or matrix of the Shady Meadow. • The lower part of the meadow is more open, and with a little more sunlight and less root competition, *Carex remota* more easily creates a carpet of soft green.

and this especially applies to any type of traditional lawn. As we become more aware of the environmental cost of such water usage, it is increasingly difficult to justify on the grounds of sustainability—if not common sense. Shade-adapted plants, on the other hand, have evolved strategies for coping with these testing conditions, and require far less by way of precious resources to do so.

The Shady Meadow consists primarily of two different low-growing sedges, and is generally a low and even-heighted planting that accepts light foot traffic. It could therefore be considered either an informal lawn or a garden meadow. *Carex remota* is a native of the United Kingdom with light green, more or less evergreen foliage and a mounding habit. Frequently found in shady conditions with some seasonal moisture, the plant's resilience is tested by the area's very dry soils. Nonetheless this sedge has made excellent cover, though it is perhaps most vibrant furthest from tree bases. *Carex* 'Silver Sceptre' has a slightly wider, quietly variegated leaf and a spreading habit that allows it to gradually colonize the toughest areas. Together they have formed the meadow's character, creating a practical partnership that is as effective aesthetically as it is durable.

Melica uniflora f. *albida* enthusiastically produces exquisite pearl white flowers resembling grains of rice, and is so well adapted to the regime of dry shade that it is at its sparkling best in the early part of the year, but will all but disappear by midsummer to await the return of adequate moisture. In such conditions, it will self-seed, and is gradually encroaching on the boundaries of the Shady Meadow, where it is a most welcome (if unplanned) addition to the duo of sedges.

As spring offers more moisture, early season bulbs and perennials populate the meadow most successfully. *Primula vulgaris* was initially planted and has subsequently found conditions sufficiently to its liking to set seed and multiply. Bulbs such as the bright white wood anemone prosper in the driest areas, while the incredibly beautiful marsh fritillary, *Fritillaria meleagris*, has taken to the more open section among *Carex remota*, gradually seeding around. Two short-lived early season perennials, foxglove and columbine, delicately place themselves around the meadow wherever they feel most appropriate. Autumn-flowering cyclamen seem to survive in the driest of shady conditions, and the first self-sown seedlings are gradually making their way into the meadow from a long-established colony at the base of a large oak nearby.

As dryness intensifies in summer, the meadow returns to its base of foliage provided by the two sedges. In prolonged dry periods, it may receive some additional water, but otherwise it is designed to cope with the prevailing conditions with little extra attention apart from some periodic weeding as required. Although in situ for some years, neither sedge has required any regular trimming, though *Carex remota* has been cut to the base on occasion to encourage fresh green growth.

Planting Palette for the Shady Meadow

GRASSES
- *Carex remota*
- *Carex* 'Silver Sceptre'
- *Melica uniflora* f. *albida*, as self-sown seedlings

PERENNIALS
- *Aquilegia vulgaris*
- *Digitalis purpurea*
- *Primula vulgaris*

BULBS
- *Anemone nemorosa* 'Alba'
- *Galanthus* 'Lady Elphinstone'
- *Galanthus* 'Sam Arnott'
- *Fritillaria meleagris*
- *Ornithogalum nutans*
- *Ornithogalum umbellatum*

Muhlenbergia is a very beautiful group well-adapted to hot, dry, desert-like conditions, and can react adversely when placed in cooler, damper environments. This firework-like display from *Muhlenbergia dubia* appears in the garden of Dave and Rainie Fross, California.

Right Grass, Right Place

PLANTS ARE HAPPIEST, and therefore easiest to look after, when growing under conditions they enjoy or at least easily tolerate. A thoughtful look at the established plant communities in natural systems shows us that plants arrange themselves into areas that best suit their needs, or to which they have become adapted. Over time, a process of natural selection matches the right plant to the right place.

In our gardens, this natural process is interrupted and replaced with a variety of other considerations that can have very little to do with matching plant with place, if anything at all. However, the more we understand our gardens' basic growing conditions, the better we will be able to match the most suitable plants with those conditions, and so the better our gardens will be.

Like any other plant, grasses have their likes and dislikes—their preferences as to sun or shade and wet or dry soils—based on the conditions to which they have become adapted in nature. Luckily for gardeners, a huge number of grasses are actually quite happy in a wide range of gardens. That said, in this chapter, we will look at some of the more specific growing conditions gardeners might encounter and explore which grasses might best suit these conditions.

Any broad categorization or list, including those in this chapter, should be viewed as a generalized starting point. The grass chosen for a specific project in a specific place needs to be a practical choice for the climate it is being asked to grow in, knowledge of local climate is key, and the use of locally appropriate species will always be the ultimate guide to long-term success.

Grasses for Sun-baked, Dry, and Drought Situations

By far the greatest number of grasses come from open, sunny, if not outrightly dry and drought-prone natural areas—so there is a significant number of grasses from which to choose for varying degrees of dryness and drought.

Drought and sun-baked conditions can be found from the harsh, arid desert of Death Valley in California to the beaches and dunes of mild, maritime England. What these environments share is a shortage of water for at least part of the year. Combined with high summer temperatures, drying winds, and often gravelly well-drained soils, such conditions will literally cook all but the most resilient of plants.

Under drought conditions, most plants will show signs of short-term stress by visibly wilting, especially those with large leaves such as *Hosta* and *Ligularia*. Grasses can be tough customers under such short-term stress, appearing hardly to notice the lack of moisture, though many will eventually roll or curl their leaves until sufficient moisture returns, so that they present less surface area to the daytime sun. For grasses that have specialized in extreme conditions like the beach grasses—the marram, *Ammophila*, or wild rye, *Leymus*—adaptations such as tough, waxy leaves and a questing root system allow them to survive and indeed, to thrive where few others can follow. Where prolonged summer droughts are a regular feature, such as in the Mediterranean, many grasses in common with other regionally adapted plants will go into summer dormancy, shutting down active growth during the hottest and driest months of the year, and starting back with the arrival of autumn rains. These include *Aristida*, *Bouteloua*, *Melica*, and *Nassella*. In even drier, desert-like conditions, where water is an unreliable and occasional luxury, grasses will remain in active growth only while there is sufficient moisture in the ground.

For the gardener, such drought adaptation can also be marked out by the presence of grey or blue foliage. *Elymus*, *Festuca*, *Helictotrichon*, *Leymus*, *Poa*, and *Sesleria* are all drought-tolerant grasses that have this signature blue-tinted foliage, which of itself has an ornamental quality much prized by gardeners, and these can be grown easily in most sunny, dry soils.

For warm climates, *Leymus condensatus*, especially in its superb form 'Canyon Prince', is perhaps unrivalled for spreading clumps of comparatively wide icy blue foliage, especially when topped by its magnificent flowers. For cooler climates, *Leymus arenarius* will contribute something very similar in effect.

Festuca is a broad and adaptable family with almost hair-like narrow leaves that may offer the greatest number of different cultivars, including numerous forms deriving from *Festuca glauca*. Of these, 'Elijah Blue' and 'Intense Blue' are perhaps among the most reliable performers. As all *Festuca* seed readily, it is important to choose cultivated selections from a reliable source, as so often inferior seedlings have

On the beach at Poole, Dorset, England, the native lyme grass, *Leymus arenarius*, has to cope with a combination of full sun; reflected heat from the sand; frequent drying winds; and ultra-dry, continually shifting ground.

become mixed with the original cultivar material. The widespread, highly adaptable, and mostly longer-lived *Festuca rubra* has some wonderful offerings, including selections of steely blue-grey *Festuca* 'Molate' and the lighter blue-grey of *Festuca* 'Patrick's Point' from the United States. In the United Kingdom, *Festuca rubra* 'Blue Haze' is a recent selection with soft blue foliage.

Happy in a range of climates, *Sesleria* is a highly adaptable and beautiful grass which offers some blue-foliaged choices. Well known for its dainty white flowers in spring, *Sesleria nitida* has stiff leaves of a powdery blue. *Sesleria caerulea* slowly forms tight mounds of evergreen bicoloured green and blue-grey leaves, as does a slightly taller selection from the United Kingdom, *Sesleria* 'Spring Dream'. A recent Californian selection, *Sesleria* 'Campo Azul', produces soft mounds of amazing blue-toned foliage.

Finally, the clump-forming *Poa labillardierei* (highlighted in previous chapter) offers mounds of hazy soft blue foliage, and even flowers of a similar shade, that gently cascade from the centre of the plant.

It should be noted that garden conditions in urban areas can present a similar set of challenges, whether small domestic gardens, roof terraces, or even in those areas that surround commercial buildings and public areas in towns and cities. Growing conditions in these places can be just as trying for plants as any natural environment. Hard, paved surfaces such as roads, parking areas, roofs, and walls all contribute to the creation of heat islands. Heat from the sun is reflected and radiated by these hard surfaces, which simultaneously prevent much-needed water from reaching and replenishing the ground. The result is a continually warm environment that is short on water—for all intents and purposes, a desert.

ARID AND DRY

Well known for its hot, dry desert location, Las Vegas, Nevada uses drought-adapted grasses to great effect. From massed plantings of *Muhlenbergia capillaris* framing architecturally distinctive buildings to *Pennisetum* 'Fairy Tails' surrounding an upscale shopping mall, a simple but refined palette of grasses provides an effective, visually pleasing solution to this city's hot, dry environments.

Muhlenbergia is a graceful and elegant group well adapted to arid and desert conditions, and can offer superb practical choices for gardens in warm and dry environments. At the Desert Botanical Garden in Arizona, for example, *Muhlenbergia capillaris* appears perfectly happy in these conditions. Other members of the family include tall *Muhlenbergia rigens* with its and architectural flower spikes, and *Muhlenbergia dubia*, which offers a similar effect at a lesser height. *Muhlenbergia rigida* produces masses of seductive soft pink flowers, while the bamboo-like woody stems and leaves of *Muhlenbergia dumosa* place it firmly in the top flight of all foliage plants in spite of its insignificant yellow flowers.

Death Valley in California has a deserved reputation for its very hot, very dry environment. Yet in one area, a colony of *Sporobolus airoides* exists seemingly in perfect harmony with its natural surroundings. Superbly adapted to this most arid place, it nonetheless performs well under more hospitable arid garden conditions such as at the Huntington Library, Art Museum, and Botanical Gardens outside Los Angeles.

TOP Large, simple blocks of grasses often work best when used in close association to large buildings, offering lightness and movement in clear contrast to impassive solidity. At a shopping mall in Las Vegas, Nevada, *Pennisetum* 'Fairy Tails' provides an almost perfect antidote to an overabundance of hard surfaces.

MIDDLE The pink muhly, *Muhlenbergia capillaris*, providing a river of fabulous flower that acts as a perfect foil for the impressive collection of cacti and succulents at the Desert Botanical Garden, Arizona.

LEFT Well adapted to its tough desert environment, *Sporobolus airoides* growing in the heart of Death Valley, California.

Sporobolus airoides in a sunny and dry position at the base of a building at the Huntington Library, Art Museum, and Botanical Gardens, California.

All fountain grasses, members of the *Pennisetum* family, revel in hot, high-sunshine areas to the extent that all demand excellent drainage and sun to grow successfully in gardens. Although the seeding potential of some, such as *Pennisetum setaceum*, is a concern in sensitive areas, there are some excellent gardenworthy forms for use in areas where this is not an issue. Pinks and whites are the flower colours favoured by fountain grasses, and these are produced in such profusion it is difficult not to be impressed by them. The foliage of fountains is not very exciting, with one or two exceptions, including *Pennisetum ×advena* 'Rubrum', whose purple foliage and long, arching flowers are exquisite; it is only hardy in warmer areas. *Pennisetum villosum* has large, fluffy, caterpillar-like white flowers that literally cascade down the light green foliage when in full flower, amply demonstrating how the common name arose. Although perhaps the least hardy of the commonly grown fountains in temperate climates, it adapts to many areas provided it has excellent drainage. *Pennisetum orientale* tends to have less vigour, but produces a

large number of delicate pink flowers in a noticeably rounded outline, and is the parent of several different worthwhile hybrids and cultivars. Two are the rather taller and more upright 'Karley Rose', whose flowers are a comparatively strong pink, and 'Shogun', with slightly softer pink flowers set off perfectly by grey-green leaves.

Pennisetum alopecuroides has given rise to many worthwhile garden cultivars so that, while the species itself can flower poorly in cooler, more maritime climates, its cultivars will perform admirably in sunny positions on well-drained soils. 'Hameln' is perhaps one of the oldest, but useful for its distinct rounded outline of foliage that is quite literally covered in small but generously produced flowers. 'Red Head' has large, dark flowers that are initially quite red, while 'Dark Desire' has almost-black cylindrical flower heads of similar size that demand attention.

SUN-BAKED AND DRY

While aridity and dryness are major limiting factors in warm climates, those areas which have the benefit of higher rainfall and cooler summer temperatures may regard such limitations as advantages. Dry, well-drained soils that provide comparatively dry conditions for roots during an otherwise wet and cold winter period will frequently make the difference between success and failure for many plants, including sun-loving grasses accustomed to warmer, drier environments. *Bothriochloa*, *Pennisetum*, *Poa*, and *Stipa* are just some of the grasses that revel in relatively hot, dry, and sunny conditions but can be grown successfully in cooler, more mild climates if given full sun and well-drained soils.

For example, although the garden at Knoll is in southern England, it forms part of a local frost pocket with poor air drainage, and at just 20 m (60 ft.) above sea level, records temperatures at least as low as -12°C (10°F) during an average winter. However, as the garden consists almost exclusively of a fine, sandy soil, most of that soil—and therefore the plants' roots—remains comparatively dry during these low

TOP Urban conditions with an excess of paving and hard surfaces create heat islands that reflect light and heat while also repelling water, mimicking harsh, arid conditions for plants. Fountain grasses such as the near-sterile *Pennisetum* ×*advena* 'Rubrum' are well adapted to such extremes, and make excellent choices in such conditions.

ABOVE In less arid environments such as the Gravel Garden at Knoll Gardens, *Pennisetum alopecuroides* 'Dark Desire' grows happily in the dry and sunny conditions with little additional water.

Springtime in the Gravel Garden at Knoll sees *Poa* and *Festuca* among the lush foliage of other early season plants before summertime dryness takes hold.

temperatures. As the combination of moisture and low temperatures causes the majority of damage to plants, this soil allows us to grow many plants that might not otherwise survive, including grasses. We can therefore enjoy the bright pink flowers of *Bothriochloa bladhii*; the amazing cascade of narrow flower spikes from *Muhlenbergia rigens*; the gold, braid-like nodding flowers of the unequalled *Miscanthus nepalensis*; and the simply stunning masses of white flowers produced by *Stipa ichu* (syn. *Jarava ichu*) with only occasional losses in more exceptional circumstances.

In heavier soils, where winter wet may limit the use of dry- and drought-loving grasses, the addition of grit and gravel is often recommended to open up and improve drainage and help dry out the soil. However, a more satisfactory technique is to raise the planting area by adding soil and organic matter, or to reshape and regrade, to provide a planting area that is at least 15 cm (6 in.) or so above the surrounding area. This will allow moisture to drain away from roots and crowns of plants, which will considerably enhance the chance of successful cultivation.

TOP The gravel garden at Beth Chatto Gardens, Essex, England combines aesthetics with horticultural experiment. Planted on dry, gravelly soil in an area prone to low rainfall, this garden is never irrigated; chosen plants survive whatever the prevailing weather conditions. Drought-loving grasses such as Spanish oat grass, *Stipa gigantea*, appear to thrive in these testing conditions.

ABOVE Gravel can be a practical, effective, long-lasting substitute for lawn grass, especially in arid areas where the high cost of watering such a sward is environmentally unsound. The shaggy outline of groups of deer grass, *Muhlenbergia rigens*, provides a fine contrast to the relative flatness of the surrounding surface even before they begin to flower.

GRAVEL GARDENS

Gravel gardens are popular and practical in dry areas that are mostly open to full sun. On a basic level, they consist of a decorative layer of gravel, or other similar natural stone material, extended to cover the surface of an area through which plants are grown. The depth can vary from 2.5 to 7.5 cm (1–3 in.), and this technique works well on relatively large areas as a cost-effective substitute for high-maintenance turfgrass or other high water-use plantings. Using an ornamental finish in this way can allow for greater spacing between individuals and groups of plants than would otherwise be acceptable.

In less arid areas, gravel gardens combine free-draining soils, full sun exposure, and low rainfall with drought-tolerant plants, drawing inspiration from naturally occurring drought-prone communities. For example, Beth Chatto's famous Gravel Garden in Essex, England is described as a horticultural experiment; based on dry, poor soils in an already dry, low-rainfall area, plants have been chosen for their ability to withstand prolonged periods of drought, as this part of the garden is never watered. Even in these very dry conditions, drought-loving grasses such as *Ampelodesmos mauritanicus*, *Stipa gigantea*, and *Nassella tenuissima* all thrive—and are arguably at their best when conditions are driest.

Attention to surface detail can add greatly to the aesthetic value of mulch in gravel gardens. While evenly sized gravel is most common, the use of different sizes and colours of material—from thimbles through to large boulders—creates an extra level of interest. The use of locally sourced materials can add significantly to the sense of place, helping to relate the garden to the surrounding environment. A further refinement of this style involves the use of reclaimed materials such as crushed brick or rubble, which not only provides an excellent foil for plants, but is also practical and reuses existing materials.

SUMMER DORMANCY

Summer dormancy in warm climates is an entirely natural response to prevailing conditions, just as winter dormancy is in cooler areas. While summer dormancy is perhaps something of an acquired taste for gardeners accustomed to green summer landscapes, it is an acceptable aesthetic in its own right. Allowing grasses and other plants to follow their customary natural pattern under garden situations offers a more genuine approach to sustainable gardening that links the right plant with the right place. Summer dormancy in the warm, dry climate of much of California is the

At the Natural History Museum of Los Angeles County, a collection of native plants is allowed go into summer dormancy as a practical example of an alternative aesthetic to water-heavy, summer green landscapes.

Right Grass, Right Place

In the Dry Garden at RHS Garden Hyde Hall in Essex, England, grasses such as **Nassella**, **Stipa**, and **Calamagrostis** have to contend with near constant wind and dry, sun-baked soil on a windy, exposed hilltop in this already-dry region.

natural state for most grassy landscapes; at the Natural History Museum of Los Angeles County, a native plant garden is allowed to follow this natural cycle, and offers a pleasing and environmentally conscious aesthetic.

Under controlled garden conditions, water is frequently available through irrigation, though the indiscriminate use of this finite and precious resource is increasingly, and correctly, coming into question. Even in the most arid of conditions, using drought-adapted grasses can significantly reduce the quantity and regularity of additional water that is needed to keep the plants alive. Embracing summer dormancy as an acceptable, even desirable aesthetic in areas where it is a natural occurrence seems a highly sensible way to conserve water where it is most precious.

Truly summer-dormant grasses, such as many needle grasses, *Nassella*, can find it hard to adapt to conditions where a plentiful supply of water avoids the necessity of a summer closedown. *Nassella cernua*, *Nassella lepida*, and *Nassella pulchra* are all exceptionally beautiful when in green and active growth, but offer just as much (if in a more restrained way) in their dried state. For such highly adapted grasses, excessive summer moisture can indeed have deadly consequences. Contrastingly, there are others like the alkali sacaton, *Sporobolus airoides*, that are quite beautiful if allowed to go into summer dormancy, but can also tolerate summer water.

Top Choices for Sun-baked, Dry, and Drought Situations

These grasses generally thrive in drought, but not all will be appropriate or hardy in every climate, and choices should always be cross-referenced with local conditions.

- Achnatherum
- Ammophila
- Ampelodesmos
- Aristida
- Bothriochloa
- Bouteloua
- Calamagrostis
- Elymus
- Eragrostis
- Festuca
- Helictotrichon
- Leymus
- Muhlenbergia
- Nassella
- Panicum
- Pennisetum
- Poa
- Sesleria
- Sporobolus
- Stipa

Grasses for Woodland and Shade

Shade is not the natural setting for most true grasses. Yet shade is found in just about every garden, with dry shade under trees in particular widely regarded as the most difficult of cultural conditions under which to plant successfully.

True grasses, which mostly have their origins in open, sunlit areas, are generally least able to cope with shady conditions found in gardens, though there are a few notable exceptions such as *Hakonechloa macra*, *Chasmanthium latifolium*, and *Calamagrostis brachytricha*. Occurring naturally in shady woodland areas, the wild oat or spangle grass, *Chasmanthium*

Korean feather grass, *Calamagrostis brachytricha*, is one of the few true grasses that can grow well in dry, shady conditions, as seen here at Knoll Gardens, Dorset, England.

latifolium, translates easily into a wide range of shady garden situations, while *Calamagrostis brachytricha* can be fairly happy in quite dry and shady conditions.

What will actually grow where depends very much on how much light and moisture is available. While confirmed sun-worshippers such as *Pennisetum* and *Stipa* are unlikely to approve of anything other than a sunny open spot, the light levels encountered in, say, Mediterranean areas will allow a greater tolerance from a larger number of grasses than would be possible in colder and less sunny climates. For example, in the comparatively warm and dry climate of California, sun-loving *Helictotrichon*, *Sesleria*, and *Festuca* can be found happily ensconced in still very dry, but far more shady conditions than they could possibly tolerate in areas of lower light and heat.

As a general rule, shade is very much the province of the grass allies, those plants that are not botanically grasses but have a superficial resemblance in one way or another to the grass family. Generally characterized by comparatively compact evergreen foliage, as well as flowers that are outshone by their foliage, the main families include *Carex*, *Luzula*, and *Ophiopogon*.

Though slow-to-establish *Ophiopogon* provides an understated elegance in even the toughest of conditions, its neat evergreen foliage seems impervious to the degree of shade or dryness of soil. Among the most popular of these grass-like plants is the black mondo grass, *Ophiopogon planiscapus* 'Kokuryu' ('Nigrescens'),

TOP Hakone grasses all do well in sun or a reasonable amount of shade. At the base of a paperbark mulberry, *Hakonechloa macra* 'Aureola' makes graceful, weed-proof, long-lasting cover in light but dry shade at Knoll Gardens, Dorset, England.

MIDDLE *Hakonechloa macra* revels in dry soils, such as at the base of large shrubs, and makes impressive, durable, and very beautiful mounds of elegantly narrow green leaves.

LEFT Wild oat, *Chasmanthium latifolium*, is one of the comparatively few true grasses that come from woodland conditions. With wide, light green leaves and an upright habit, and producing masses of distinctive flattened flowers, it is very effective in open or shady spots in gardens.

which seems equally happy in sun or shade. Its foliage is about the closest to pure black available in the plant world, and it has tiny, bluish-white flowers, and occasional fruits nearly the same colour as the foliage. The best performer for shade is the more infrequently seen green form, *Ophiopogon planiscapus*,

RIGHT In warmer climates that benefit from higher light levels, such as at the Natural History Museum of Los Angeles County in California, plants like *Festuca rubra* 'Patrick's Point' and *Sesleria autumnalis* will be successful in more shade than would be possible in cooler areas with lower light levels.

BELOW Sun-loving, drought-tolerant, blue-foliaged grasses such as *Helictotrichon sempervirens*, *Festuca*, and *Sesleria* grow happily in the very dry and comparatively shady conditions to be found in the Mediterranean climate of Dave and Rainie Fross' garden in Arroyo Grande, California.

which has tighter clumps of foliage that hardly (if ever) need attention, so that it comes as close to maintenance-free as any plant can. Some years ago at Knoll, we planted narrow drifts of *Ophiopogon planiscapus* at what was then the edge of a large silver maple's leaf canopy. As the tree has grown, so the *Ophiopogon* has continued to grow and flourish in the dry, rooty shade, and has yet to require any maintenance other than occasional raking of fallen leaves from the maple.

Carex, the sedges, are such a large and adaptable group that they can be difficult to characterize. They frequently inhabit various levels of damp to wet soils, and can be found growing in quite dense shade to open sun, but can also be found in very dry places. They can be clump forming, or they can have a running nature. They are frequently but not exclusively evergreen. And they tend to be foliage- rather than flower-based garden choices, though again, there are exceptions. With such a valuable set of characteristics, sedges can form a major constituent of meadows and open, grassy spaces, sometimes in association with grasses, but frequently taking over the role of grass-like groundcover where true grasses might find conditions not to their liking. *Carex pensylvanica*, for example, in its native woodland setting will create a relatively even green sward that will cover significant areas in generally shady and dry environments, sometimes wet. Other North American woodland species that translate to broadly similar environments in a garden setting include *Carex laxiculmis* and *Carex flaccosperma*, both with rather wide blue-green leaves. Like many of its family, the palm sedge, *Carex muskingumensis*, is found in moist soils in its native North America, but it is also fairly drought tolerant, and this ability to adapt has seen it widely planted in European and American gardens.

In testing dry shade conditions within the canopy of mature trees at Knoll Gardens, England, the evergreen mondo grass, *Ophiopogon planiscapus*, gradually makes a dense carpet of dark green strap-like foliage that needs virtually no aftercare.

Right Grass, Right Place

A Japanese mound-forming species inhabiting dry wooded areas, *Carex oshimensis* is credited with many of the modern foliage-based selections freely available today. All make mostly trouble-free garden plants, and while happy in sun, they are especially useful in open shade, where conditions are dry or with some moisture. *Carex oshimensis* 'Evergold' is one of the longest established, but many of the newer selections also have merit. 'Everlime', 'Everest', 'Everglow', 'Everillo', and 'Evercream' are all deservedly popular and offer an impressive variation of foliage colours.

Shade itself can come in many different forms. It ranges from the light, open shade cast by fence line or single-story building; deepening levels and rain shadow in the lee of larger buildings and distant woody plants; to the severely limiting dry and dark conditions found under the canopies of established trees and within reach of their questing root systems. Damp shade, on the other hand, can offer soils that are either constantly wet or periodically wet and dry depending on the season. Plants that have learned to cope with such difficult conditions in nature usually prove to be highly adaptable to similar garden environments.

OPEN SHADE

The comparatively open shade cast by fences, buildings, and other non-living objects is often easier to accommodate as there are no moisture-sucking root systems from trees or shrubs with which new plants have to contend. What's more, while direct access to the sun may be physically denied, the surrounding area can still be relatively open so that light levels are frequently sufficient to sustain a wide range of plant growth. In such situations, not only will the

TOP Often found in relatively moist habitats, *Carex muskingumensis* translates easily to shady, dry conditions in cultivation.

MIDDLE *Carex pensylvanica* will carpet large areas in dry and shady conditions that true grasses find difficult to colonize.

LEFT *Carex divulsa* translates well to the testing, sometimes dry and shady city environments that can mirror the sedge's native habitat.

Nearly all *Miscanthus* grow best in open positions away from the root systems of woody plants, and where sunlight levels are sufficient to stimulate effective flowering. However, some of the more compact Yakushima Dwarf selections such as these Miscanthus 'Starlight' at Knoll Gardens, Dorset, England appear reasonably happy with open shade.

shade-tolerant grasses and allies such as *Chasmanthium*, *Carex*, *Luzula*, and *Melica* do well, but some of the main groups of grasses such as *Calamagrostis*, *Deschampsia*, *Miscanthus*, *Molinia*, and *Sesleria* may also find sufficient light to grow successfully. In fact, *Miscanthus* such as the more compact selections of the Yakushima Dwarf group may be quite happy with a level of open shade. One such selection, *Miscanthus sinensis* 'Starlight', grows well at Knoll in the sun shadow of large shrubs, and while not cut off entirely from any direct sunshine, it contends successfully with dry soils and the established root systems of other plants.

Always adaptable, many forms of *Sesleria* will cope with some open shade, especially in warmer climates where light levels are higher. The two-tone blueish foliage of *Sesleria caerulea* will be happy in such conditions, and while *Seleria autumnalis* may not take on such intense golden yellow hues as it does in sun, it will still perform well in open shade, as will *Sesleria* 'Greenlee Hybrid', *Sesleria argentea*, and *Sesleria* 'Campo Verde'.

Right Grass, Right Place

DRY SHADE

Shade cast by established trees and shrubs is the most difficult in which to plant successfully, whether with grasses or other plants. This is because the lack of light is combined with extreme dryness at the root, usually during the active growing period when moisture is needed.

Under deciduous trees and shrubs, there can often be adequate moisture in the spring period, after winter rains occur and before trees leaf out. Spring-flowering bulbs take advantage of this period to flower, and then close down as woody plants wake up and soil starts to dry out. Several grasses have copied this strategy, including the wood melics, *Melica*, and wood millets, *Milium*, which are at their best before the dry summer period, when they also close down until the return of wetter winter conditions.

One of the toughest sedges for dry shady conditions is *Carex morrowii* 'Ice Dance', which gradually forms spreading mats of dense, weed-proof, durable cover comprised of creamy white-striped green leaves that appear entirely indifferent to dryness and lack of sun. It is especially useful in spaces with severe competition from mature trees and shrubs, such as in public

RIGHT The green leaves and tiny, enthusiastically produced white flowers of *Melica uniflora* f. *albida* are a springtime favourite. It is happiest in very dry soils and various levels of shade, even within the canopy of larger woody plants.

BELOW The gradually spreading habit of *Carex* 'Ice Dance' makes it a practical and durable cover as part of a public planting in New York.

open spaces in New York City. Another more recent selection is *Carex morrowii* 'Vanilla Ice', which has much the same weed-smothering habit, but with a more noticeable soft yellow variegation that lightens up dark, austere places.

Where tree roots have not entirely taken over the soil, or under smaller or less established trees and shrubs, the hakone grasses, *Hakonechloa macra* and its cultivars, can make wonderful, long-lasting mounds of elongated, elegant foliage. Initially somewhat slow-growing, they are very long lived and durable once established. At Knoll, a most satisfying combination has resulted from planting *Hakonechloa macra* 'Aureola' in a 3–4 m (9–12 ft.) circle around the base of a paperbark mulberry. While not the deepest shade, the conditions of sandy soil and roots of the mulberry ensure frequent dryness during the summer months, which the hakone grass simply shrugs off. The combination of the grass and bark's textural qualities with the tree's leaves is as immensely satisfying as it is undemanding to maintain. 'Samurai', with its creamy white-striped leaves, behaves in a similar fashion, although the even slower-growing 'All Gold', while happy in open and generally dry shade, is not as durable as other forms under tough conditions.

Among the most useful spring flowerers is the snowy woodrush, *Luzula nivea*. Its tight mounds of green leaves are covered in soft white hairs and topped by the most subtly beautiful spikes of white or off-white flowers, at their best before soils become too dry. Amazingly adaptable, this woodrush will grow in reasonably open shade or sun, from almost boggy to fairly dry.

For conditions ranging from full sun to dry shade in dry soils, the pheasant grass, *Anemanthele lessoniana* (formerly *Stipa arundinacea*), is a most adaptable choice, very tough but also very beautiful and quick growing, if comparatively short-lived and disliking of wet soils. While its average lifespan may only be a few years, pheasant grass will, if happy, produce a fair amount of seed, so it is possible to establish a colony whereby as the older plants die away, they are replaced with younger seedlings.

ABOVE LEFT *Luzula nivea* or snowy woodrush is a rosette-forming plant producing masses of white flowers early in the season. Happiest where the soil is not too dry, its common name refers to the noticeable silvery hair on its younger leaves.

LEFT Pheasant grass is good for most levels of shade except in wet soils. *Anemanthele lessoniana* is fast growing, with rather wider than high mounds of evergreen leaves that, with enough light, are continually changing their colours from reds and oranges to greens and yellows. In the Fross garden in California, these well-spaced plants cope admirably with dry shady conditions.

DAMP SHADE

For rather wetter conditions in shade, the woodrushes are among the most reliable performers, seemingly adept at coping with seasonal variations of flood and drought that these particular areas frequently face. *Luzula acuminata* and *Luzula multiflora* are two North American species that excel in this respect. By and large, the woodrushes are not the most attention-grabbing of plants, but their ability to tolerate damp, wet, and sometimes dry conditions in shade makes them most useful for covering areas that other plants would find too extreme. *Luzula sylvatica*, for example, creates rosettes of green leaves that are truthfully not very exciting, but amazingly tough, and although the attractive variegation in the form 'Marginata' is delicate, the plant's ability to cover ground in tough conditions is almost unmatched. Several European selections have been chosen for their distinctive wide leaves, including 'Bromel'. The lighter forms such as 'Aurea' and 'Solar Flair' offer more interesting foliage. Especially vibrant in spring, their bright golden yellow leaves can light up the darkest of corners.

Arguably at its best with some moisture and shade, and especially in warmer climates, *Acorus gramineus* is a slow-growing, long-lived, grass-like plant that gradually produces mounds of elegant, slightly pendulous foliage in damp to wet soils in various levels of shade. While not the fastest to establish, it will make impressive cover in heavy soils and shade where few other grass-like plants would be happy. 'Ogon' and 'Variegatus' are two excellent selections that have withstood the test of time.

Luzula sylvatica 'Marginata' offers quietly attractive, gradually spreading mounds of ground-covering foliage that will survive where few other plants would be happy.

Top Choices for Shade

These grasses generally thrive in shade in the conditions listed, but not all will be appropriate or hardy in every climate, and as always, choices should be cross-referenced with local conditions.

OPEN SHADE

- Acorus
- Anemanthele
- Calamagrostis
- Carex
- Chasmanthium
- Deschampsia
- Elymus
- Hakonechloa
- Liriope
- Luzula
- Melica
- Milium
- Miscanthus, some, especially compact forms
- Molinia
- Ophiopogon
- Sesleria

DRY SHADE

- Anemanthele
- Carex
- Chasmanthium
- Hakonechloa
- Liriope
- Luzula
- Melica
- Milium
- Ophiopogon

DAMP SHADE

- Acorus
- Carex
- Luzula

Grasses for Wet and Waterside Positions

Most true grasses do not appreciate wet, boggy, watery conditions. The very demanding nature of some of the more watery environments has given rise to a specialized group of plants whose specific qualities have not always been appreciated by gardeners. In nature, the transition zone where the land meets water is in many ways a unique habitat. A brief look at any estuary or river mouth will show a mix of habitat from sandy beaches to boggy soils along with marshland, complete with plants that have adapted to cope with these conditions, as well as a whole ecosystem of associated wildlife evolved to thrive there. Often in a state of permanent flux, with the regular and sometimes rapid changing of water levels in times of flood or drought, the plants that have adapted to these marginal areas are mostly grass allies such as sedges, rushes, and reeds.

Comparatively few true grasses have adapted to really wet environments, though the so-called common reed, *Phragmites australis*, is one very notable exception, covering vast areas of land and water's edge with equal facility. Like the common reed, all such

truly adapted grasses—and grass-like plants such as *Glyceria*, *Juncus*, and *Schoenoplectus*—have a running rootstock that can move swiftly in order to survive in the constantly changing conditions of their natural homes. However, this strategy can make them less than welcome in the more controlled conditions of the average garden, unless they are used in wet environments such as stream sides, boggy areas, or lakes and ponds.

For practical purposes, grasses that can tolerate wet soils could be placed in one of two broad categories: those that prefer to paddle and those that don't mind swimming. Paddlers are those grasses able to thrive with a fair amount of moisture in the ground for extended periods. While they tolerate heavy soils that are often waterlogged, on the whole they prefer solid ground. Swimmers, on the other hand, will be happy in permanently wet soil to almost open water conditions. By definition, most swimmers also make happy if enthusiastic paddlers.

Several moisture-lovers such as *Juncus*, *Luzula*, and various species and cultivars of *Carex* are recommended for being able to cope with rather dry and shady conditions, which initially appears as something of a contradiction considering their native habitats. But most wet soils in various situations can become drier—and sometimes even dry out completely—as

TOP Vast areas of river mouths, wetlands, lakes, estuaries, and open water play host to a relatively small number of species, such as reeds and rushes. These thrive in wet conditions, from stagnant to fast flowing, that are permanently in limbo; somewhere between solid ground and open water.

ABOVE *Deschampsia cespitosa*, *Carex divulsa*, and *Luzula nivea* are among the several grasses and sedges that will easily tolerate various levels of soil moisture in gardens, ranging from very wet to very dry.

part of an annual cycle, and as a result many damp-loving plants have had to adapt to occasional extended periods of drought. This has led to great success with such plants in rain gardens (see next chapter), and other stormwater management systems, where the sometimes wet, sometimes dry cultural conditions mirror that of their native habitats.

Right Grass, Right Place

PADDLERS

Many of these plants can be perfectly happy as paddlers: sedges such as *Carex stricta*; cotton grasses such as *Eriophorum angustifolium*; moor grasses such as *Molinia caerulea*; feather reed grasses such as *Calamagrostis epigejos*; as well as *Deschampsia*, *Glyceria*, and *Juncus*. They grow primarily in soil rather than water, but are at home in a range of soil conditions, from sometimes dry, to damp, to wet, to waterlogged.

In the inspirational gardens of Beth Chatto at Elmstead Market in England, the waterside plantings include *Carex elata* 'Aurea', which is a native selection that is happy in marginal conditions, and also *Miscanthus sinensis* 'Zebrinus'. Planted just a little further away from the usual water level, the *Miscanthus* no doubt draws on the relatively high water table and perhaps copes with occasional flooding, but nonetheless remains on comparatively solid ground.

Over a period of time, some sedges that are adapted to swamps, river banks, and other areas subject to occasional or regular flooding will develop a trunk of old root and stem that can make an attractive feature quite apart from the qualities of the actual foliage. These include the North American *Carex stricta*, European *Carex paniculata*, and Australasian *Carex secta*.

Common cotton grass, *Eriophorum angustifolium*, thrives in the open yet boggy conditions of a nature reserve a short distance across open water from the busy urban centre of Poole, Dorset, England.

ABOVE At the Beth Chatto Gardens, Essex, England, *Miscanthus* 'Zebrinus' and *Carex elata* 'Aurea' are used in successful association with moisture-loving plants such as *Gunnera*, *Iris*, and *Eupatorium*, which are happy in the usually damp soils at the water's edge.

LEFT Some larger sedges to be found at the water's edge such as *Carex paniculata*, *Carex stricta*, and *Carex secta* gradually produce ornate stacks of old roots and stems that can be an ornamental feature in their own right.

NATIVE TOLERANCES

Given grasses' wide range of tolerance and adaptability, it is also quite possible to find some among the true grasses, like *Molinia* and *Panicum*, growing in very wet soils, including heavy clay, and right up to the edge of open water. A grass is usually most tolerant within its native habitat, and may consequently be less forgiving when used as an exotic in a garden or designed space. For example, the prairie switch grass, *Panicum virgatum*, is tolerant of wet conditions, and can be found growing with its feet in water in the New Jersey Pine Barrens, where it is locally native—but is unlikely to be as tolerant in the maritime conditions of Europe and the United Kingdom. The European *Molinia caerulea* exhibits a similarly wide range of tolerance within its native areas and can be seen, for example, growing perfectly happily in soils that are summer dry and extremely wet in winter on Ferndown Common, Dorset, England. This ability to tolerate a wide variation of cultural conditions can make regionally adapted native grasses a very practical choice for garden use.

SWIMMERS

The swimmers include reeds and rushes such as *Juncus*, *Phragmites*, *Typha*, and *Schoenoplectus*, whose strong, mobile root systems are equally at home in solid ground but have evolved to deal successfully with the shifting ground, or lack of it, in a watery environment. Their ability to travel over such a variety of conditions gives many coastal and lakeside areas their characteristic look and feel, and is the prime reason for their successful and increasing use in stabilization and erosion control projects. While some, such as *Phragmites australis*—even in its comparatively restrained variegated form *Phragmites australis* 'Variegata'—will not be suitable for smaller gardens, several make the perfect accent in ponds and smaller water features. These species also come in comparatively restrained ornamental forms, such as *Schoenoplectus lacustris* subsp. *tabernaemontani* 'Albescens', with its unique light green and cream longitudinal stripes on brittle rounded stems. For a still bulky but more controllable plant, the attractively variegated *Spartina pectinata* 'Aureomarginata' is a good choice to associate with other moisture-loving garden perennials such as *Eupatorium*, *Lythrum*, and *Filipendula*. Some species of land-based *Carex*, such as *C. riparia* and *C. stricta*, can also be found in virtual open water in native habitats.

ABOVE LEFT In the Pine Barrens of New Jersey, the adaptable native switch grass, *Panicum virgatum*, even appears happy with its feet in water.

LEFT *Panicum virgatum*, the prairie switch grass, has a wide-ranging tolerance of conditions from drought to water's edge. With the latter, its stout root system can help prevent erosion, as with this practical, ornamental planting on the lake edge at Chicago Botanic Garden, Illinois.

Used historically for matting and thatching, the common club rush, *Schoenoplectus tabenaemontani*, makes dense colonies in rivers and open water, providing cover and forage for wildlife as well as an ornamental feature for the local human population in Wimborne, Dorset, England.

Top Choices for Wet and Waterside Positions

These grasses generally thrive in the wet conditions listed. Not all will be appropriate or hardy in every climate, and choices always should be cross-referenced with local conditions.

PADDLERS
- *Carex*
- *Cyperus*
- *Deschampsia*
- *Eriophorum*
- *Juncus*
- *Luzula*
- *Miscanthus*
- *Molinia*
- *Phalaris*
- *Rhynchospora*

SWIMMERS
- *Arundo*
- *Carex*
- *Cyperus*
- *Glyceria*
- *Juncus*
- *Phragmites*
- *Schoenoplectus*
- *Spartina*

Grasses for Pots and Containers

Easy to grow on the whole, grasses are no less obliging when grown in containers, provided their basic needs such as water, light, and adequate root run are met. Indeed, for many gardeners, some of the slower-to-establish grasses perform better in pots than in open ground, at least in their early years. One example is Japanese blood grass, *Imperata* 'Rubra', which can be very slow to establish in open ground; in its native Japan, it has been grown for many decades in shallow dishes as a companion to bonsai.

In many respects, container-grown grasses demand the same considerations as other container-grown plants. Drought-loving grasses may tolerate a little less water than moisture-lovers, and those slower growers like the hakone grass, *Hakonechloa macra* and its forms, will survive happily for longer without being repotted. However, attention to irrigation, pot size, and growing medium is necessary for successful container growing. A key element is the size of the container in relation to the plants to be grown in them. The greater the volume of soil that the pot holds, then the better the root system, and so ultimately the better the final plant growth will be. By definition,

RIGHT An eclectic mix of grasses in containers creates a constantly varying scene as part of an outdoor seating area at Knoll Gardens, Dorset, England.

BELOW Long-lived but slower-growing grasses such as *Hakonechloa* 'Aureola' (shown here) and *Imperata* 'Rubra' can be happy in containers for several years without the need for repotting.

due to the restricted root run of all but the largest containers, it is unlikely that many grasses will attain their full height, and this applies especially to the tall deciduous grasses such as *Miscanthus*, *Arundo*, and *Panicum*.

Some grasses that are grown primarily for their foliage are especially effective in taller containers, as this allows the foliage to gradually trail downwards and develop a more pendulous habit than the grasses would manage planted in the ground. For example, the purple-tinged foliage of *Eragrostis* 'Totnes Burgundy' deepens in colour as the season progresses, and if grown in a sufficiently tall container, it gradually develops a distinct weeping habit that is quite special. The flowers of this wonderful form, especially when grown in pots, can distract from the foliage, and are often best removed for maximum impact.

Certain evergreen sedges can also develop this habit. For instance, the tan-coloured leaves of *Carex testacea* seem to extend much further than their normal length when given the opportunity. Generally the evergreen sedges make good container plants, as their compact habit and relatively slow-growing nature allow them to be happy in pots for a number of years with minimum care. The various foliage-based forms of *Carex oshimensis*, such as 'Everillo', Everglow', and 'Everlime' excel in this respect.

A collection of plants in containers, whether entirely grasses or a mix of plants in differing shapes and sizes, can make for a satisfying display in a relatively limited space over a long period of time. Individual containers can be rearranged or replaced,

ABOVE Given the opportunity in a tall pot, the foliage of *Eragrostis* 'Totnes Burgundy' gradually extends down towards the ground.

MIDDLE A strong linear outline allows grasses to contrast effectively with any more solid surface, especially those made from a natural material. Tall, elegant containers allow certain grasses to display traits that would be lost at ground level, such as *Carex testacea* with its bronzed evergreen foliage that appears to gradually creep ever downwards.

LEFT *Muhlenbergia dumosa* can make a most gorgeous, soft, and tactile container plant.

allowing for a constantly changing matrix of flower and form to delight and refresh the senses.

Grown in containers that can be moved at short notice, grasses which are borderline or distinctly non-hardy for the area where they are growing can be more easily protected from frost, so that plants are kept warm and/or dry as required during the colder months. For example, *Pennisetum ×advena* 'Rubrum', and *Muhlenbergia dumosa* are two architectural grasses that can be grown successfully in cooler climates using containers.

On hard surfaces where soil or space is lacking like terraces close to the house, roof gardens, or balconies, the thoughtful use of containers is a successful way to provide a home for plants. And with a little ingenuity, the containers can be as interesting as the plants themselves. Whether of horticultural origin or not, any suitable receptacle can be pressed into service as long as it will hold growing medium and allow water to drain.

Containers made of wood, stone, or other natural material usually make the most satisfying associations with plants, particularly with the strong linear outline of grasses. The simpler geometric outlines of circles and squares combined with finishes that develop an ever-changing patina with increasing age—rusty metal for example—provide perhaps the greatest satisfaction in terms of contrast between plant and container.

In the relatively austere, even harsh, surroundings of a busy San Francisco street, the repeated use of *Acorus* 'Ogon' in containers brings a welcome respite to the eye weary of concrete and paving.

ABOVE Most grasses with fibrous root systems are happy in containers provided they are watered when dry and repotted when needed. Container growing is also an excellent, easy way of growing plants in areas that might otherwise be considered at risk if grown in the open ground, such as this *Stipa ichu* forming part of the entrance container display at Knoll Gardens, Dorset, England.

RIGHT The strong linear outline of most grasses contrasts effectively with more solid objects, especially when made of natural materials such as terracotta pots and wood. The association is no less effective, even through the quieter but no less important winter period.

Top Choices for Pots and Containers

Virtually all grasses work well in pots, but several stand out as especially suitable. While container-grown grasses may be more forgiving of inhospitable climatic conditions, some may struggle nonetheless. As always, knowledge of local conditions is key.

- *Anemanthele*
- *Carex*
- *Cyperus*
- *Eragrostis*
- *Festuca*
- *Hakonechloa*
- *Imperata*
- *Miscanthus*
- *Muhlenbergia*
- *Pennisetum*
- *Stipa*

Using Natives in Our Landscapes

Historically, gardening literature and even culture is littered with references to native plants as weeds, regardless of whether they are grasses or other plants. And it is possible to understand this long-established link between weeds and natives; historically, gardens were intentionally artificial creations filled with exotic introductions. Imposed on the natural landscape, these exotics necessarily displaced native species which were regarded simply as unwanted plants. As one of the most common groups of wild plants, grasses in particular have historically been removed in favour of non-natives.

These days, however, as we wake up to the true value of our natural systems and our collective impact on them, the definition of a weed is coming full circle to include many of those introduced exotic species—especially those that have aggressive tendencies to colonize, displace, or disrupt the original communities of plants. An old saying has it that 'a weed is a plant in the wrong place', and for all its simplicity, this has to remain among the most valid and accurate of gardening observations.

Grasses are present in just about every natural system in virtually every part of the world, and as such can adapt to as many differing garden conditions. While not all native grasses will have gardenworthy qualities, those that do offer an opportunity for gardeners to choose plants that have not only ornamental qualities but also a connection to the area of their intended use. What's more, where locally adapted native options exist, their use in our gardens lowers the risk of gardeners introducing exotic escapees (more weeds), simply as those plants will have already been present as natives.

Using suitable native grasses for their ornamental qualities in gardens offers several significant advantages, including reducing the risk of non-native garden escapes. For example, at Knoll Gardens in Dorset, England, two forms of the native *Molinia caerulea* make a most ornamental contribution while presenting negligible risk to the wider environment.

DEFINING NATIVE

At first glance, a native plant could simply be regarded as coming from a distinct geographical area—Europe, for example, or Germany more specifically—while 'exotic' or 'alien' would describe a plant that did not naturally occur in a given area, but had been introduced there, usually through human agency. A further category, that of a 'naturalized' species, describes an exotic that has been in its new home for sufficient time to be regarded, at least by some, as almost native.

However, given the vast areas, differing climates, and local conditions they describe, these broad terms can often be effectively meaningless and even counterproductive when it comes to the practice of garden-making and the process of choosing plants. For example, a grass may be said to be a European native, but this does not necessarily mean it is a native of the United Kingdom, and it is even less likely to be a native of a local, coast-adapted community, say, in the county of Cornwall. In his excellent and thought-provoking *Bringing Nature Home*, Douglas Tallamy offers a far more useable definition by suggesting that "a plant can only function as a true native while it is interacting with the community that historically helped shape it." Therefore, to be of greatest benefit to the wider environment, grasses and any other plants chosen should be locally native and form part of the relevant plant community.

Plants that are native to an area are often the best choices for specific tasks that mirror their natural surroundings. For example, the beach grass, *Ammophila arenaria*, is ideally suited to stabilizing dune banks or other areas prone to slip, as it is superbly adept at colonizing similar areas in its natural environment.

Wrong Grass, Wrong Place

When we accept the principle of 'right plant, right place', it is a short step to the appreciation that long-established native plants already thriving in a given area will be part of that local environment, and therefore make a sensible informed choice for garden use. Taking this principle one small step further, it follows that an introduced plant that has the ability to disrupt precious local systems is a clear example of the wrong plant in the wrong place: a weed.

Much of our built environment seems so far removed from original plant systems destroyed in the process of its construction that it is arguable whether the use of exotic plants has any less an environmental value than the original natives. In these situations, simply creating a functional environment with plants (be they native, non-native or a mix of both) has great value in combating environmental considerations such as heat islands, stormwater mismanagement, and air pollution—to say nothing of our simple human need for green space.

However, in other areas where natural systems still remain intact to any degree, the spread of invasive, non-native plants is a deeply serious issue. Our recent history is replete with examples of introduced plants escaping into native systems. Not all of those introduced plants have the capacity to become a major issue by any means, but many are causing disruption and damage. These introductions were sometimes undertaken for seemingly practical large-scale applications, or simply for the plant's ornamental value. Take, for example, the common reed, *Phragmites australis*, which has a worldwide distribution. As a hugely successful grass, it is of major wildlife value in all areas that it is a native. However, the European form was introduced into North America for various tasks such as erosion control, and has since been found to have negligible value in its new home. What is more, growing unchecked by its normal, natural controls, it is rapidly outcompeting the North American reed, and has become a serious invasive exotic. This in spite of the fact that in its original European home, that same reed has great wildlife value.

High on Figueroa Mountain, California, a meadow of *Elymus elymoides* successfully survives in an area of serpentine soil in which alien grasses originally introduced to improve grazing, and seen here covering the background slopes, have difficulty penetrating.

Vast expanses of locally native common reed, *Phragmites australis*, are positive havens for wildlife in the Neretva Delta in Croatia. This grass is also native to the U.S., and appears identical to the human eye; however, when the European version was imported to the U.S. and introduced in similar conditions, its wildlife value was found to be substantially less than its American counterpart. The European form has since become an invasive pest in those areas.

Pennisetum setaceum comes from warm climates, and has been introduced to many areas of the world as a pretty ornamental plant. To reseed, it requires a relatively warm environment, so in much of mainland Europe and the United Kingdom, for example, it does not survive winter—though with the continuing global rise in temperatures, it is difficult to forecast how this may alter that dynamic in the near future. It is a different story in warmer climates such as the Canary Islands or in Arizona, for example, where this grass has become a serious threat to native communities, and requires continued effort to control and remove it.

On the Pacific coast of California, pampas grass has escaped from gardens, and is rapidly invading and disrupting long-established coastal communities of native plants. It continues to spread in spite of significant efforts to remove it.

Pennisetum setaceum, though undoubtedly pretty in gardens, has escaped into the wider environment, and in warmer climates such as the delicate desert environment of Arizona, its ability to rapidly colonize new areas has seen it threaten native plant communities.

Environmentally Sensitive Plant Choice

- Gardens and built landscapes are an increasingly significant percentage of the planet's green space, and as environmentally aware gardeners, we should encourage a sensitivity to the wider environment and the collective effect of the plants we choose as individuals may have on it.

- Plant choice is not just a matter of personal preference. 'Right plant, right place' is as valid an ethos when applied to the wider environment as it is to the conditions of an individual garden.

- While an enduring approach to plant selection for our gardens has historically seen flower and colour as the governing factors, both our gardens and the environment in which they sit would benefit from a more considered, longer-term approach to the plants we use in our gardens.

- We should be aware of local conditions, consider the area in which the garden sits, and the risk our ornamental plant choices might pose to any sensitive areas nearby.

- There are few 'bad' plants, just bad positioning.

- We should take advantage of relevant resources such as botanic gardens, conservation bodies, and native plant organizations to gain the necessary information to make informed and sensitive plant selections.

A meadow approach to open green space surrounding the visitor centre at the Apple Campus, Cupertino, California sees the use of native *Carex praegracilis* to provide a resource-conscious and highly effective aesthetic.

Grasses for a Greener World

IT IS AN EXCITING TIME TO BE INVOLVED in horticulture as we come to understand more clearly how essential plants are in shaping and maintaining not only our gardens but also the wider environment. We have long appreciated the aesthetic beauty of flower and form, and perhaps now we are coming to an equal appreciation of other more practical qualities that plants, including grasses, have to offer us.

Lawn replacement, rain gardens, green roofs, erosion control, and habitat restoration can all be said to be practical, environmentally useful applications that may also be high in aesthetic value, both in the garden and wider landscape. While a detailed account of such processes is rather beyond the scope of this book, given the amazing versatility and adaptability that grasses exhibit, it will be no surprise to see them figure highly in these practical and often environmentally based horticultural applications, whatever the size of the project.

Don't Mow It—Grow It: the Alternative Approach to Lawn Culture

Found across many cultures and under most climatic conditions, lawns are among the most enduringly popular garden features. Traditional, high-quality lawns can be impressive. For instance, when surrounding historic buildings, they create a clear feeling of open space and provide easy access for foot traffic—though ironically, many of the best lawns prohibit foot traffic to preserve their pristine appearance and display them as horticultural showpieces. Regardless of quality, most lawns are very demanding in terms of time and resources needed to maintain them.

Alternatives to regularly cut grass swards are especially valuable when environmental or financial costs of maintaining the traditional lawn are unacceptably high, or where cultural factors such as deep shade or dry, arid conditions prohibit the successful establishment of a more traditional green sward.

Another powerful argument for an alternative approach comes from a purely aesthetic standpoint: there is little value in maintaining an unsatisfactory or

OPPOSITE AND ABOVE In the subtropical conditions of Tenerife, one of the Canary Isles, this lawn (above) prohibits foot traffic and needs regular watering and attention to maintain. By comparison, the carpet of sedge (opposite), *Carex pensylvanica*, is a naturally occurring 'lawn' that requires absolutely no maintenance.

average traditional lawn when a looser, less formal finish (often termed 'the meadow look') makes for a more stimulating feature with much less effort on the part of the gardener. Many unsatisfactory lawns probably linger today simply because their owners are unaware of the alternative possibilities.

Other than creating open space that is generally tolerant of foot traffic, the average traditional lawn can be said to serve little purpose, and offers poor value considering the level of attention and resources lawns demand. In mild and often wet conditions such as those found through much of the United Kingdom, the average lawn may only need cutting during the summer months, and possibly a few waterings if not left to go dormant in dry summers (which would lessen the need for regular mowing, if also lessening the aesthetic value). Though still performing no real function, such a lawn may be less burdensome than one in warmer, drier conditions in, say, southern California, where lawns require far more irrigation (and therefore mowing), in an area that is already short of precious water resources. While often serving little use from either a design or a practical viewpoint, collectively these traditional lawns consume a vast amount of resources in water, fuel, and time, which is becoming increasingly difficult to justify in a resource-conscious environment.

Replacing the mown lawn with a more relaxed meadow-style planting, selecting alternative species for an informal lawn or low meadow effect, or even adopting an altered maintenance regime for an existing sward will all reduce the use of precious resources while increasing the aesthetic and the wildlife value of the same space.

For a looser, meadow-style approach, simply swapping the usual lawn grasses with a locally appropriate mixture of generally low to mid-height grasses and sedges creates an open, grassy place—a meadow—which, together with bulbs and perennials, can become a sensory delight, a home for wildlife, and an exciting place for play or simply passing through. On a larger, public scale, and perhaps especially in water-conscious climates, such meadows offer a significant saving on precious resources while achieving a vastly improved aesthetic. Even on a small scale, such an approach can turn a staid patch of lawn grass into something infinitely more dynamic and resource friendly.

LEFT Although a beautiful flowering plant, *Bouteloua gracilis*, can also be used as a low-water lawn replacement that requires relatively infrequent trimming, as seen here at the Santa Barbara Botanic Garden in California.

BELOW Where the open green space does not necessarily require frequent access, a variety of low to mid-height grasses can recreate an open, grassy feel at a fraction of the maintenance cost. In this Californian housing development, the lawn-based ethos has been replaced with a softer and more resource-conscious approach using a mix of grasses.

Where a more restrained feel might be desired, the best choice for an informal lawn or low meadow may not be true grasses, but sedges. Suitable *Carex* are characterized as generally compact and evergreen. Those with spreading rootstocks that can effectively renew themselves to maintain a good, even cover, much like typical lawn grass, prove to be excellent alternatives to those more traditional lawn species.

A good example is the western meadow sedge, *Carex praegracilis*. Native to a large part of the western United States in a range of situations from coastal sand dunes to inland meadows, this plant is grown successfully in many areas across its native country. Like other forms of *Carex*, this spreading sedge makes dense cover, remains green with enough water, and eventually goes summer dormant in prolonged drought. Its adaptability has seen its use in many private gardens where it can be cut on a regular basis,

TOP AND ABOVE Western meadow sedge, *Carex praegracilis*, has a well-established reputation as a successful lawn substitute. Native to much of western United States in a variety of conditions, its durable nature and spreading rootstock allow it to adapt well to the sometimes equally testing conditions found in the built environment.

Grasses for a Greener World

CLOCKWISE FROM TOP LEFT Avoiding a more resource-heavy approach to creating a green space in their Californian back yard, Dave and Rainie Fross have created a meadow based on *Carex praegracilis* that echoes the soft and uncut feel of the sedge's natural habitat. • In this private garden in Los Angeles, California, the regularly maintained lawn is composed of *Carex praegracilis*, and is irrigated as necessary with recycled grey water from inside the house. • Of necessity, and in common with *Carex praegracilis*, *Carex arenaria* has developed a fast-rooting strategy that frequently sees offsets appearing in discernable straight lines. • At Knoll Gardens, in the relatively tough garden conditions of dry, sandy soil, part shade, and root competition from large woody plants, *Carex arenaria* has formed a low-growing meadow of green foliage that will tolerate light foot traffic, and requires only occasional water and an annual trim to maintain. • In coastal areas of the U.K., *Carex arenaria* occupies a similar ecological niche to its counterpart *Carex praegracilis* in the U.S. Adapted to the harsh conditions of coastal life, it is also proving adaptable under garden conditions.

Practical Choices for an Alternative Lawn or Meadow

These grasses generally work well as lawn or meadow. Not all are appropriate for or hardy in every climate. Lawn choices should always be cross-referenced with local conditions.

- Bouteloua
- Briza
- Carex
- Deschampsia
- Festuca
- Koeleria
- Schizachyrium
- Sesleria
- Sorghastrum
- Sporobolus

to the point it becomes virtually indistinguishable from a more traditional sward. However, it is arguably at its most eloquent as a shaggy evergreen cover that is cut as rarely as once or twice each year.

Eschewing a more traditional layout, Dave and Rainie Fross have planted a private garden in Arroyo Grande, California, with a system of informal pathways threading their way unhurriedly though grassy plantings. The result is a superlative essay in achieving the natural meadow effect, where plantings of *Carex praegracilis* are allowed to grow unchecked by the lawnmower, requiring perhaps a once-a-year trim, to produce a lush and pleasing sward. On a rather larger scale, the open space surrounding the visitor centre of the Apple Campus in Cupertino has used the same sedge to create a meadow style that is entirely appropriate to its place and function.

In the maritime climate of the United Kingdom, another sedge, *Carex arenaria*, occupies a similar coastal ecological niche as its American counterpart, is equally tough and resilient, and appears to react similarly when used in our gardens as a lawn alternative. At Knoll Gardens, *Carex arenaria* was planted in a testing combination of dry soil with root competition from large woody plants, and has nonetheless formed a practical and effective low meadow that is as high on effect as it is low in aftercare.

In San Francisco, an altered care regime offers an attractive 'natural' feel to a grassy feature that appears entirely comfortable set against the urban hardscape.

Festuca rubra is a major component of many lawns, and like all regularly mown grass, will turn brown without the requisite water in dry periods. Simply altering the regime for this grass to accommodate less frequent mowing reduces the use of resources while creating a new, less formal, more tactile aesthetic—the shaggy look—as can be seen in numerous gardens and public spaces such as the Huntington in southern California, the Gothenburg Botanical Garden in Sweden, and downtown San Francisco.

Grasses for Erosion Control

As our homes and gardens extend outwards, they creep ever closer to beaches and their shifting sands. Consequently, plants once regarded as 'weedy' beach grasses of no real value are now seen as valuable tools, which can solve a problem without recourse to often unsuccessful, always expensive engineered solutions of block and concrete. For instance, *Panicum amarum*, a coast-adapted species from the eastern seaboard of the United States, is both a beautiful and practical choice for stabilization in these areas.

While a vigorous, self-renewing, densely spreading root system may not characterize the ideal garden plant, it is essential if that plant is to deal effectively with unstable sand or soil. Lyme grass, *Leymus arenarius*, for example, as well as other specially adapted beach grasses like marram, *Ammophila arenaria*, help to stabilize the movement of the sand dunes on beaches around Poole in Dorset, England. In the process, they also create a more stable environment for themselves and wildlife.

Not all of us can live on a beach, but many gardens have soil banks of varying degrees of steepness, which in many respects are similar to the shifting sands; soil banks are known for their tendency to slip, especially in wet weather. Such problems are often controlled by engineered solutions such as retaining walls, which are never cheap, frequently ugly, and difficult to disguise. In many situations, even steep banks can be controlled and stabilized by the use of dense-rooting, mat-forming plants such as *Carex praegracilis*, *Phragmites australis*, or *Leymus arenarius*, which cover the surface, and whose robust root systems will bind the soil together.

With banks that are less steep, a wider range of grasses such as *Panicum*, *Miscanthus*, *Festuca*, and *Calamagrostis* can be used successfully—not necessarily those with vigorous, spreading root systems. Often in such situations, especially in dry soils, erosion is principally wind-driven in that the wind will gradually carry off the top layers of soil over an extended period. Establishing any kind of cover with woody plants, grasses, or perennials will help stop or slow this process.

Practical Choices for Erosion Control

These grasses are known to help prevent erosion. As ever, not all are hardy or appropriate in every climate or site—especially considering the vigorous nature of a few—so choices should be cross-referenced with local conditions.

- *Ammophila*
- *Carex*
- *Leymus*
- *Luzula*
- *Panicum*
- *Phalaris*
- *Phragmites*

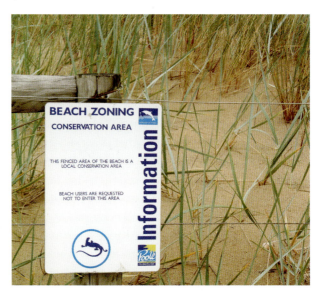

Grasses with spreading root systems can provide a valuable function in erosion control. This lyme grass, *Leymus arenarius*, on a sandy beach in Dorset, England, helps stabilize and conserve the sandy dunes. The grasses themselves sometimes need protection from too much foot traffic.

Planting a bank is not much different from any other garden planting. For best results, consider the following:

- The steeper the bank, the more a vigorous root system is needed.
- Always use beach grasses for shifting sand, as they are adapted to such extreme conditions.
- Quick establishment is always the goal, so plant at greater densities, perhaps using twice the usual recommended number of plants per square metre.
- A greater number of smaller plants will often establish and make a complete cover more easily than fewer larger plants.
- On steeper banks, or where loose soil is inclined to move around, use a covering mulch of matting that can be pegged down onto the soil. Netting can also be used if appropriate.

A steep bank between a private garden and public highway in Monterey, California is prevented from slipping or eroding by the use of a native sedge, *Carex praegracilis*, which in its summer dormant state mirrors the surrounding hillsides almost perfectly.

Grasses for Habitat Restoration

The term 'habitat restoration' usually describes the return of an area to the vegetative population that occupied it at some point in the recent past. Often this involves removing existing aggressive exotic species and replacing them with native plants that were gradually displaced by the colonizing exotics. This is often carried out in areas where there has been direct, frequently short-term human interference, such as laying of pipelines, civil engineering work, or even new home construction. After these projects end, it is desirable to return the area (or what might be left of it) to something resembling its original natural state. Sometimes 'site-specific' projects are carried out; when an area is due to be disrupted, plants (usually natives) are collected, propagated, and later returned to the site once work has been completed.

On the coastal fringe of Monterey, California, in the narrow strips between a golf links and the ocean, garden designer Fred Ballerini and his team undertook a successful scheme to turn an overlooked area back into its valuable habitat. The area had become covered with aggressive exotics such as the ever-popular ice plant. While perhaps aesthetically pleasing to the casual eye, this exotic ground cover had effectively stifled everything else in its path. As a first step, the ice plant covering much of the area's 40 acres was mechanically bulldozed and buried, with any regrowth spot-sprayed and left as a mulch. As a result, many native plants made a determined and almost immediate comeback, including the saltgrass, *Distichlis spicata*. New plants germinated from the seed bank that was dormant but still viable in the underlying soil, and were quick to take advantage of the opportunity to recover lost ground. Some years later, the area has a healthy mixed population of natives including grasses, sedges, and rushes that are largely self-sustaining, and

Where the built environment intrudes into natural systems, the use of locally native plants, such as *Aristida purpurea* in this Californian garden, can create a link to the wider landscape and help restore some of what was lost during the building process.

Grasses for a Greener World

ABOVE Stabilized sand dunes adjoining a coastal golf links at Monterey, California were overgrown with exotics such as ice plant, to the detriment of native plants and grasses. A rigorous planned programme of restoration has witnessed the successful return of many native grasses, sedges, and rushes.

RIGHT Roof gardens such as this in downtown San Francisco, California are increasingly popular, as their benefits begin to be fully realized. *Festuca* and *Carex* combine in an attractive mosaic designed by Dave Fross.

make a far greater contribution to the area's biodiversity. The biggest threat to continued long-term success remains the return of the exotic ice plant.

Historically, habitat restoration has been seen as the province of nature reserves and natural parks rather than gardens and designed spaces. But as more and more homes infringe on natural areas, and as we gain greater understanding of the importance of preserving the natural landscape and maintaining biodiversity, the blurring of the lines between natural and designed areas will see the value and relevance of restoration projects increase many times over in the coming years.

Grasses for Green Roofs

In use for almost as long as humans have been building houses, green roofs—where living plant material is used as a roof covering for homes and buildings—are not exactly new. As urban, industrial areas take up ever more space, green roofs have seen increased popularity for their eco-friendly ability to modify and control major environmental issues such as the general loss of biodiversity, creation of heat islands, and increased risk of stormwater flooding.

The 2½-acre green roof at the California Academy of Sciences is an impressive example of the functional, aesthetic, and environmental value of green roofs in the urban landscape.

With the construction of any building, from basic garden shed to multi-storey parking lot, the ground it occupies becomes unable to support any biodiversity. Installing a green roof helps to replace at least part of that loss, and this can be furthered through the appropriate use of locally native plants. Apart from their aesthetic appeal, such roofs' demonstrable benefits include reduced energy consumption, as well as the control of stormwater runoff—established green roofs behave like sponges, gradually releasing water over a much longer period than a traditional roof would.

Practical Choices for Green Roofs

In general, these grasses work well as components of green roofs. Not all will be appropriate or hardy in every climate, and choices should always be cross-referenced with local conditions.

- *Bouteloua*
- *Briza*
- *Carex*
- *Deschampsia*
- *Festuca*
- *Nassella*
- *Ophiopogon*
- *Poa*
- *Sesleria*
- *Sporobolus*

A variety of locally appropriate plants including grasses and sedges make excellent green roof subjects, though as conditions can be difficult—extreme dryness, a shallow root run, and searing temperatures in many cases—toughness is perhaps the plants' prime requirement. Similar in some respects to lawn alternatives, a spreading, self-renewing, compact habit is a distinct advantage as this helps to create a dense, self-sustaining mat that binds the roof together.

As with banks and lawn replacement schemes, a great number of smaller plants makes a more satisfactory cover than a lesser number of larger plants. Planting density depends partly on the actual size of the plants so that while larger plants may be used at, for instance, fifteen per square metre or yard, smaller plug-sized plants might be used at twice that number.

On a domestic scale, with a little knowledge and preparation, green roofs can be fitted to small outbuildings, garden sheds, and even kennels relatively easily. As a green roof can add considerable weight to the loading of a roof structure, it is advisable to consult building professionals or specialist green roof firms before commencing any project.

Green roofs are frequently described as either 'extensive' or 'intensive'. Extensive roofs tend to cover larger areas, but with a shallow depth of substrate that restricts plant choice. Intensive roofs tend to be smaller in area but have a greater depth of substrate, which allows a wider choice of plants; these are somewhat reminiscent of traditional roof gardens.

Grasses for a Greener World

Set against a background hardscape of urban building and pavement, the valuable green aesthetic, practical purpose, and change in ground level of rain gardens create a distinctive feature, even while still fairly new.

Grasses for Rain Gardens

Along with green roofs, rain gardens offer a highly practical alternative approach to water use in our gardens and designed spaces. Rain gardens challenge the more traditional view of water, so often regarded as either as an individual 'feature' effectively divorced from the rest of the landscape, or especially in the case of urban stormwater, simply an irritation to be drained or culverted away at the earliest opportunity.

In essence, rain gardens are planted areas of lower-lying ground, swales, dips, or depressions into which water collects during rainfall or flood. The rain garden then acts as a temporary holding area for the water, which gradually seeps into the ground. As with a green roof, a rain garden can be seen as a natural sponge, soaking up excess water in a relatively short space of time to release it more slowly over a longer period. Rain gardens are therefore periodically both very wet and very dry, which in horticultural terms may appear as something of a contradiction. But in the natural world, such changeable conditions are frequently encountered where water and land coincide, and so a range of plants such as *Carex*, *Juncus*, *Luzula*, and *Deschampsia* have adapted to take advantage of these sometimes-challenging environments. In our natural systems, these plants are generally found in damp and wet areas such as water meadows and stream sides. Such places are frequently wet, but as the seasons alter, streams and wet areas can become quite the opposite until moisture returns. To successfully colonize these places, these plants have learned to cope with the sometimes wet, sometimes dry environment, and this successful strategy can be used to great effect in our designed spaces, especially when planting rain gardens.

The principle of the rain garden can be applied successfully to almost any scale or project, whether in a city centre or a private backyard. Commercial and urban rain garden projects of significant scale require the same level of planning and expertise as any in the public realm but offer tangible benefits in return, including green space in the urban hardscape,

TOP Rain gardens mirror naturally occurring lower land, depressions, or swales, which during wet periods will become very wet, and even hold open water. A range of grasses have evolved to cope with this environment, and have proved equally adaptable under similar cultivated conditions.

ABOVE Rain gardens such as this one at the Mt. Tabor School in Portland, Oregon are so called as they are designed to catch and absorb runoff from buildings and other structures. This avoids the need for expensive stormwater runoff systems and allows water to infiltrate into the soil rather than be removed from the area it was most needed.

Grasses for a Greener World

a commodity that is always valuable. Rain gardens can be part of a cost-effective solution to stormwater run-off and thereby help to mitigate the heat island effect as well. They support biodiversity by creating habitat for a range of wildlife. And they can help engage the public by offering a narrative of a greater understanding and interest in the wider environment.

On the smaller scale of private gardens and landscapes, creating a rain garden can be a simpler process that involves utilizing or altering ground levels to ensure water will collect in the desired places. Creating swales or depressions will provide different growing conditions that can be aesthetically attractive as well as practical. For example, in my own garden at Knoll, as part of a recent project, we created a series of four linked swales to make the Rain Garden immediately adjacent to the Dry Meadow. For the most part, the garden soil is a dry sand, though with heavy rainfall, local flooding can occur, and the Rain Garden was sited in part to help alleviate this problem. Since it sits at a lower level than the Dry Meadow, any excess water flows off the meadow and into the Rain Garden.

RIGHT Environmentally efficient deep-sided rain gardens populated by *Muhlenbergia* and *Juncus* make an attractive aesthetic feature at the Apple Campus Visitor Centre, Cupertino, California.

BELOW *Carex divulsa* is just one of many ornamental sedges that are proving well adapted to the periodic wet and dry conditions to be found in rain gardens, providing both a functional and aesthetic value.

Practical Choices for Rain Gardens

These grasses tend to work well in rain gardens. As always, not all will be appropriate or hardy in every climate. Choices should always be cross-referenced with local conditions.

- Acorus
- Calamagrostis
- Carex
- Deschampsia
- Eriophorum
- Juncus
- Luzula
- Molinia
- Panicum
- Schoenoplectus
- Typha

OPPOSITE Early season in one of the swales of the Rain Garden at Knoll in Dorset, England sees the fresh green foliage of *Calamagrostis*, *Deschampsia*, *Luzula*, and *Carex* set against the bright flower colour of spring-flowering woody plants.

RIGHT At Knoll Gardens, Dorset, England, a mix of *Carex oshimensis* 'Everlime' and *Luzula nivea* 'Snowflake' form an evergreen base to one of the swales that runs alongside the Dry Meadow.

BELOW *Acorus gramineus* 'Golden Edge' and *Luzula sylvatica* 'Solar Flair' (submerged), are among a range of adaptable plants that will cope with the ebb and flow of a rain garden cycle.

Each of the four separate-but-linked swales were planted with a different mix of plants, including *Acorus*, *Carex*, *Calamagrostis*, *Juncus*, *Luzula*, and *Deschampsia*. Although the Rain Garden palette differs radically from that of the Dry Meadow, plants from both areas were allowed to mingle at the margins to help merge one area into the other. Planting was completed in the early autumn, and winter rainfall soon proved the garden's value. Flooding of nearby pathways was virtually eradicated, and while often full, the individual swales collectively held the volume of water, releasing it into the ground over a period of time.

Simply by altering the ground levels, this project proved a low-impact solution to local flooding, and created a distinctive growing environment as attractive to wildlife as it is to the gardener.

With deciduous grasses, leaving last year's growth on the surface of the border as a mulch (suitably shredded) offers practical benefits. These first few weeks after being cut back are the least interesting for this group, and when the structural value of woody plants including evergreens becomes clear.

Looking After Grasses

GRASSES ARE GENUINELY easy to look after. With a little annual attention, they will generously repay in the form of a very long display that is as short on work as it is high on value. Tuning in to what your grasses need, and planning accordingly, will make things easier still.

Routine Maintenance

In caring for grasses, the annual routine will depend very much on whether the grasses are deciduous or evergreen. Because they can resent disturbance during dormancy, most tasks are best carried out once grasses come into active growth. In mild climates, this is from early spring onwards, when the worst winter weather has passed. For warmer areas where summer dormancy is prevalent, these tasks can be completed at the end of autumn in preparation for autumn rains and the general greening of the landscape.

As a general rule, few of the usual tasks often associated with garden plants, such as staking and deadheading, are necessary with grasses. While individual circumstance may dictate some mid-season treatment, for the most part, grasses will be happy with attention just once a year.

DECIDUOUS GRASSES

Deciduous grasses are those whose stems last only one year, producing a new sheaf of growth at the start of each season. This type—which includes many of the true grasses we see in gardens like *Andropogon*, *Bouteloua*, *Calamagrostis*, *Eragrostis*, *Miscanthus*, *Molinia*, *Panicum*, and *Pennisetum*—stops growing and shuts down for winter in temperate climates, or for summer in warmer climates. In common with many other perennials, grasses' stems and flowers are retained virtually intact, gradually drying and changing colour through myriad subtle tones of brown and beige in tune with the seasons. It is largely this ability to retain the dried outline of stem, leaf, and flower that gives this group of grasses such a long season of interest in the garden.

For deciduous types, the annual routine consists of simply removing the old dried stems to prepare for the

Deciduous grasses are those whose stems last only one year, producing a new sheaf of growth at the start of each season. Under natural conditions, the old growth is effectively removed by a combination of elements, including wind and fire. In garden conditions, this role is usually undertaken by the gardener.

CLOCKWISE FROM TOP   A variety of tools can be used for maintenance, all of which have some value. As with many garden tools, it is a question of personal preference. Mechanical or electric trimmers are certainly faster, while hand tools can offer a greater degree of control for more delicate tasks. • Old stems are cut back as close to ground level as is practical, leaving a light and airy base from which new shoots will emerge. • Shorter-handled trimmers are sometimes more adept at cutting around finer growth. • Remove cut growth from the crown of the plant either by hand or rake, then leave in situ as a surface mulch or remove and compost.

new season's rapid growth. Under natural conditions, this removal is accomplished through a combination of elements including wind and fire; in the garden, this role is more conveniently undertaken by the gardener. Where a more natural look is desired, this annual routine could be applied less frequently.

Cutting back can be achieved by a variety of different tools, from hand-held scissors to motorized flail mowers. It is chiefly a question of convenience for the user, though undoubtedly mechanized trimmers are more efficient for larger areas. Removal of stems close to ground level allows for the new growth to show through quickly; cutting through any existing new growth in the process does no harm to the plant.

Subsequent disposal of cut stems is also largely a matter of personal preference. The old stems can be physically removed from the area to be composted, or they can be left in situ as a valuable, labour-saving mulch. To create a practical and pleasing mulch layer, the stems will need reducing into much smaller pieces, either by initially chopping into smaller sections if using shears or trimmers, or by running a rough rotary grass cutter over the areas once cut down. The cut stems can also be passed through a garden shredder to create a fine mulch, and flail mowers can be a useful alternative for larger, unobstructed areas where the flailing action cuts and macerates the old growth in one simple operation.

In agricultural situations, a long-established alternative to cutting is the controlled burning of old growth, mimicking the cycle of some natural systems. While undoubtedly effective in skilled hands, this option is potentially hazardous, especially within the confines of a garden setting, and is not normally recommended.

The 'Chelsea chop' is a technique that can reduce the ultimate height of fast-growing deciduous grasses, and some perennials, that regularly become too tall for a given situation. Cutting new growth back to the

In the Mediterranean climate of the Santa Barbara Botanic Garden, California, the famous meadow receives its annual cut and removal of debris in advance of the winter rains.

ground is carried out in late May, around the time of the famous Chelsea Flower Show, and reduces the amount of time the stems have to grow before flowering is initiated, thus reducing the overall height of the plant. Although it involves extra work, this can be an effective technique in certain situations—for instance, where very rich soils regularly create fast, green growth that is inclined to flop later in the season.

SUMMER-DORMANT GRASSES

Summer-dormant grasses are found in warmer climates such the Mediterranean and areas with similar conditions, like California, where without supplemental irrigation, plants would usually close down due to heat and a lack of moisture, rather than winter cold and wet. With respect to maintenance, the process is very similar to that of winter-dormant grasses in that old stems can be cut down at some point during dormancy, either late in the season and before autumn rains (so their strawy silhouette can be enjoyed), or earlier in the season to reduce possible fire risk in sensitive areas.

EVERGREEN GRASSES

Caring for evergreens can be slightly more complex than for the deciduous group in so far as the attention they may require will depend on whether they are by nature shorter- or longer-lived grasses.

When well sited, longer-lived evergreens such as *Acorus*, *Carex*, *Juncus*, *Luzula*, and *Ophiopogon* tend to be slower growing, and will need very little subsequent attention to keep them happy for a good number of years. In this respect, they could be regarded as

When well-sited, many of the foliage-based *Carex* can require virtually no after care. These *Carex oshimensis* 'Evergold' at Knoll Gardens have been growing happily in a dry, shady spot for more than a decade with virtually no attention.

TOP When happy, shorter-lived evergreens such as this *Nassella tenuissima* may require little attention for a season or two. Combing through in the spring with a rake or other toothed implement may keep plants looking fresh, though eventually foliage will need to be cut back to stimulate new growth.

ABOVE AND LEFT Shorter-lived evergreens such as this *Festuca* 'Elijah Blue' can be cut hard back to remove old, tired growth, but ideally should be only cut once the plant has come into active growth in spring to minimize risk of damage. Hand tools are often easiest for this task, leaving a tidy ball or 'hedgehog', which produces new growth within days.

virtually maintenance free, requiring only periodic removal of fallen debris, such as autumn leaves.

Shorter-lived evergreens like *Festuca* and *Nassella*, for example, will also possibly need very little attention for the first few seasons. However, these generally grow quickly, and so even when well sited, after a season, their freshness and overall appearance can suffer. Initially, the appearance of these finer-leaved evergreens can be improved by combing or raking through the foliage and removing much of the old, tired, or dead leaves and flowers. Even domestic rubber gloves can be useful, as debris will adhere to their semi-adhesive surface when passed, comb-like, through the foliage. Where this no longer has the desired result, these evergreens can be cut back, quite hard in many cases, but in most climates, this should only be carried out while the plants are in active growth.

Hard pruning of both shorter- and longer-lived types stimulates new growth from the base, but evergreens in general can take severe exception to heavy pruning, especially when in dormancy. Cutting back during active growth minimizes this risk by stimulating an almost immediate response in the form of new shoots.

The extent to which old foliage is removed often depends on a combination of garden conditions, individual plants, and personal experience of what works best. Removal of between a third to half the old foliage is a practical option in most areas; taking the plant almost to ground level can also work successfully, especially in warmer climates with good light levels.

Most *Festuca* and other fine-leaved evergreens will take a tight pruning on an annual basis; after being cut back early in the season, they quickly put on vigorous new growth. These quick-growing evergreens can be cut at almost any point during the active growing period as they will start regrowth immediately—sometimes within hours of trimming. As a further refinement, and with sufficient daylight hours, *Nassella tenuissima* will accept being cut back more than once annually when used in applications where the green foliage is desired, but not the comparatively top-heavy flowers.

SEMI-EVERGREEN GRASSES

While evergreen in more favourable climates, semi-evergreen grasses such as *Elymus* and *Sesleria* can frequently become effectively deciduous by the end of the winter period in mild and damp environs such as the United Kingdom. On the whole, this group will tolerate being cut back relatively hard, even to the ground, on a regular springtime basis, provided plants have begun active growth.

The 'No Maintenance' Option?

In reality, there is no such thing as 'no maintenance' in a garden situation. In certain instances, however, there can be varying degrees of low maintenance that come close. For example, some of the longer-lived evergreens such as *Ophiopogon* and *Carex*, when happy, will require virtually no attention once established. For most plants in nature, 'pruning' and 'cutting back' is only enacted by a combination of wind, animals, and other physical agencies; otherwise, grasses lose old growth that either gradually breaks away or is covered by emerging new growth. Perfectly adapted as this process is in our natural systems, under garden conditions, often with less well-balanced plant communities, the results of such an approach can appear messy and unworkable. But with a well-chosen plant palette and a desire to experiment, grasses can come very close to that highly desirable 'no-maintenance' ideal.

Mulching and Feeding

Renowned for their general ability to grow in nutrient-poor soils in the wild, grasses' natural fastidiousness is carried over to garden conditions, where most require very little to no feeding.

Indeed, in extreme circumstances, it is possible to overfeed grasses to the detriment of flower in favour of foliage, and using grasses from nutrient-poor areas in high-nutrient garden soils can result in a similar alteration to the plants' growth habit. In practice, however, this not usually a major concern, although in some situations—for instance, when carrying out habitat restoration or in other sensitive areas—nutrient levels may be an issue.

Mulching, the laying of an organic or inorganic material on top of the soil and around plants, is recommended practice in most garden situations. Mulch material is usually bark, garden compost, manure, spent hops, or other organic material, though the use of stone, gravel, and other inorganic substances such as crushed brick rubble should not be overlooked. The depth to which a mulch should be applied is often a matter of preference and material availability, but generally 25–50 mm (1–2 in.) is a workable guideline. To be most effective, the mulch should cover the entire planting area (not just the area immediately adjacent to the plants), though care should be taken to avoid covering the crowns of the plants to any depth, as this may lead to rot. If the old growth of deciduous grasses is cut and left in situ, this in itself provides a self-sustaining mulch with very little effort from the gardener.

Aesthetic considerations and reduced need to weed are two excellent reasons for applying mulch, though it could be argued that the single most important reason is water conservation. Mulch helps retain moisture in the soil over an extended period, much to the advantage of young, thirsty roots that are prone to drying out in the early stages of life.

Looking After Container-Grown Grasses

With their fibrous root systems, so many grasses lend themselves easily to pot and container growth. Annual routines for pot-grown grasses do not differ from those grown in the ground, except that pot-grown grasses' root systems will demand more regular attention.

Grasses' fibrous root systems frequently necessitate an annual potting—exceptions include the slowest growing, such as *Hakonechloa* and *Imperata*. If roots slow down due to lack of fresh soil or space to grow, inevitably the top growth will follow, leading quickly to disappointing performance and senescence. Potting on into a larger container each year is a simple procedure using any well-balanced potting

As with most other plants in containers, grass roots soon outgrow available space, often in one season for vigorous plants such as the *Pennisetum* 'Hameln' shown here. Cutting back and removing roots allows new soil to be placed in the existing container, and ensures a fresh root run for another growing season.

medium, though eventually it becomes impractical to pot into yet a larger container; while dividing the plant solves this issue, it also reduces the size of the plant left for display. Where a mature size is desired, remove the bottom third (or even half) of the old root ball in spring, along with a section of the side growth if necessary, and replace it with fresh growing medium to allow the plant to be replaced intact in the old container, where it will grow with renewed vigour with its roots in contact with the fresh soil. This technique can be repeated on an annual basis, seemingly many times, though eventually the plant will require division to maintain vigour.

Planting and Renewal

With such a diverse group as grasses, which successfully colonizes almost every conceivable climatic condition, there is no one perfect time for planting. It is often said among gardeners that while spring is the preferred period for people to plant, autumn is nature's favourite time. Both can be true; there is no better way to determine the optimum planting time than consulting local practices and tuning in to surrounding conditions.

In the relatively mild dampness of maritime climates like that of the United Kingdom, most times of year can be suitable for planting. In the Mediterranean climate of California, on the other hand, planting after

Spring is a favoured time for planting, though it is often said that autumn is nature's favourite moment. Grasses grown in containers can be planted at almost any time of year, so much will depend on local conditions as to the best practice for a given area.

the onset of the first winter rains would likely be best practice. And yet in much of the United States, autumn planters are wary of 'frost heave', the process by which frost and ice pushes young plants out of the ground, to the extent that spring may be the better choice.

PREPARATION

While choosing the right plants to suit the garden's conditions is no doubt the most important aspect of successful planting, ensuring the soil is in suitable condition to receive those plants is arguably second most important. Although grasses in particular are tolerant of a wide range of cultural and soil conditions, common sense dictates that plants finding themselves in aerated, weed-free conditions will establish more successfully than those that have to fight for their survival from the moment of planting.

Best practice under garden conditions involves ensuring the prior removal of unwanted plants, including, critically, their root systems. Where soils have been heavily compacted, preventing the free movement of water and air through the soil, it is usually essential to break this compaction before continuing with any further preparation. A variety of different tools are available for this purpose, including machinery with hydraulic arms attached to digging buckets that can make such a task relatively straightforward.

While digging over and relevelling the soil as part of the preparation process has long been regarded as best practice, the 'no dig' option has always found favour with many gardeners. By not disturbing the soil more than is necessary, arguably the soil is kept in better health, requires less work to prepare, and any viable weed seed stored there is not brought to the surface to germinate. Where the ground is not severely compacted, such an approach has clearly demonstrated its ability to deliver good results.

HOW MANY PLANTS?

Most experienced gardeners will have developed their instincts when it comes to deciding how many plants should fill a given space. But whatever your level of

When planting large areas, it is often easiest to work in terms of plants per square metre or square yard. This step is not only a convenient method of calculating the number of plants needed, it can also help crystallize planting patterns and even palette.

experience, it is often useful to have a strategy when dealing with large areas.

Breaking up a planting area into square metres or square yards can not only help to calculate the number of plants needed, it can also aid in design and layout by crystallizing plant patterns and even plant choice. In doing so, it becomes easier to determine plant density and anticipate quantity, which can be adjusted and recalculated to allow for budgets or design considerations. (See next chapter for recommended plant densities.)

MAKING NEW

Grasses are propagated either by seed or through division. For annuals, seed sowing is the only option—and in addition to being relatively cheap, it is the time-honoured way to ensure genetic diversity among different species.

Division, the splitting of a mature plant into smaller pieces, is used for cultivars or those plants that will not necessarily retain their unique characteristics if reproduced from seed. It is also the most

Looking After Grasses   145

Most deciduous grasses will at some point benefit from division and renewal. This *Miscanthus*, while still healthy after eight years in the ground undisturbed, has begun to show dead space in the centre. Simple division by spade is enough to reenergize the plant.

convenient method in garden situations where the lifting and dividing of an existing plant rejuvenates that plant at the same time as providing a ready supply of new plants for little cost or effort. While requiring only the annual removal of dead stems for many years, most deciduous grasses will eventually benefit from division and renewal. The timespan for this depends mostly on planting conditions and species involved; often, an individual will begin to show a marked dead space in the centre, which is not producing the same level of new growth that can be seen on the outside of the plant once it has been lifted. A simple division by spade is enough to reenergize the plant, replanting or discarding the newly split sections as needed.

Deciduous grasses are ideally lifted and split in early spring, just as they are breaking into growth. Evergreens can be divided at the same time, though in many cooler climates it is best to delay until the plants are actively growing. Evergreens can also be split at virtually any time during active growth in the summer.

A few grasses do not take kindly to division. One example is the pheasant grass, *Anemanthele lessoniana*, which is best raised from seed. Others, like *Stipa gigantea*, the Spanish oat grass, can also object to unnecessary disturbance. In such cases, best results are usually achieved by dividing the plant while it is still in the ground, cutting off and lifting smaller sections with a sharp spade, while leaving the majority of the plant undisturbed.

Nearly all grasses can set seed in favourable circumstances—some, such as the shorter-lived grasses, more easily than others. This seed can be collected while still on the plant in early autumn and stored in paper envelopes or bags in a cool, dry place until spring, when it can be sown under controlled conditions much as with any ornamental plant. (As a general rule, seed collected from garden cultivars will not come true to type, so cultivars should not be propagated by seed.)

Where seed is not collected, or eaten during winter by other garden inhabitants, some may germinate in spring. Applying an early mulch controls unwanted grass seed as it would any other type. Unwanted seedlings that result can be used as stock to replace old plants, or as fresh supply for new plantings. Sowing directly onto prepared ground can work well, especially with annuals, but in a garden setting where conditions are not controlled, results for most grasses will vary, and success is not guaranteed.

Pests and Diseases

RUST

On the whole, under garden conditions, grasses are remarkably free from disease, with only foliar rusts appearing regularly. Frequently resulting from cultural conditions, these rusts are usually only temporary, and easy enough to ignore in all but the most delicate of situations, where a chemical solution may be employed. Alternatively, cutting back the foliage to encourage fresh new growth is often easier.

The Burning Question

Periodic wildfire has always been an essential feature of the natural grassland cycle; during hot, rainless summers, grass becomes tinder dry and catches alight, clearing away tired old growth and allowing vigorous new growth to start again. In managed areas of natural beauty, reserves and preserves, fire is something that must be contended with and planned for. Under relatively controlled conditions, it is even an effective agricultural tool. But for most domestic gardeners it is hardly a safe option—and for those gardening in drier parts of the world, the threat of fire can be a real issue, especially when homes and gardens are in close proximity to areas that are part of a naturally occurring fire cycle.

Some gardeners in high-risk areas are taking steps to protect their gardens from the threat of fire. In Mediterranean California, for example, the use of native *Aristida purpurea* as a meadow allowed to come close to the residence is part of a generally accepted design contingency to combat the threat of fire. Many grasses in Mediterranean areas will go summer dormant; without summer irrigation, they cease growth, turning brown until autumn rains come. (Some will even go summer-dormant regardless of how much water they are given.) Using summer-dormant grasses such as *Aristida purpurea* rather than woody plants for a given distance surrounding a house—the 'defensible area'—can help to reduce the amount of available fuel for a fire. In areas at risk, trimming grasses in midsummer, just before the highest threat of naturally occurring fire, can also help to reduce the danger.

SAP SUCKERS

While grasses can play host to a variety of sucking insects such as aphids, in general they are relatively free from all but the most extreme infestations. When infestation by sucking insects occurs, physical removal or spraying can be undertaken if letting nature take its course is undesirable.

Some forms of *Carex* can suffer from aphids which colonize the leaf bases and root systems of the plant, remaining almost invisible in the dense foliage or below ground. More often seen in pot-grown plants, a lack of vigour characterizes a severe attack, which can be dealt with through chemical treatment or physical removal.

One species of mealybug, *Miscanthicoccus miscanthi*, has been a recent pest of *Miscanthus*, especially in the United States, causing stunted growth and twisting of flowerheads. Difficult to spot in the early stages, it is usually addressed with chemical control or disposal of infected plants.

GRAZERS AND BURROWERS

A wide range of grazing animals will choose grasses as food sources. Deer, rabbits, and a selection of rodents—not to mention domestic cats and dogs on a smaller scale—browse the top growth. Still others such as voles, gophers, and moles burrow underground, where they eat the root systems, and frequently cause severe damage and death to the plants attacked.

Browsing animals' tastes vary, with regional differences sometimes emerging so that, for example, *Panicum* may be unpalatable in one area only to become a favoured food item in another. No reliably browser-proof grasses seem to exist, and physical prevention or control of the animals involved appear the only viable options when the damage becomes unacceptable. Planting larger quantities of the same plant can allow for a higher level of damage before aesthetic considerations are compromised.

Looking After Grasses

The massed flowers of *Molinia caerulea* 'Dauerstrahl' marking the end of the Decennium border and the beginning of the Long Walk at Knoll Gardens, Dorsett, U.K.

Directory of Grasses and Grass-Like Plants

Rushes are round,
sedges have edges,
and grasses have nodes
from the top to the ground.

—from an oft-quoted ditty

AMONG THE GRASSES AND GRASS-LIKE PLANTS described here, you will find choices that are ornamental, some with biodiversity value, others that play a part in erosion control, and quite a few with all of these traits. With more than ten thousand different species of grasses existing today, as well as over three thousand species of sedges alone—not to mention many other allied species and innumerable garden selections—it would be impossible to include all of them. Instead, listed here are a carefully chosen and wide-ranging selection of plants that in some way or another bring value to the garden.

You can simply browse this directory for something eye-catching, or look up a specific plant that has caught your interest in the past. In each entry, I have tried to shed light on whether a given plant is likely to thrive in your garden and how it might be used to best effect.

Clumpers, Runners, and Seeders

When choosing a grass, it is useful to understand how it might 'behave' in the garden. From a gardener's perspective, grasses and grass-like plants can be categorized according to how they spread. There are those whose roots form effectively stationary clumps, and others whose roots travel or otherwise spread through the soil. Finally, there are annual grasses that reproduce exclusively from seed.

CLUMPERS

Clump-formers, also known as bunch grasses, generally have the best garden manners in that their fibrous root systems produce relatively tight clumps of stems that will never stray very far from their original planting position. Over a period of time, these clumps can attain significant size, sometimes eventually dying out in the congested centre, as can happen with *Cortaderia* and *Miscanthus*. But they can be rejuvenated by lifting and dividing whenever necessary, almost ad infinitum.

RUNNERS

Runners are those whose roots move through the soil away from the original planting position, frequently with the ability to cover large areas of ground over a short period of time. These root systems are a successful adaptation for grasses like the marram grass, *Ammophila*, so often seen on sandy beaches where the ability to move around is advantageous. But grasses with these continually questing roots are more prone to outstaying their welcome in the relatively controlled conditions of a garden. However, for applications such as lawns and green roofs, where a close carpet of growth is required, having a mobile and self-renewing root system becomes a distinct advantage.

Some plants that are widely regarded as clump-forming technically have spreading roots, but do so comparatively slowly, so that from a horticultural standpoint they can usually be regarded as clump-formers. For example, although most *Miscanthus* are regarded as clump-forming, *Miscanthus sacchariflorus* has the ability to spread—though in most climates it makes only moderately spreading patches which, to a gardener's eye, can be seen as rather large clumps. It is only in warmer climates when this spreading ability becomes more pronounced.

SEEDERS

Like most other plants, most grasses will seed given the right conditions. However, it is primarily the annuals, ephemerals (those with lifespans of under one year), and short-lived perennials that make up this third group: the seeders.

By definition, an annual must set seed to survive; the more copious the seed produced, the better the chances of success. Such free-seeding annuals can outstay their welcome in the garden and should be introduced with appropriate caution. Short-lived perennials such as *Nassella tenuissima* and *Anemanthele lessoniana*, for example, can set significant amounts of seed in the right conditions, although with some thoughtful care, such seeding can be used to replace older plants as they senesce and die away.

Warm-Season or Cool-Season?

Across most of the plant world, the terms 'warm-season growers' and 'cool-season growers' are used to describe basic technical differences between how plants obtain their energy. Complicated in detail, these differences can be important from a gardener's point of view in that warm-season grasses such as *Arundo*, *Miscanthus*, *Panicum*, and *Pennisetum* are at their best in warm conditions. They tend to start into growth relatively late in the season, and are capable of doing so speedily when soil conditions and air temperatures are warm and to their liking. Contrastingly, cool-season grasses such as *Calamagrostis*, *Festuca*, *Milium*, and *Stipa* fare better at cooler temperatures, will start into growth much earlier in the spring, and are frequently at their best when conditions are moister, usually in late winter to spring.

Sun or Shade? Wet or Dry?

In nature, plants are mostly adapted to specific conditions such as sun or shade, wet or dry, and this general advice is given in the descriptions. This tendency to adapt, however, is a constantly evolving, dynamic process, and in practice most plants have a range of tolerances that the gardener can use to advantage. For example, *Carex secta* is happy in sun and under wet conditions, where it makes a magnificent dark green mound. But under much drier conditions in some shade, it can still perform satisfactorily, though perhaps not as exuberantly. As with all living things, experimentation is key to success.

Maximum Heights, Planting Densities, and Lifespans

The heights shown in these descriptions refer to the heights the grass can generally be expected to achieve under average-to-good conditions. In difficult conditions or where a plant is at the edge of its tolerances, this maximum height might easily be significantly reduced. Maximum heights are approximate; the height that a specific plant will achieve depends on the specific conditions in the garden.

The heights given will include any flowers, which typically make up a significant part of a grass's overall height. For example, *Stipa gigantea* is listed as up to 2.4 m (8 ft.) tall when in full flower, although the basal foliage itself is less than half than height.

When planning the garden, the distance that should be left between plants can vary quite significantly depending on the size and vigour of the plants themselves, the soil conditions, and the desired effect. For suggestions on planting densities, see the section that follows in this chapter called Planting Distances and Densities.

As with any other diverse group, grasses' lifespans vary tremendously. They range from annuals, which last a season, through short-lived perennials that can be expected to live anywhere from two to five years, to long-haul perennial grasses that live for ten years and often much longer.

The Naming of Plants

The naming of plants, or plant nomenclature, is an often complex and confusing subject that is well beyond the scope of this book. Modern identification techniques are providing results that can challenge long-held traditional views, with taxonomists suggesting a plethora of name changes that are not always welcome to the gardener unconcerned with the background science. My approach to naming plants in this directory and throughout the book is purely intended to match plants with current accepted names, and should not be taken as an opinion on the botanical validity of those names used.

If a plant's scientific name appears to be missing from this alphabetical listing, it may be because the name has been changed by taxonomists. To find the current name, look up the 'missing' name in the index. Cultivar names are enclosed by single quotation marks, and any synonyms for cultivars follow the current name and are enclosed in parentheses. Unless otherwise indicated, cultivars can be assumed to share the approximate maximum height and frost-hardiness of the species under which they are classified.

Planting Distances and Densities

The following chart offers suggestions for the number of plants that might be used per square metre or square yard of planting area.

Thinking in terms of the number of plants per square of planting can be very useful in calculating (and recalculating!) the total number of plants needed, especially for a significant area. Simply multiply the number of plants needed per square metre or yard by the total number of square metres or yards available to plant.

These suggestions are based on the assumption that complete cover is required (no bare ground between the plants once established), of a particular grass over a given area.

Numbers of plants that might be needed have been given a suggested range. Both lower and higher densities should achieve cover once the grasses mature. The higher number will achieve cover sooner but will cost more initially in term of plants, whereas the lower number will cost less initially but take a little longer to achieve the same cover.

Where complete cover of the ground is not required, such as with gravel gardens, where an ornamental surface mulch forms part of the aesthetic, then the minimum suggested number can be reduced appropriately in order to achieve the desired effect.

If smaller plants such as plugs are being used, for a lawn replacement scheme for example, then a higher density of plants may be needed than is suggested here. Consult the supplier for appropriate guidelines.

Climatic conditions affect plant growth, so numbers needed may be less in more favoured warmer areas.

SUGGESTED NUMBER OF PLANTS PER SQUARE METRE OR YARD

Achnatherum	1–3		Ampeledesmos	1–3
Acorus	3–7		Aristida	3–5
Agrostis	7–11		Arrhenatherum	3–7
Alopecurus	3–7		Arundo	1–3
Ammophila	3–5		Austrostipa	1–3
Anemanthele	1–3		Bothriochloa	3–5
Andropogon	3–5		Bouteloua	3–5

Briza	5–7
Bromus	3–5
Calamagrostis	1–5
Carex, small forms such as C. flacca	7–11
Carex, medium forms such as C. oshimensis 'Evergold'	3–5
Carex, large forms such as C. pendula	1–3
Chasmanthium	3–5
Chionochloa	1–3
Cortaderia	1–3
Deschampsia	3–7
Desmoschoenus	3–5
Distichlis	7–9
Elymus	3–5
Eragrostis	3–5
Eriophorum	5–7
Festuca, small forms such as F. rubra	7–9
Festuca, medium forms such as F. glauca	5–7
Festuca, large forms such as F. mairei	1–3
Glyceria	1–3
Hakonechloa	5–7
Helictotrichon	3–5
Holcus	3–7
Hordeum	7–9
Imperata	7–9
Jarava (Stipa)	3–5
Juncus	5–7
Koeleria	5–7
Leymus	3–5
Luzula	5–7
Melica	5–7
Melinis	5–7
Milium	5–7
Miscanthus	1–3
Molinia caerulea	3–5
Molinia caerulea subsp. arundinacea and its cultivars	1–3
Nassella	3–7
Ophiopogon, most forms	7–11
Ophiopogon, small-leaved forms such as O. japonicus 'Minor'	11–15

continued →

(cont'd)

Panicum	1–5
Pennisetum	1–5
Phalaris	3–5
Phragmites	1–3
Poa	1–5
Rhynchospora	5–9
Saccharum	1–3
Schizachyrium	3–7
Sesleria	5–9
Sorghastrum	1–3
Spartina	1–3
Sporobolus	3–7
Spodiopogon	3–5
Stipa, small forms such as *S. ichu*	3–5
Stipa, large forms such as *S. gigantea*	1–3
Tridens	3–5
Typha	1–5
Uncinia	7–9

Hardiness Zones

A plant's tolerances extend to its ability to cope with widely differing temperature regimes. In the following entries, Hardiness Zones are given as a guide as to how a plant may perform. Zone numbers refer to the lowest cold-hardiness zone in which the plant is likely to survive.

Local weather conditions, soils, and microclimates are all likely to have a substantial impact on a plant's hardiness, and due weight must be given to these other factors when evaluating whether a plant is likely to be hardy in the garden.

MINIMUM TEMPERATURE (CELSIUS)	ZONES	MINIMUM TEMPERATURE (FAHRENHEIT)
below -45	1	below -50
-45 to -40	2	-50 to -40
-40 to -34	3	-40 to -30
-34 to -29	4	-30 to -20
-29 to -23	5	-20 to -10
-23 to -18	6	-10 to 0
-18 to -12	7	0 to 10
-12 to -7	8	10 to 20
-7 to -1	9	20 to 30
-1 to 4	10	30 to 40
above 4	11	above 40

Achnantherum
SILVER SPEAR GRASS

Achnatherum calamagrostis
Syn. *Stipa calamagrostis*

Dense clumps of bright green foliage that host numerous, subtly arching stems, weighted by freely produced needle-like flowers to create a wonderfully light and feathery appearance. Tolerant of drought, sunshine, and poor soils, but less happy under warm, humid conditions. From Europe. To 90 cm (3 ft.). Z5.

'Lemperg'. A selection that is more compact in stature but otherwise retains a similar habit and the same free-flowering nature. To 60 cm (2 ft.).

Acorus
SWEET FLAG

Although not botanically true grasses, this useful group of grass-like evergreens has narrow, iris-like foliage that is slowly spreading, tough, and long lived. *Acorus calamus*, the sweet flag, is even more iris-like; *Acorus gramineus* is the most widely used in gardens.

Acorus gramineus

Produces compact, tightly-formed clumps of evergreen foliage that slowly attain more bulk over time. Found in damp to wet waterside conditions, this small species has given rise to many cultivars, usually distinguished primarily by leaf

Acorus gramineus 'Golden Edge'

Acorus gramineus 'Ogon'

Acorus gramineus 'Variegatus'

colouration. From Japan, India, and China. To 40 cm (16 in.). Z5–7.

'Golden Edge'. A more recent cultivar which in habit and appearance is very similar to 'Ogon'. Similarly excellent in containers.

'Ogon'. The most widespread cultivar, with bright gold-, yellow-, green-, and even cream-striped leaves forming the typical slowly spreading mounds. Leaf colouration can vary, perhaps due to seasonal or even cultural conditions, leading to speculation as to whether the form now commonly grown is in fact the original correctly named plant. Regardless, 'Ogon' is reliable for damp areas, but will also survive happily under drier conditions such as in containers.

'Variegatus'. Slow-growing but quietly attractive, with narrow evergreen foliage in creamy white and grey-green, which can be slightly pendulous towards the tips.

Agrostis
BENT GRASS

A genus of widely occurring, and diverse cool-season deciduous grasses, *Agrostis* contains more than two hundred annual and perennial species, some used as components of lawn grass. Originates from a widespread area, especially northern-hemisphere temperate climates.

Agrostis capillaris

Common bent has a creeping rootstock and is a frequent component of both amenity turf as well as meadows, where its open airy panicles provide an attractive soft pink haze during early summer. From Eurasia but widely introduced elsewhere. To 60 cm (2 ft.). Z5.

Agrostis nebulosa
CLOUD GRASS

A pretty annual with an apt common name. Covers itself in delicate, airy flowerheads. Like most annuals, it is quick growing and prefers generally open sunny conditions. Reseeds if happy. From Spain, Morocco, and Portugal. To 30 cm (1 ft.). Z5–7.

Agrostis capillaris

Alopecurus
FOXTAIL

A group consisting of cool-season deciduous grasses, both annuals and perennials. Not so often seen as garden plants, foxtails are mostly constituents of pasture and other meadow areas. The common name refers to cylindrical flowerheads produced early in the season.

Alopecurus pratensis 'Aureovariegatus'
GOLDEN MEADOW FOXTAIL

Although naturalized over large areas of North America, the species is most commonly seen in this attractive golden-foliaged form, brightest at flowering time and in full sun. Old growth can be cut back to encourage fresh growth after flowering ends. From Eurasia. To 60 cm (2 ft.). Z4.

Ammophila
MARRAM, BEACH GRASS, DUNE GRASS

Confined to coastal sand dunes, these salt-tolerant, warm-season deciduous beach grasses have highly adapted fast-moving root systems that have made them essential elements in the control and stabilization of sand dunes. Successfully used in restoration and erosion control schemes. Where the European species has been used outside of its natural range, such as in North America, it has been found to outcompete and displace native species.

Ammophila arenaria

Ammophila arenaria
MARRAM, EUROPEAN BEACH GRASS

A coast-hugging species whose rapidly spreading root system makes it superbly effective for stabilizing sand dunes. Has tough grey-green foliage and strongly upright buff flowerheads. Often seen in association with *Leymus*, from which it can be differentiated by its smaller leaves and distinct clumping appearance. From Europe and North Africa. To 90 cm (3 ft.). Z5.

Ammophila breviligulata
AMERICAN BEACH GRASS

A highly adapted beach grass that is an essential stabilizer on coastal sand dunes due to its impressive rhizomatous root system. Several selections such as 'Cape' and 'Hatteras' have been made for their regionally adapted qualities. From the coastal eastern U.S. To 90 cm (3 ft.). Z5.

Ammophila breviligulata

Ampelodesmos

Ampelodesmos consists of a single species of clump-forming, warm-season evergreen grass whose foliage superficially resembles that of pampas grass. Once used for tying vines.

Ampelodesmos mauritanicus

VINE REED, ROPE GRASS

Imposing mounds of tough evergreen foliage support tall pale stems of striking one-sided drooping flowerheads, creating a distinctive outline in the best forms. Can vary considerably as most production is from seed. Requires a sunny, well-drained position to do well. From North Africa and Mediterranean Europe. To 2.4 m (8 ft.). Z7–8.

Ampelodesmos mauritanicus

Andropogon

BEARDGRASS

A large and wide-ranging group including some of the best-known and most numerous prairie grasses, all warm-season deciduous. A much smaller number of cultivated species are valuable clump-forming garden plants, generally upright in habit with stems and leaves offering a wide selection of warm oranges, cinnamons, and reds, especially during autumn. Originates from a mix of tropical and temperate climates.

Andropogon gerardii
BIG BLUESTEM, TURKEY FOOT

'Turkey foot' describes the shape of the often 'three-toed' flowers appearing atop elegant tall stems in an array of subtle colours ranging from green to almost blue—perhaps the plant's primary feature. This warm-season species is an important component of tallgrass prairie, and has produced noteworthy cultivars for gardens that accentuate its vertical habit and potential for spectacular autumnal pageants of colour. Long-lived, tough, and hardy in wet to dry soils. Requires open, sunny conditions for best performance. Too rich a soil or shade can incline the plants to flop as the flower stems extend. From North America, including Mexico. To 2.4 m (8 ft.). Z3.

'Blackhawks'. A distinctive selection from Intrinsic Perennial Gardens offering deep purplish-green spring foliage, and deeper tones of burgundy to almost black as cooler nights set in. To 1.5 m (5 ft.).

'Dancing Wind'. A free-flowering form selected for its later season mix of green and red that darkens to scarlet shades in September as the fall progresses. Best in full sun. Selected by Intrinsic Perennial Gardens. To 1.8 m (6 ft.).

'Holy Smoke'. This distinctive selection from Intrinsic Perennial Garden forms mounds of silvered foliage that offers luscious, smokey purple and red tints to the leaves and stems over a long period. To 2.1 m (7)'.

'Lord Snowden's Big Blue'. An especially upright selection that combines possibly the tallest and bluest of stems and leaves, though still

Andropogon gerardii 'Dancing Wind'

Andropogon 'Holy Smoke'

offering myriad purple, orange, and copper hues on cool fall days. To 2.1 m (7 ft.).

'New Wave'. A striking selection from seed, with strong reddish stems that are distinctly upright, holding the flowers quite clear of purple-tinged clumps of green foliage. To 1.8 m (6 ft.).

'Red October'. A selection from Intrinsic Perennial Gardens with an upright habit and red-tinted green foliage that deepens to a darker, more vibrant red as fall approaches. To 1.8 m (6 ft.).

Andropogon glomeratus
Syn. *Andropogon virginicus* var. *abbreviatus*.
BUSHY BEARDGRASS

Naturally occurs in wet places like marshes and bogs, with relatively short (though still upright) flower stems, noticeably fluffy when in seed. The stiff stems of *A. glomeratus* var. *scabriglumis* are a little taller; it is limited to warmer areas. Both make excellent garden plants, especially in prairie or meadow plantings, preferring full sun. From North America. To 90 cm (3 ft.). Z5.

Andropogon ternarius

Andropogon gerardii 'Red October'

Andropogon glomeratus

Andropogon ternarius
SPLIT BLUESTEM

From eastern parts of the U.S., this upright clump-forming grass is relatively unassuming in spring but becomes highly noticeable when summer flowers appear. Tiny spikelets appear to hang from stems, and reflect and sparkle in the sunlight. Will flop in shade, too rich or wet a soil. Variable to 1.5 m (5 ft.).

'Black Mountain'. A durable selection more compact in habit, so less prone to flopping. Clumps of grey-green foliage and flower stems offer pink and red hues later season. To 90cm (3ft).

Andropogon virginicus
BROOMSEDGE

Tough and adaptable, occurring over a wide area and under greatly differing soil conditions.

Anemanthele lessoniana

Especially valuable when used en masse, such as in meadows, where its bright autumnal and winter colourations ranging from orange to dull copper create the most striking of effects. At its best in poor soils and full sun. From North America. To 90 cm (3 ft.). Z3.

Andropogon virginicus var. *glaucus*
CHALKY BLUESTEM

Less cold-hardy but more heat tolerant than the species, this geographically limited variety is distinct for its glaucous blue summer foliage, and it has given rise to several cultivars with more intense blue colouration. Especially useful in drought-prone areas in full sun. From the southern U.S. To 90 cm (3 ft.). Z7.

Anemanthele

Native to both North and South Islands of New Zealand from hilltop to sea level, this genus comprises just one species of ornamental cool-season evergreen grass—long known to gardeners as *Stipa arundinacea*.

Anemanthele lessoniana
Syn. *Stipa arundinacea*
PHEASANT TAIL, WIND GRASS

A most graceful and useful clump-forming evergreen that happily tolerates a range of conditions from full sun to fairly deep shade. Happy in most dry soils but dislikes wet. Forms graceful mounds of leaves gently cascading from a tight central clump that does not split easily. Leaves follow a constantly changing pattern of greens, tans, oranges, and reds, though in deepest shade, they tend to remain green. Quick-growing but short-lived with lifespan between three to five years. With enough sun, masses of tiny pinkish-red flowers on lax stems are produced, covering the plant in a gauzy cascade of pink. Reseeds when happy. To 75 cm (2½ ft.). Z8.

Aristida

THREE AWN

A very large and wide-ranging group of warm-season deciduous, mostly clump-forming bunch grasses, often a major constituent of dry grasslands such as savannah in North America, Africa, Asia, and Australasia.

Aristida purpurea

Aristida purpurea
PURPLE THREE AWN

A common element of Californian dry grasslands, named for its flowers which are produced in some profusion over a long period. Can provide a vivid sense of drama when used en masse as in meadow plantings or large drifts. Bright green bunches of leaves support the flowers for the earlier part of the year, with stems, leaves, and flowers all gradually drying and bleaching during dry summers, though in coastal areas growth may continue to be active all season. Reseeds easily under the right conditions. Tolerates a wide variety of soils, though mostly dry, and always requires full sun. From the southern U.S. To 60 cm (2 ft.). Z6.

Arundo donax

Arundo

REED

Only three species comprise this small but well-known group of warm-season semi-evergreen grasses. All have a running rootstock and can be mistaken for bamboo at a casual glance.

Arundo donax

GIANT REED

Despite having naturalized over a wide area—especially in warm climates where there is sufficient moisture to fuel its phenomenal rate of growth and sunlight to allow it to set fertile seed—the giant reed remains a valuable garden plant in areas where its vigour is at least partially restrained by climatic conditions. Tall, strongly upright stems and long grey-green leaves tapering to a point make it the biggest grass, reaching around 5 m (15 ft.) in warm areas where it remains evergreen. In cooler climates, the stems and leaves become so bedraggled after winter that it is frequently best cut to ground level, and in this case, it can still reach heights of 3–4 m (10–14 ft.) in a single season. Not picky about soil conditions, it will tolerate various levels of drought and moisture, and while aggressively colonizing in the warmest areas, it is content to make slowly spreading (though still large) clumps where it is colder. Always prefers sun. From Africa, Asia, and Eurasia. Z6.

    'Golden Chain'. A golden-variegated form with the same striking patterns as 'Versicolor' but with a less robust growth rate and even less cold-hardy. Needs sun and shelter. To 2.4 m (8 ft.). Z8.

    'Macrophylla'. An excellent garden form that has wider, greyer leaves and thicker stems that are almost vertical and not nearly so tall. As hardy as the species. To 2.7 m (9 ft.). Z6.

    'Versicolor' ('Variegata'). Possibly among the most striking of variegated plants, with large wide leaves and stout stems all strikingly striped in creamy white and green, occasionally marbled with many shades of pink. Noticeably less hardy than the type, it will need some protection over winter in colder areas. To 2.4 m (8 ft.). Z8.

Arundo donax 'Golden Chain'

Arundo donax 'Macrophylla'

Arundo donax 'Versicolor'

Arundo formosana
TAIWANESE REED GRASS

Smaller in all parts than the giant reed, this downsized version has a daintiness absent from *Arundo donax*. Forms tighter clumps with more regularly produced pink-suffused blooms. Not overly fussy about soil, but requires sun. From Asia. To 2.4 m (8 ft.). Z6.

'Green Fountain'. A selection from China with a more rounded form.

'Oriental Gold'. Very distinctive, with bright green- and yellow-striped foliage. Occasionally produces bright pink flowers.

Bothriochloa
BEARDGRASS

The perennial warm-season deciduous to semi-evergreen grasses in this relatively small group are used in agriculture, and include some species with distinctive ornamental value. Widely distributed in temperate and tropical areas.

Bothriochloa barbinodis
Syn. *Andropogon barbinodis*
SILVER BEARDGRASS

A highly attractive bunchgrass producing slender flower stalks topped with initially slender silvery white flowers that gradually dry and open with age. Prefers an open position, though copes with light shade, and is reasonably drought tolerant. From the southern U.S. to Mexico. To 1.2 m (4 ft.). Z7.

Bothriochloa bladhii
Syn. *Bothriochloa caucasica*
BEARDGRASS

Delicate-looking clumps of narrow light green foliage which can turn deep red autumnal colours. Flower spikes consist of widely spaced silvery red flowers, creating a light and airy effect. Needs full sun and warm, well-drained soils. From Asia and Africa. To 1.2 m (4 ft.). Z7.

Bothriochloa bladhii

Bothriochloa ischaemum
YELLOW BLUESTEM

A clump-forming grass with light green to almost yellow foliage, generally upright and topped with attractive red flowers that gradually dry to silver. Needs sun and warm, well-drained soils. From Europe and North Africa. To 90 cm (3 ft.). Z6.

Bouteloua
GRAMA GRASS

A dry-loving group of annual and perennial warm-season semi-evergreen to deciduous grasses, many important for forage, present in both North and South America in open grasslands, including shortgrass prairie.

Bouteloua curtipendula

Bouteloua curtipendula
SIDE OATS GRAMA

Relatively erect and distinct in appearance, with noticeably one-sided flowers, initially purplish and coming from generally upright stems. Can also have purplish maroon-tinted leaves. In cooler temperatures, it needs full sun. Extremely drought-tolerant. From North and South America. To 90 cm (3 ft.). Z4.

Bouteloua dactyloides
Syn. *Buchloe dactyloides*
BUFFALO GRASS

This low-growing warm-season grass has spreading grey-green foliage that forms a dense, compact turf, and is an important constituent of the shortgrass prairie. Its durability, low water requirement, and ability to withstand considerable foot traffic has made it a natural choice for meadows and a replacement for more traditional lawns in many parts of the United States. Has given rise to several forms specifically for lawn replacement. Requires good drainage and will turn brown in periods of drought. From central North America. To 20 cm (8 in.). Z4.

Bouteloua gracilis
BLUE GRAMA, MOSQUITO GRASS

Daintier than side oats, with maroon-purple flowers that gradually curl with age arranged at right angles to the stem. When planted in quantity, the effect is almost magical. Tolerates a wide range of conditions but always prefers sun, and may stay evergreen with sufficient moisture. Tough and adaptable, it is a successful lawn substitute that can be mown to a height of a few inches or left as an effective unmown meadow. From the southern U.S. To 60 cm (2 ft.). Z3.

   'Blonde Ambition'. An impressive selection with good vigor and bluish-green leaves topped by masses of distinctive light blonde-yellow flowers produced during summer. To 90 cm (3 ft.).

   'Honeycomb'. An Intrinsic Perennial Gardens introduction. Similar in stature to 'Blonde Ambition', producing many delicate eyelash-like yellow-pollened flowers in early summer. To 90 cm (3 ft.).

Bouteloua gracilis

Bouteloua gracilis 'Blonde Ambition'

Bouteloua gracilis 'Honeycomb'

Briza
QUAKING GRASS

A genus of annual and perennial, temperate, cool-season semi-evergreen grasses grown principally for their spikelets of heart-shaped flowers. The annual *Briza maxima*, with comparatively large flowers, is commonly grown but often regarded as a weed in gardens due to its generous production of viable seed.

Briza media
QUAKING GRASS, PEARL GRASS, RATTLE GRASS, TOTTER GRASS

Late spring sees the arrival of the dainty spikelets of this easygoing clump-forming grass. Tolerates a wide range of soils, from heavy, wet clay to light, dry sand, but prefers reasonably sunny open conditions. Frequently found in meadows and easily adapts to garden use. Flowers are purple at first, dancing in the slightest breeze. Once dried, they rustle and rattle with the wind, but do not generally persist through winter. From Eurasia. To 75 cm (2½ ft.). Z4.

'Golden Bee'. A selection with flowerheads of a distinctive golden yellow hue as they mature. Perhaps a little more compact than the species.

'Limouzi'. With blue-green foliage, this selection may be a bit slower to flower than other quaking grasses.

'Russells'. A pretty variegated form with white- and green-striped foliage that can be tinged pink at cooler temperatures. This colouring extends to the flower stem, making an attractive overall ensemble. Sets viable seed that reverts to the species.

Briza media 'Limouzi'

Briza media

Briza media 'Golden Bee'

Calamagrostis

REED GRASS

A large and diverse group of cool-season deciduous grasses distinguished by their usually upright, sometimes feather-like flowers. An adaptable group, many cope happily with a mix of soils, including moist to wet, in full sun to part shade. Variegated forms tend to show best colour in the first part of the year, then fade. Widely distributed in northern temperate Eurasia, the U.K., and North America.

Calamagrostis ×*acutiflora*
FEATHER REED GRASS

A naturally occurring if seldom seen hybrid between *C. epigejos* and *C. arundinacea*, mostly represented by *C.* ×*acutiflora* 'Karl Foerster', named after the famous German nurseryman. Tough and adaptable, most forms prefer open positions, and will tolerate a wide range of soil moisture except very dry. Z4.

'Avalanche'. Has clear wide white bands down the centre of each leaf and makes healthy mounds of foliage which are topped by silvery tan plumes on strongly vertical stems. Tolerates light shade. To 1.5 m (5 ft.).

'Eldorado'. Slightly less hardy than the type, with bright golden-yellow-and-green-striped leaves. Takes light shade. Flowers may be less upright than other forms. To 1.5 m (5 ft.).

Calamagrostis ×*acutiflora* 'Avalanche'

Calamagrostis ×*acutiflora* 'Eldorado'

Calamagrostis ×*acutiflora* 'Karl Foerster'

Calamagrostis ×*acutiflora* 'Overdam'

Calamagrostis ×*acutiflora* 'Waldenbuch'

Calamagrostis brachytricha

'Karl Foerster' ('Stricta'). One of the most popular and easily recognizable of grasses, with tall, firmly upright, narrow flower stems that are unremarkable individually but are packed together in such numbers on established plants they become impossible to miss. Most effective planted in drifts or masses where it provides a startling vertical accent. Also effective as an informal hedge or screen. Fresh green growth starts early in the season, with initially green flower stems arising from vigorous mounds around midseason with dark purple flowers gradually turning the trademark beige from high summer onwards. Stems are brought to the ground by heavy rainfall, only to spring up again when dry weather returns. Virtually sterile, it is a wise choice for large-scale plantings with little risk to surrounding sensitive natural areas. To 1.8 m (6 ft.).

'Overdam'. From the excellent Danish nursery of the same name, this cultivar has bright mounds of green-and-white-striped leaves setting off pinkish feathery plumes of flower. Best colour in cooler climates. To 1.5 m (5 ft.).

'Waldenbuch'. Clumps of bright green foliage support masses of tall narrow upright stems with a slightly splaying habit that creates a more open feel than the similar 'Karl Foerster'. Flowers initially open and airy. Late-season green leaves, tan stems, and beige flowers create a distinctive effect. Best in sunny open spot. Will take some moisture. To 1.8 m (6 ft.).

Calamagrostis brachytricha
Syn. *Calamagrostis arundinacea* var. *brachytricha*

KOREAN FEATHER REED GRASS

From mounds of strong green foliage come large upward-pointing arrow-like heads of flowers, initially purple-tinted before quickly fading to a striking buff and beige. Generally unfussy about soil type, in its native range it prefers some moisture, whether in sun or the shade of the woodland edge. In gardens, it is one of the few true grasses that can tolerate relatively shady conditions. From Asia. To 1.2 m (4 ft.). Z4.

Calamagrostis emodensis
CHINESE REED GRASS

With soft-textured bluish green leaves and gently nodding heads of feathery flowers, this is a very pretty if comparatively short-lived grass. Can slowly spread from its original position and will reseed in favourable conditions. Plant in sunny, well-drained soils for best performance. From China. To 1.2 m (4 ft.). Z8.

Calamagrostis epigejos
FEATHER REED GRASS

A variable and strongly spreading species forming thick mats of upright stems topped by flower spikes that typically curve. Self-sows readily and ideal for erosion control or for covering large areas. Will tolerate sun or shade and most soils, though prefers some moisture. From Europe, the U.K., and Asia. To 1.5 m (5 ft.). Z5.

Calamagrostis foliosa
MENDOCINO REED GRASS

Gentle mounds of soft blue-green foliage—occasionally streaked purplish red—make this geographically limited species quietly attractive, especially covered in spring-blooming flowers, which accentuate the rounded habit of mature specimens. Tolerant of sea spray and winds; a good choice for gardens exposed to coastal conditions. Happy in light shade or full sun with enough moisture. Does not respond to being cut back, and may require dividing every few years to maintain vigour. From California. To 45 cm (1½ ft.). Z8.

Calamagrostis 'Little Nootka'

From Calflora Nursery, this evergreen selection is thought to be a possible hybrid between *C. foliosa* and *C. nutkaensis*, similar though more compact in habit to the latter, with gently arching flowers. To 60 cm (2 ft.).

Calamagrostis nutkaensis
PACIFIC REED GRASS

Coarse arching green leaves form healthy clumps from which upright to slightly pendulous flower stems emerge during spring; these persist for some time. Semi-evergreen in mild locations.

Calamagrostis emodensis

Found in grasslands, swales, and open woodland with some moisture. Adapts to either shade or sun and quite dry soils under garden conditions. From the North American Pacific coast. To 1.2 m (4 ft.). Z7.

'The King'. An especially good form of the species from the King Range mountains selected by Roger Raiche for its free-flowering nature and overall habit. Happy in sun or shade and dry soil. To 1.2 m (4 ft.).

Calamagrostis varia
REED GRASS

Slowly spreading roots make large tussocks of bright green foliage that support upright flower stems and slightly pendulous pinky purple flowers in early summer. Copes with a variety of soils including damp, and prefers sun but tolerates light shade. From Europe. To 1.2 cm (4 ft.). Z5.

Calamagrostis nutkaensis

Calamagrostis nutkaensis 'The King'

Calamagrostis varia

Carex
SEDGE

Carex is a genus of mostly evergreen grass-*like* plants: not in fact true grasses, but members of a huge plant family commonly referred to as sedges, which includes several thousand species and almost innumerable cultivars. Clump-forming or rapidly running, and capable of adapting to a variety of soil types and climatic conditions as wide as the species are numerous, sedges have become a major part of the gardener's plant palette. Many occur naturally in moist soils in sun or shade, but the ability of others to withstand drought and dry shade is invaluable. Clump-forming types offer foliage in myriad hues with flowers mostly (though not exclusively) of secondary consideration. Running types are especially valuable for testing applications such as erosion control, lawn replacement, and green roofs. Widely distributed in temperate areas.

Carex alba
WHITE SEDGE

Gradually spreading, finely textured mounds of bright green foliage make quietly attractive ground cover in conditions from full sun to damp shade. From Europe. To 30 cm (1 ft.). Z5.

Carex alba

Carex appalachica

Carex arenaria

Carex albicans
WHITETINGE SEDGE

Tough, low-growing, and tolerant of shade, this clumping semi-evergreen sedge is a sensible fine-leaved choice for woodland areas. From North America. To 20 cm (8 in.). Z4.

Carex amphibola
GREY SEDGE

A most adaptable clump-forming sedge from eastern United States. Though it comes from moist conditions, like many sedges it can adapt to drier conditions in the garden. Mounds of green foliage, semi-evergreen in warmer climates, provide a pleasing shaggy effect. Will reseed noticeably when happy. To 45 cm (18 in.). Z4.

Carex appalachica
APPALACHIAN SEDGE

A graceful long-leaved evergreen sedge of relatively fine texture from generally shady areas. The slowly spreading clumps prefer average to dry soils and are happiest with some shade, especially in warmer areas. Often used as a lawn substitute. Native to North America. To 30 cm (1 ft.). Z4.

Carex arenaria
SAND SEDGE

Found on stabilized sand dunes, this sedge has solid green leaves and is distinctive for the often noticeably straight lines created by its far-reaching running habit. Tolerant of sun and a level of shade, though not too wet a soil. Makes excellent lawn alternative. From Europe and the U.K. To 45 cm (1½ ft.). Z4.

Carex berggrenii
NUTBROWN SEDGE

Low-growing with gradually spreading clumps of reddish-brown leaves. Happy in sun but soil should not be too dry. From New Zealand. To 10 cm (4 in.). Z5.

Carex brunnea
BROWN SEDGE

A widely distributed clump-forming evergreen, usually represented in gardens by shorter-growing variegated cultivars. From Australia and Asia, especially China and Japan. Z8.

'Jenneke'. Tidy mounds of narrow evergreen foliage, brightly striped greenish-yellow to cream- and green-edged. Best in sun or part shade if not too dry. To 40 cm (16 in.).

'Variegata'. Has similar small mounds of evergreen foliage, but with green-centred creamy white edges. To 40 cm (16 in.).

Carex buchananii
LEATHERLEAF SEDGE

A striking, bright copper bronze-foliaged plant forming tufted erect mounds with characteristically curled leaf tips. Looks stunning when contrasted well. Drought-tolerant. Comes easily from seed with minor variations, which have given rise to several seed strains such as 'Red Rooster' and 'Viridis'. All can be comparatively short-lived. From New Zealand. To 60 cm (2 ft.). Z7.

Carex cherokeensis
CHEROKEE SEDGE

Slowly spreading clumps of evergreen foliage make this an especially useful sedge for a variety of applications such as rain gardens, meadows, and woodland ground cover. Preferring shade and moist soils, it will tolerate some sun and average soils. From the southeastern U.S. To 60 cm (2 ft.). Z6.

Carex comans
HAIRY SEDGE

Possibly the most commonly grown brown-foliaged sedge, Carex comans has given rise to several selections, all differing somewhat in colouration but broadly forming wider-than-high mounds of evergreen foliage and insignificant flowers. All brown-foliaged sedges can be relatively short-lived (lasting three to five years), though timely division can rejuvenate established plants. Will reseed if happy, allowing for the gradual replacement of older plants. Best in full sun and well-drained soils, but will tolerate part shade. From New Zealand. To 50 cm (20 in.). Z7.

'Bronze'. Probably an all-inclusive name for any of the darker forms of the species that come easily from seed.

'Frosted Curls'. A distinctive light form, with pale silvery green foliage curling prettily towards the ground. Best in a sunny, open spot.

'Milk Chocolate'. Has warm chocolate-brown leaves. Of uncertain origin.

Carex conica
HIME-KAN-SUGE

With glossy green leaves forming dense mounds of tufted foliage, this is usually only seen in gardens in the variegated form. From Japan and the Korean Peninsula. Z5.

'Snowline' ('Variegata', 'Marginata'). Attractive sedge with slowly growing mounds of white-margined deep green leaves. Can be relatively long lived. Happy in open, sunny positions or light shade if not too dry. To 40 cm (16 in.).

Carex comans

Carex comans 'Milk Chocolate'

Carex dipsacea

Carex dipsacea 'Dark Horse'

Carex dipsacea
AUTUMN SEDGE

Forms evergreen clumps of dark bronzy olive-green leaves with almost-black flowerheads appearing from within the foliage. Best colour in full sun where not too dry. From New Zealand. To 60 cm (2 ft.). Z7.

    '**Dark Horse**'. Has rather darker, more dramatically coloured foliage in many shades of deep green and olive. Prefers full sun and soil that is not too dry.

Carex divulsa
GREY SEDGE

Beautiful and adaptable, with long dark green leaves forming gracefully drooping mounds of evergreen foliage. Invaluable for garden and wider use. Dainty soft yellow flowers, if individually unremarkable, are produced in sufficient numbers to contrast with the foliage's colour and form. Happy in sun or shade, and dry to damp soils. From Eurasia and the U.K. To 45 cm (1½ ft.). Z4.

Carex elata
TUSSOCK SEDGE

Forms dense tussocks of grey-green leaves that slowly make larger stands in wet, marginal places such as marshes and riversides. This tough species is not usually seen in gardens other than in its very popular golden-foliaged forms. From Eurasia and the U.K. Z5.

'Aurea'. One of the most striking of all sedges during spring, when its bright golden leaves, variably striped light to dark green, are freely produced—upright at first, then gradually cascading outwards to the ground. Flowers are also freely produced, and most attractive up close; can add considerably to the overall effect of a mature plant. Best in the early part of the year with enough moisture. Foliage will gradually crisp, especially if dry, though cutting back at this time can stimulate a fresh crop of less bright but still effective leaves. To 75 cm (2½ ft.).

Carex divulsa

Carex elata 'Aurea'

Carex elata 'Knightshayes'

Carex flacca 'Blue Zinger'

'Knightshayes'. A less robust form, named for the famous British garden, with leaves lacking any green. To 60 cm (2 ft.).

Carex flacca
CARNATION GRASS, GLAUCOUS SEDGE

The narrow, pointed glaucous blue foliage of this gradually spreading sedge resembles that of a garden carnation. Found among sand dunes and marshes, it is tough but attractive—a desirable ornamental, useful as a green roof plant. Occasional dainty purple-black flowers are sometimes numerous enough to be noticeable. Good in sun, drought, or light shade. Various selections have been made. From Eurasia, the U.K., and North Africa. To 30 cm (1 ft.). Z4.

'Blue Zinger'. Selected for its blue-toned foliage and happy in similar conditions to the species.

Carex flagellifera
MOP HEAD SEDGE

A brown sedge—similar in its generally rounded outline to *Carex comans* and *C. testacea*—with a range of foliage colour that has led to several selections including 'Toffee Twist' and 'Coca Cola'. Like other browns, it can be short-lived and will seed where happy. Best in full sun and not-too-wet soils. From New Zealand. To 40 cm (16 in.). Z7.

Carex flava
YELLOW SEDGE

Has subtly attractive light greenish-yellow leaves topped with unusual orange-brown flowers that turn to spiky yellow seed heads late in the summer. Occurring naturally in marshes and wet woods, it will also tolerate quite dry conditions. From Eurasia and the U.K. To 60 cm (2 ft.). Z5.

Carex grayii
MACE SEDGE

Most noticeable for its comparatively large club-like seed heads in light greenish yellow, produced from mounds of bright green foliage in late spring. Happy in some sun or light shade with not too dry a soil. From North America. To 90 cm (3 ft.). Z7.

Carex laxiculmis
WOODLAND SEDGE

An attractive clump-forming sedge having relatively wide evergreen leaves of a rather glaucous blue. Tolerant of a range of conditions including dry shade, it will cope with sunny, more open positions if soil is not too dry. From North America. To 30 cm (1 ft.). Z6.

'Bunny Blue'. A selection with good blue foliage and similar robust garden performance.

Carex morrowii
Syn. Carex fortunei
KAN SUGE

Easygoing, with gradually spreading mounds of evergreen leaves. Tolerant of a wide range of conditions and usually seen in gardens as one of the following selected forms. From Japan. Z5.

'Everglow'. Quietly attractive mounds of green and creamy white leaves with a distinctive basal tint of orange. Effective in sun or shade. To 50 cm (20 in.).

'Fisher's Form'. Fresh, attractive yellow-white and green foliage on compact rosette-forming plants. Equally happy in sun or light shade. To 50 cm (20 in.).

Carex grayii

Carex laxiculmis

Carex laxiculmis 'Bunny Blue'

Carex morrowii 'Everglow'

'Ice Dance'. A spreading form which makes dense, durable, and long-lived cover, with light green leaves narrowly margined pale creamy white. One of the best for inhospitable dry shade. To 50 cm (20 in.)

'Silk Tassel'. Technically a cultivar of a markedly different subspecies, *C. morrowii* var. *temnolepis*, this form has very narrow leaves with a refined variegation that is white-centred, green-edged, and gives an overall impression of grey. Happy in sun or part shade. To 30 cm (1 ft.).

'Vanilla Ice'. Spreading mounds of attractive, bright creamy white leaves boldly edged in green. Happy in sun or shade, and makes excellent cover in dry shade. To 50 cm (20 in.).

Carex morrowii 'Fisher's Form'

Carex morrowii 'Ice Dance'

Carex muskingumensis

Carex muskingumensis 'Little Midge'

Carex muskingumensis 'Oehme'

Carex muskingumensis 'Silberstreif'

Carex nigra 'Online'

Carex muskingumensis
PALM SEDGE

Slowly increasing, long-lived clumps of narrow, architectural semi-evergreen leaves of light green that taper to a point. Topped with brown pompom-like flowerheads during summer. From wetter areas, but tolerates quite dry soils in sun or part shade. From North America. To 60 cm (2 ft.). Z4.

'Little Midge'. A lovely and genuinely dwarf selection, similar in most respects to the species except smaller in all its parts. Perfectly formed to 15 cm (6 in.).

'Oehme'. Green-foliaged, with subtle narrowly yellow margins gradually appearing as the season progresses.

'Silberstreif'. Slightly more compact, with attractive green-and-white-striped variegated foliage. Best in light shade. To 45 cm (1½ ft.).

Carex nigra
BLACK SEDGE

Found in bogs, waterways, and marshy areas, this variable species can be clump forming or running, with foliage in various shades of glaucous green. Flowers are interesting, if unshowy. An excellent ground cover for wet areas, it has given rise to several cultivated forms. From Europe, the U.K., and coastal North America. To 75 cm (2½ ft.). Z5.

'Online'. Forms slowly creeping mounds of grey-green foliage narrowly margined in creamy yellow. To 45 cm (1½ ft.).

Carex obnupta

Carex obnupta 'Golden Day'

Carex oshimensis 'Evercream'

Carex oshimensis 'Everest'

Carex oshimensis 'Evergold'

Carex obnupta
SLOUGH SEDGE

Makes large clumps of tough, bright green, sharp-edged leaves. Can spread to cover large areas under suitable conditions, such as in wet soils or by the water's edge. Has highly attractive purplish-black flowers. Best in sun or reasonable shade. From the U.S. West Coast. To 1.2 m (4 ft.). Z7.

'Golden Day'. A seed-raised selection with entirely golden foliage. Less robust than the species. To 1.2 m (4 ft.).

Carex oshimensis
OSHIMA KAN SUGE

A clump-forming, tough, and hardy evergreen sedge often found in woodland areas in its natural range, and most commonly encountered in cultivated forms, which have become deservedly popular for their combination of durability and effectiveness in our gardens. From Japan. To 50 cm (20 in.). Z5–6.

'Evercream'. Subtle, creamy yellow-and-green-striped foliage. Gradually creates tough and long-lived rounded mounds. Tolerant of most soils in sun or shade. To 50 cm (20 in.).

'Everest'. Mounds of dark green with white stripes that are at their brightest and most effective in shady areas. Most soils in some sun or part shade. To 50 cm (20 in.).

'Evergold'. ('Old Gold', 'Variegata'). Individual leaves are brightly variegated with variable creamy white to yellow centres and dark green marginal stripes, gradually forming gracefully cascading mounds. Happy in shade, or sun if planted in not-too-dry soils. To 50 cm (20 in.).

Carex oshimensis 'Everillo'

'Everillo'. A distinctive clump-forming sedge producing lime green to yellow foliage that can gradually deepen to golden yellow as temperatures drop. Best in light shade with soil not too dry. To 60 cm (2 ft.).

'Everlime'. Quietly variegated limey yellow-and-green-striped leaves. Gradually creates understated and refined mounds of evergreen foliage. Part shade or some sun. Soil not too dry. To 50 cm (20 in.).

'Feather Falls'. Lovely selection with boldly striped creamy white and green leaves. Can make large, pendulous mounds of foliage, especially noticeable when grown in containers. To 50 cm (20 in.).

Carex oshimensis 'Feather Falls'

Carex panicea

Carex pellita

Carex paniculata

Carex pendula

Carex pansa

'Gold Strike'. A variegated selection from Kurt Bluemel with similar dark green margins and uniformly creamy yellow centres. To 50 cm (20 in.).

Carex panicea
CARNATION SEDGE

Similar to (and often confused with) carnation grass, *Carex flacca*, this pretty sedge has blue-green foliage and dainty flowers. Tolerates a wide variety of conditions, from full sun to shade and wet to quite dry soils. From Eurasia and the U.K. To 60 cm (2 ft.). Z7–8.

Carex paniculata
GREATER TUSSOCK SEDGE

Resembling in habit and habitat the North American *Carex stricta* and the Australasian *Carex secta*, this large trunk-forming sedge grows in various levels of damp to wet soils, including by open water. Happiest in open conditions but may tolerate some light shade. From Eurasia and the U.K. To 1.5 m (5 ft.). Z6.

Carex pansa
CALIFORNIA MEADOW SEDGE

This tough, spreading evergreen sedge is very similar to *Carex praegracilis*—very adaptable, and frequently used in meadows, for lawn replacement, and restoration projects throughout its widespread range. Happy in sun or some shade, in a wide variety of soil types and in most levels of moisture. From the western U.S. To 40 cm (16 in.). Z6.

Carex pellita
WOOLLY SEDGE

A variable sedge that is widely distributed across much of North America in damp and wetland areas, but can also be found colonizing disturbed ground. Forms spreading mounds of green foliage that will cope with some sunshine or shade. To 75 cm (2½ ft.). Z4.

Carex pendula
PENDULOUS SEDGE

Makes dense clumps of tough dark green pendulous foliage from which emerge tall graceful flowering stems with drooping yellow catkin-like flowers. Can reseed heavily. Tolerates a wide range of conditions, including sun or shade in wet or dry soils. Commonly encountered throughout its range. From Europe, the U.K., Asia, and North Africa. To 1.8 m (6 ft.) in flower. Z7.

'Moonraker'. Not often seen, with bright golden yellow young shoots and foliage that gradually returns to the usual green after the spring flush. To 1.5 m (5 ft.).

Carex pendula 'Moonraker'

Carex pensylvanica

Carex pensylvanica
PENNSYLVANIA SEDGE

Mostly evergreen, spreading, and variable, this widespread species can be found covering large areas with an even, lawn-like sward under trees or in more open conditions. Very drought- and shade-tolerant but will not withstand regular foot traffic. Can be winter dormant in coldest areas. From eastern North America. To 20 cm (8 in.). Z4.

'Straw Hat'. Generally similar in habit to the species, this well-named selection from Intrinsic Perennial Gardens has more noticeable flower clusters in late spring. Part shade is best. To 20cm (8 in.).

Carex phyllocephala
CHINESE PALM SEDGE

This unusual species is not often cultivated in gardens, though it is seen in a variegated form. From China. Z7–8.

'Sparkler'. This stunning sedge resembles a starburst, with its cream, green, and white foliage on tall, almost cane-like stems that are often blotched deep maroon purple. Disliking of cold areas, and ideal with adequate moisture and some shelter. To 60 cm (2 ft.).

Carex plantaginea
BROADLEAVED SEDGE

Clump-forming, with distinctive wide, pale green leaves, almost rosette-like. From open woodland in damp areas. Can be evergreen, and needs moisture to be happy. From North America. To 40 cm (16 in.). Z5.

Carex praegracilis
WESTERN MEADOW SEDGE

A most adaptable North American sedge. Widespread in its natural range and slowly making its way from West to East Coast North America, this strongly spreading species makes dense mats of almost indestructible, usually evergreen foliage that may go summer- or winter-dormant depending on prevailing conditions. From coastal sand dunes to inland meadows, from wet to dry, its tough adaptability makes it a first choice for meadows, lawn replacement, and green roofs. When cut on a regular basis it will produce a close sward of foliage that can be kept just a few inches tall. From western North America. To 45 cm (1½ ft.). Z5.

Carex phyllocephala 'Sparkler'

Carex plantaginea

Carex praegracilis

Carex remota
REMOTE SEDGE
Compact mounds of bright green leaves, and in spring, widely spaced pale yellow flower spikes. Found in shady and often moist areas. Good for shade conditions and adaptable to more open situations where soil not too dry. From Eurasia and the U.K. To 45 cm (1½ ft.). Z6.

Carex riparia
GREATER POND SEDGE
Found in slowly moving or still water and often forming large drifts over time, this aggressively colonizing pond sedge is usually seen as a variegated form in gardens. Best in sun or light shade. Widespread in the Northern Hemisphere. To 1.2 m (4 ft.). Z6.

Carex remota

Carex siderosticha 'Variegata'

Carex secta

Carex 'Silver Sceptre'

'Variegata'. Gracefully arching leaves are boldly striped white and green. Shares the species' running ability.

Carex secta

NEW ZEALAND TUSSOCK SEDGE

A beautiful evergreen sedge, with nicely coloured clumps of narrow bright green leaves, gradually forming fountains of gently arching foliage. Especially effective near open water. Will slowly form trunks from the old roots and leaf bases, increasing the height of the plant. Prefers sun and adequate moisture but will tolerate some shade if not too dry. From New Zealand. To 1.2 m (4 ft.). Z8.

Carex siderosticha

BROADLEAF SEDGE

Low, dense, slowly creeping masses of wide green leaves make excellent durable cover even in dryer woodland conditions, though some sun and moisture are preferred. Has given rise to several mostly variegated forms. Deciduous in winter. From China and Japan. To 20 cm (8 in.). Z5.

'Banana Boat'. Bold and attractive with dramatic yellow-centred variegation. Can lack the other forms' vigour.

'Variegata'. Occasionally pink-tinged, strongly marked white-striped leaves make this the most popular form in gardens. Tolerates relatively dry situations.

Carex 'Silver Sceptre'

'SILVER SCEPTRE' SEDGE

Gradually creeping mounds of compact, neatly variegated leaves with broad, creamy white margins, this is an excellent sedge for garden use, tolerating wide-ranging conditions from sun to shade and wet to dry. Of uncertain origin in Japan. To 25 cm (10 in.). Z8.

Carex spissa

Carex tenuiculmis 'Cappuccino'

Carex spissa

SAN DIEGO SEDGE

Broad, toothed leaves in steely blue-grey with noticeable midribs are produced in stout clumps in sun or shady areas where there is sufficient moisture. Light brown flowers are freely produced in spring. Non-invasive and drought-tolerant once established. From California and Mexico. To 1.5 m (5 ft.). Z7.

Carex stricta
TUSSOCK SEDGE

Widespread in North America, this dense tussock-forming sedge offers bright green foliage that is often connected by underground runners to make large stands in wetlands, marshes, and wet woods. Freely produces yellow-brown arching flower stems. Can tolerate drier conditions. From the northeastern U.S. To 90 cm (3 ft.). Z4.

Carex tenuiculmis
BROWN SEDGE

A graceful semi-arching open habit and distinctive chocolate-coloured foliage make this a useful addition to the brown range of sedges. Prefers sun or light shade and not-too-dry soils. From New Zealand. To 60 cm (2 ft.). Z6.

'Cappuccino'. Selected for its attractive, warm, milky coffee–coloured foliage.

Carex testacea
ORANGE SEDGE

A most ornamental sedge forming loose clumps of orange-green foliage that changes subtly throughout the seasons. The arching habit is even more pronounced in tall containers. Best colour in full sun. From New Zealand. To 60 cm (2 ft.). Z6.

Carex testacea

Carex texensis

TEXAS SEDGE

A fine-textured sedge that gradually forms dense colonies from slowly spreading clumps. Will tolerate light foot traffic when used as a lawn replacement. Especially useful in dry shady situations, but will adapt to a level of sun and soil moisture. From eastern and midwestern North America. To 30cm (1 ft.). Z5.

Carex trifida

NEW ZEALAND BLUE SEDGE

One of the bigger sedges, with large keeled green leaves with glaucous undersides, most noticeable in sun. Unusual chunky flowerheads of light brown are especially striking in the early season. Prefers sun or light shade. Drought tolerant, but dislikes cold areas. From New Zealand. To 90 cm (3 ft.). Z8.

'Rekohu Sunrise'. Striking, with attractive warm yellow, gold, and grey-green variegated foliage. To 75 cm (2½ ft.).

Carex trifida 'Rekohu Sunrise'

Chasmanthium

WILD OAT

Growing happily in shady conditions, the warm-season deciduous upright perennial grasses that make up this small group are especially useful in gardens. Originally part of the genus *Uniola*.

Chasmanthium latifolium

WILD OAT SPANGLE GRASS

With wide, ribbon-like, bright green leaves on perky upright stems, this grass is happy in relatively dry shady conditions, though stems may be a little more lax than in more open and sunny conditions, where foliage is a lighter green. Almost-flat spikes of nodding flowers are highly attractive and turn a procession of green to gold and brown, as does foliage as autumn approaches. Clump-forming and tolerant of clay soils and drought, it is versatile for use in many garden applications. Self-seeds in wetter conditions. From North America. To 1.2 m (4 ft.). Z5.

Chasmanthium laxum

SLENDER WILD OAT

Clump-forming and taller than wild oat, with smaller flower spikes held clear of the leaves. Happy in light shade and not-too-dry soils. From North America. To 1.5 m (5 ft.). Z6.

Chionochloa

This small group of tussock-forming cool-season evergreen grasses are closely related to *Cortaderia*, and cover large areas of grassland in their native Australasia.

Chionochloa conspicua

PLUMED TUSSOCK GRASS

Often found near streamsides and other wet places, producing large, open, airy flower stems from relatively coarse and rough foliage. Prefers sun. From New Zealand. To 2.1 m (7 ft.). Z8.

Chionochloa flavicans

TUSSOCK GRASS

More common in gardens than than *Chionchloa conspicua*, with tough evergreen foliage. Very long-lived and drought-tolerant. Distinctive, light green-yellow flowerheads are attractive when grown well. Happy in sun or light shade and not-too-dry soils. From New Zealand. To 90 cm (3 ft.). Z8.

Chionochloa rubra

RED TUSSOCK GRASS

Grown for its wonderful warm, brassy brown to gold evergreen leaves. Forms mounds of gently arching foliage that moves in the slightest breeze. Happy in sun and drought-tolerant once established. From New Zealand. To 1.2 m (4 ft.). Z8.

Cortaderia

This group of warm-season evergreens includes the popular—and sometimes overused—pampas grass, as well as more than twenty different species that can offer flowers of amazingly airy gracefulness. All have tough and relatively coarse semi-evergreen leaves and make substantial clumps with age. Tolerant of a wide range of garden conditions, nearly all perform best in sunny, open positions. Its adaptability and ability to escape from gardens has led to it being regarded as an invasive species in sensitive areas.

Chionochloa flavicans

Chionochloa rubra

Chasmanthium latifolium

Cortaderia richardii

Cortaderia richardii
TOETOE

Arguably the most graceful of all *Cortaderia*, with relatively early, freely produced brown to tan and beige flowers on nodding, gently pendulous stems that fan outwards to create tall, airy fountains that are distinctive and beautiful. Leaves can be pale grey-green with distinct midribs, and form quite significant mounds over time. Versatile in its tolerance of wet to fairly dry soils and full sun or semi-shade. From New Zealand. To 2.7 m (9 ft.). Z8.

Cortaderia selloana
Syn. *Cortaderia argentea*
PAMPAS GRASS

A major constituent of the iconic South American grasslands—the pampas that inspired its common name. Most gardeners are only too familiar with the ability of its tough, sharp-edged leaves to cut skin. In late summer, stiff, robust, upright flower stems produce the often-huge feather duster-like blooms that have made this grass such a widely used (and frequently misused) plant. Drought-tolerant and adaptable, its ability to set copious seed makes it a serious weed in some areas. Most forms are happy in full sun to part shade and most soil types. From South America. Z6–8.

'Albolineata' ('Silver Stripe'). An old cultivar with bright white-striped leaves. To 2.1 m (7 ft.).

'Evita'. Chiefly of interest for its very compact free-flowering habit. Mounds of typical green foliage are topped by large, fluffy white flowers on very short stems from high summer onwards. To 1.8 m (6 ft.).

Cortaderia selloana 'Patagonia'

Cortaderia selloana 'Gold Band'

Cortaderia selloana 'Pumila'

'Gold Band' ('Aureolineata'). The pampas with possibly the brightest yellow-gold and green stripes. Of modest size, though occasional specimens can make large mounds. To 1.8 m (6 ft.).

'Monstrosa'. Possibly the largest selection yet made, with massive flowers produced on very tall stems. To 3 m (10 ft.) or taller.

'Patagonia'. A first-class introduction with blue-grey leaves and pinkish plumes on compact plants. Noticeably resistant to cold temperatures. To 2.1 m (7 ft.).

'Point du Raz' (also known as 'Pointe du Raz'). Mid-green leaves edged creamy white, and consequently a little slower in growth. Fairly free-flowering. To 1.8 m (6 ft.).

'Pumila'. Arguably one of the best-performing selected forms of pampas and certainly one of the hardiest, with many handsome heads of freely produced typical flowers in late summer. Good grey-green foliage. To 2.4 m (8 ft.).

'Tiny Pampa'. Among the most compact forms, this green-leaved selection is free flowering, with typical blowsy plumes in later summer. To 90 cm (3 ft.).

'Rendatleri'. The best-known purplish-pink-flowered form of *C. selloana*. To 2.7 m (9 ft.).

Cortaderia selloana 'Silver Feather'

'Silver Feather'. Most attractive and comparatively compact selection with a regular white-striped variegation that is very bright and effective. To 2.1 m (7 ft.).

'Splendid Star'. A recently introduced dwarf pampas with gold-streaked green leaves topped with white flower plumes in late summer. To 1.5 m (5 ft.).

'Sunningdale Silver'. The best-known selection among larger pampas. Can make massive, fountain-like mounds of grey-green foliage from which arise numerous tall, stately flower spikes at about 3 m (10 ft.).

Cortaderia toetoe

TOETOE

A less well-known species found on New Zealand's North Island. Very similar to *Cortaderia richardii*, with which it shares many characteristics as well as its common name. To 2.7 m (9 ft.). Z8.

Cortaderia selloana 'Sunningdale Silver'

Deschampsia

HAIR GRASS

This widely distributed group of clump-forming cool-season deciduous to semi-evergreen grasses includes some invaluable forms for garden use. Found in a variety of conditions from meadow to woodland and in wet to dry soils, all have delicate, freely produced flowers that can obscure the relatively plain foliage.

Deschampsia cespitosa
TUFTED HAIR GRASS

Preferring moist, open areas from boggy meadows to edges of woodland, this adaptable grass forms mounds of dark green leaves that are completely obscured by billowing masses of cloudlike flowers, varying from purplish to greenish yellow before gradually fading to a fine lace-like beige that stands virtually intact well into winter. Can be short-lived and will last longest with some moisture and sun. Can be rejuvenated by periodic dividing. Comes easily from seed, partially explaining why some established cultivars have become mixed in the trade. Seed-raised strains continue to be developed for use as low resource-use turfgrass. From the temperate U.S., Asia, Eurasia, and the U.K. To 1.2 m (4 ft.). Z6.

'Bronzeschleier'. Chosen for its fresh-looking flowers, greenish bronze upon opening. To 90 cm (3 ft.).

'Goldgehange' Selected for its relatively gold pendant-like flowers that are held above clumps of dark green leaves. To 1.2m (4ft).

'Goldtau'. A highly regarded, relatively compact form with finely textured flowers. To 80 cm (2½ ft.).

'Mill End' Masses of tall light-coloured flowers produced from mounds of dark green foliage. To 1.5 m (5 ft.).

'Schottland'. Robust dark green clumps of foliage support relatively tall, initially purple, light and airy flowers. A selection made in Scotland. To 1.2 m (4 ft.).

'Tardiflora'. Possibly slightly later to come into bloom and produces masses of initially bright green flowers. To 90 cm (3 ft.).

Deschampsia cespitosa 'Goldtau'

Deschampsia cespitosa 'Mill End'

Deschampsia cespitosa 'Schottland'

Deschampsia cespitosa 'Tardiflora'

Deschampsia cespitosa 'Tautrager'

Deschampsia cespitosa 'Waldschatt'

Deschampsia cespitosa var. *vivipara*

Deschampsia cespitosa subsp. *holciformis*

'Tautrager'. Masses of light green flowers that gradually fade as they age. To 60 cm (2 ft.).

'Waldschatt'. A good selection making clumps of green foliage topped with light green flowers that turn bronze as they age. To 90 cm (3 ft.).

Deschampsia cespitosa var. *vivipara*
TUFTED HAIR GRASS

Uncommon but distinctive, producing live young plants on the flowers' ends, which are weighted down in consequence. Sometimes referred to as 'Fairy's Joke'. To 75 cm (2½ ft.).

Deschampsia cespitosa subsp. *holciformis*
PACIFIC HAIR GRASS

Often found on coastal bluffs or in open grasslands. Much more compact in all its parts than the species. Low-growing, with distinctive, more densely packed spikes of flower. For a range of soils. Drought tolerant and prefers sun. Several selections have been made for gardens, including 'Marin' and 'Shell Beach'. From the western U.S. To 40 cm (16 in.). Z7.

Deschampsia flexuosa
HAIR GRASS

A finer textured and drought-tolerant species, well adapted to dry shade. It is also more compact than its more robust cousin, though less often seen in gardens. Will seed where happy. From temperate North America, Eurasia, and the U.K. To 60 cm (2 ft.). Z6.

Deschampsia flexuosa

Desmoschoenus
GOLDEN SAND SEDGE

This genus comprises just one species, an evergreen grass-like sedge from New Zealand.

Desmoschoenus spiralis
GOLDEN SAND SEDGE

This New Zealand version of marram or dune grass has suffered a decline due to being outcompeted by introduced European species. Tough yellow-green leaves arise from questing fibrous root systems that survive and help to stabilize coastal sand dunes throughout its native habitat, where restoration schemes are helping this species to make a comeback. From New Zealand. To 90 cm (3 ft.). Z8.

Distichlis
SALT GRASS

This small group of tough warm-season semi-evergreen grasses tolerates many coastal situations, mostly in North and South America but also in Australasia.

Distichlis spicata
SALT GRASS

Tough and adaptable, salt grass copes with a variety of coastal as well as inland conditions from dry to distinctly moist, where its creeping habit allows it to make dense ground-hugging mats of spiky foliage. Useful for erosion control, in bioswales, and as a lawn replacement that will tolerate light foot traffic. Prefers open conditions. From North and South America. To 45 cm (1½ ft.). Z4–7.

Distichlis spicata

Elymus
WILD RYE, WHEATGRASS

Grown in gardens primarily for their attractive foliage ranging from soft, glaucous grey-green to strong, steely blue, this large group of mostly cool-season, largely perennial grasses can be either clumping or spreading. Found in a wide variety of mostly open habitats including coastal dunes, prairies, and meadows; some may even be found in light woodland. The common name of wheatgrass refers to the flowerheads which are characteristically spiky and open with a strong resemblance to well-known cereal crops. Widely distributed in temperate areas.

Reclassification of *Elymus* species

Elymus is closely related to *Leymus*, to which several species have recently been reclassified: *Elymus arenarius* is now *Leymus arenarius* (page 229); *E. cinereus* now *L. cinereus* (page 229); *E. condensatus* now *L. condensatus* (page 230); *E. mollis* now *L. mollis* (page 230); and *E. racemosus* now *L. racemosus* (page 230).

Elymus canadensis
CANADA WILD RYE

Found widely throughout much of North America, where it is happy in conditions ranging from moist streamsides to dry sandy soils. Relatively short-lived but fast-growing, this clump-former has rather coarse foliage ranging from glaucous green to blue, topped with nodding rye-like flowers. Its ability to seed makes it well placed for meadow or restoration work, but perhaps less so for garden situations. From North America. To 1.8 m (6 ft.). Z3.

Elymus elymoides
SQUIRREL TAIL

Adapted to a wide variety of different soil types from dry mountain to desert and grassland, always preferring sunny open positions. Its common name refers to the tight *Hordeum*-like flowers that are often noticeably pinkish red. From North America, including Mexico. To 45 cm (1½ ft.). Z6–8.

Elymus hystrix
BOTTLEBRUSH GRASS

One of few true grasses that will happily tolerate reasonable levels of dry shade, though also happy in sun and even moist soils. From clumps of relatively coarse greenish foliage and stiff stems come very showy upright-pointing bottlebrush-like flowers in summer. Known by many gardeners by its synonym *Hystrix patula*, it has been transferred to *Elymus* as its ability to hybridize with other members of this group suggests a strong family tie. From North America. To 90 cm (3 ft.). Z3.

Elymus magellanicus
Syn. *Agropyron magellanicum*
BLUE WHEATGRASS

Valued for its intense silvery blue clumps of slowly spreading semi-evergreen leaves that are among the bluest of garden grasses. Dislikes high, humid night temperatures and requires sunny, well-drained soils. From South America. To 60 cm (2 ft.). Z6.

Elymus elymoides

Elymus hystrix

Elymus magellanicus

Elymus solandri
Syn. *Triticum solandri*
WHEATGRASS

Rather wider than high, and with a slowly spreading habit, this interesting wheatgrass often has very blue foliage which is always at its best in full sun. Coming from well-drained but not too dry coastal rocky sites to higher mountain elevations, it is happy in similar garden situations and excellent in containers, where it can develop its trailing habit. From New Zealand. To 45 cm (1½ ft.). Z7.

Eragrostis
LOVEGRASS

This very large group of more than three hundred annual and perennial species, often-warm-season deciduous grasses, are found in a variety of usually sunny areas worldwide. Those most commonly used in gardens are perennials that will seed easily under suitable conditions and can be invasive in sensitive areas. Most dislike damp and wet soils. Widely distributed in temperate to tropical areas.

Eragrostis chloromelas
Syn. *Eragrostis curvula* var. *conferta*
BOER LOVEGRASS

Although now classified by many botanists under the variable species *Eragrostis curvula*, this form is clearly identifiable in gardens by its attractive silvery glaucous blue foliage and by being noticeably less cold-tolerant than *E. curvula*. Happy in a reasonable range of soils and drought tolerant, though always best in sun. Masses of delicately airy flowers offer a gently cascading effect when in full bloom. Comes true from seed, so may be considered a strain. From Africa and Asia. To 90 cm (3 ft.). Z7.

Eragrostis chloromelas

Eragrostis curvula

Eragrostis curvula 'Totnes Burgundy'

Eragrostis spectabilis

Eragrostis curvula
AFRICAN LOVEGRASS

A graceful species. Long used not just for ornamental purposes but also for stabilization and even forage, it has been widely introduced to different areas for those purposes. Better behaved in cooler climates, where it has proved more tough and hardy than its South African origin might suggest; it can seed aggressively, becoming a weed in warmer areas. Rounded tussocks of fine hair-like bright green leaves, highly ornamental in themselves, support many finely arching flower stems and delicate, airy flowerheads that can cover the foliage in a haze of light green fading to tan and beige. Prefers sun. From South Africa but widely naturalized. To 1.2 m (4 ft.). Z6.

'Totnes Burgundy'. A wonderful selection with mature leaves turning a stunning deep burgundy-red from the tips down and long arching sprays of insignificant beige flowers. Seedlings will revert to the straight species. Excels in containers, where its gradually pendulous foliage habit can be best appreciated. To 90 cm (3 ft.).

Eragrostis elliottii
LOVEGRASS

Not often seen in cultivation, the true species is found in coastal pine and oak woodland. Has relatively bluish-green leaves and compact spikes of flower. Many of the plants in cultivation, especially in the United States, are likely to be forms of *Eragrostis chloromelas*, which itself is now regarded as a form of *Eragrostis curvula*. From North and South America. To 75 cm (2½ ft.). Z8.

'Tallahassee Sunset'. A selection from John Greenlee with particularly glaucous blue leaves.

Eragrostis spectabilis
PURPLE LOVEGRASS

Named for its spectacular clouds of pinkish-purple flowers, freely produced on relatively compact clumps of basal foliage when happy. Can be short-lived but will reseed. Always happiest in sun; may be disappointing in mild, maritime areas with lower light levels. Widely distributed on sandy soils. Dislikes wet soils. From North and South America. To 60 cm (2 ft.). Z5.

Eragrostis trichodes

Eriophorum vaginatum

Eriophorum angustifolium

Eragrostis trichodes
SAND LOVEGRASS

Of similar height to African lovegrass and coming from sandy open areas, sand lovegrass is attractive, easy growing, and very drought tolerant. Produces masses of spectacular shimmering reddish-pink panicles that can cover the basal clumps of green foliage. Dislikes wet soils. From the U.S. To 1.2 m (4 ft.). Z5.

    'Bend'. With less robust stems that bend under the weight of freely produced flowers. To 90 cm (3 ft.).

Eriophorum
COTTON GRASS

The common name for this family of grass-like sedges refers to the cotton-like, woolly, often white but occasionally tan flowers that all species produce profusely. Clump-forming or spreading, all twenty or so species prefer the cooler conditions of wet, boggy, acidic soils mostly open to full sun. Individually beautiful and quite spectacular en masse. Occurs mostly in the Northern Hemisphere.

Eriophorum angustifolium
COMMON COTTON GRASS, COTTON SEDGE

Can be breathtaking in autumn when the white flowers, which are actually more bristle-like than cottony, are in full bloom. Over time, long running roots can form large masses of narrow grass-like leaves that cover open boggy areas. From Eurasia, the U.K., Greenland, and North America. To 60 cm (2 ft.). Z3.

Eriophorum latifolium
BROADLEAVED COTTON GRASS

Wider-leaved than its more commonly encountered cousin *Eriophorum angustifolium*, and often occurring on richer soils. Slowly spreading, with the usual white cotton heads of flower. From Eurasia and the U.K. To 60 cm (2 ft.). Z4.

Eriophorum vaginatum
HARE'S TAIL

Distinguished by single flower spikes. Slowly spreading, with densely tufted clumps. Common in peaty moorlands. From Eurasia, the U.K., and North America. To 60 cm (2 ft.). Z4.

Eriophorum virginicum

Eriophorum virginicum
TAWNY COTTON GRASS, VIRGINIA COTTON GRASS

Distinctive for its often-tan-coloured cotton flowers produced from long spreading roots. Widespread and common throughout its range in moist meadows, bogs, and other wet areas. From North America. To 90 cm (3 ft.). Z3.

Festuca
FESCUE

A huge group of characteristically perennial, fine-foliaged, generally evergreen grasses coming from sunny, open areas ranging from mountains to meadows. Being cool-season, they are not adapted to hot, humid climates. Fescues can seed easily, and so a procession of interesting new selections are a feature of the group. Garden forms are mostly clump forming, though some are spreading, including those used as turfgrass and in traditional lawns. Relatively short-lived as a group, regular division will maintain youth and vigour, while most species will come easily from seed. Generally happiest in sun and some soil moisture in warmer climates. Widely distributed in temperate areas.

Festuca amethystina
TUFTED FESCUE

Tidy rounded clumps of finely rolled, usually mid- to dark green leaves support gently pendulous flower stems that can vary in shades of pinkish red. Initially violet-tinted to purple, flowers are particularly effective in early parts of the year. Variable from seed, which has given rise to several selections. From Central Europe. To 60 cm (2 ft.). Z4.

Festuca amethystina

Festuca californica
CALIFORNIA FESCUE

Frequently dormant during the dry season in warm climates; the onset of autumn rain sees new silvery blue-green stiffly arching leaves appear from the resting mounds, to be followed by delicate, airy blue-grey spikes of flower that fade beige. Drought-tolerant and happy even in light shade in high-sunlight areas. Has given rise to several bluish-grey leaved cultivars such as 'Phils Silver' and 'Serpentine Blue'. From the western U.S. To 90 cm (3 ft.). Z7.

'**Scott Mountain**'. Mounds of relatively stiff and erect blue-green foliage with similarly upright flower spikes. A Native Sons selection from Siskiyou County, California. To 90 cm (3 ft.).

Festuca glauca
BLUE FESCUE

This species has given rise to various commonly seen, tufted, mound-shaped cultivars and forms valued for their fine, narrow leaves in myriad shades of grey and silver to blue. With their propensity for setting viable seed, the older

Festuca glauca 'Boulder Blue'

Festuca glauca 'Cool as Ice'

Festuca glauca 'Elijah Blue'

Festuca glauca 'Intense Blue'

Festuca glauca 'Sunrise'

cultivars' original material has likely been adulterated so that some are now simply regarded as seed-raised strains, many of which have reasonable garden merit. Most will produce upright flower stems, initially blue-grey but quickly drying a strawy beige. Where foliage colour is of primary interest, a regular pruning or shearing of old growth in spring will often prevent flowering and maintain foliage quality. From southern France. To 40 cm (16 in.). Z4.

'Boulder Blue'. Well adapted to steppe-like conditions, producing mounds of steely blue-grey foliage. To 40 cm (16 in.).

'Cool as Ice' Selected by Intrinsic Perennial Gardens. Lighter bluish-green spring foliage turns a softer blue-grey in summer and offers a greater tolerance to heat in warm areas. Vigorous plants turn blue later in summer. To 40 cm (16 in.).

'Elijah Blue'. Long established selection forming spikey mounds of bright silvery blue foliage and occasional flowers. To 40 cm (16 in.).

'Intense Blue'. An excellent selection forming neat mounds of very blue foliage. To 40 cm (16 in.).

'Golden Toupee'. A yellow-foliaged form, with attractive warm yellow leaves and flower stems. Very short-lived if not happy. To 30 cm (1 ft.).

'Sunrise'. A distinctive selection from Szkółka Słowińscy that offers mounds of green foliage and freely produced bright orange-red flowers and stems during summer. To 70 cm (2 ft. 4 in.).

Festuca 'Hoggar'

Sometimes listed as a selection of *Festuca cinerea*, which itself is now frequently regarded as belonging to *Festuca glauca*. While there is some uncertainty as to the plant's origin, its tight clumps of very narrow leaves and comparatively tall flower spikes make it a distinctive selection. Probably of Eurasian origin. To 75 cm (2½ ft.). Z6.

Festuca idahoensis
IDAHO FESCUE

One of the most widely distributed and common fescues within its range, preferring mostly open dry habitats from sea level to mountain meadow. Variable from seed, so has given rise to several selections, which generally form neat clumps of blue-grey leaves and flower stems, eventually fading to straw, sometimes flushed pink. From western North America. To 60 cm (2 ft.). Z4.

'Stony Creek'. Mounds of steely blue-grey leaves mark this Californian selection from S.W. Edwards. Tolerates most soil types in sun or some shade. To 30 cm (1 ft.).

'Tomales Bay'. A wonderful blue-grey-leaved selection, forming relatively compact mounds of strong, healthy foliage. To 40 cm (16 in.).

Festuca mairei
ATLAS FESCUE

Slower-growing and longer-lived than most other fescues, forming relatively large mounds of rather tough grey-green leaves. Individually somewhat indistinguishable, when planted en masse, the narrow flower stems add considerably to the charm of this underused species. Best planted sufficiently far apart to appreciate the plants' distinct rounded outline. Prefers sunny, open positions and dislikes winter wet soils. From Morocco. To 75 cm (2½ ft.). Z5.

Festuca rubra

Festuca ovina
SHEEP'S FESCUE

Common on poor moorland and upland soils where it can become a popular fodder crop, this species has limited ornamental value. Many of the blue garden fescues ascribed to *Festuca ovina* quite possibly belong to the wide-ranging *Festuca glauca*. From Eurasia and the U.K. To 60 cm (2 ft.). Z5.

Festuca rubra
RED FESCUE

Often used as lawn or turfgrass, with many seed-raised strains identified explicitly for this purpose. As a lawn substitute, unmown or even infrequently mown, it can produce loose meadow-like swards of fine hair-like foliage that will accept some foot traffic. Widely distributed and ubiquitous throughout its range, it comes easily from seed, and has provided numerous regionally adapted cultivars for garden and green roof use. Slowly spreading clumps tolerate wide-ranging soil conditions, including drought. Prefers sun but will tolerate light shade. From Eurasia, the U.K., and North America. To 40 cm (16 in.). Z4.

'**Blue Haze**'. A drought-tolerant Knoll Gardens selection slowly forming mats of attractive bright powdery blue foliage.

Festuca rubra 'Blue Haze'

Festuca 'Siskiyou Blue'

Festuca rubra 'Patrick's Point'

Glyceria maxima var. *variegata*

'Jughandle'. A compact Californian coastal selection with dense blue-grey foliage.

'Molate'. Named after Point Molate in California, this comparatively large selection has grey-green leaves that slowly form drought-tolerant mats.

'Patrick's Point'. Ideal for green roof and lawn use, with fine grey-green leaves in slowly spreading tight clumps.

Festuca 'Siskiyou Blue'

An impressive hybrid introduction from the Berkeley Botanic Garden, gradually making large, lax mounds of relatively long silvery blue leaves. To 60 cm (2 ft.).

Glyceria
MANNA, SWEET GRASS, SWEET REED GRASS

These warm-season deciduous grasses are found in wet places such as marshes and on the edges of open water. The common name of sweet grass refers to the tasty seeds and foliage that waterfowl and livestock respectively find to their liking. Widely distributed in temperate areas.

Glyceria grandis
AMERICAN MANNA GRASS

Can form extensive masses of mid-green leaves with summer-blooming upright flowers. Native to marshes, rivers, and swampy areas, it prefers permanently damp to moist conditions and open sun. Widely distributed in North America. To 1.5 m (5 ft.). Z3.

Glyceria maxima
MANNA GRASS

Aggressively spreading roots establish large patches of green foliage that support tall, graceful panicles of flower in shallow water such as ponds or lakes. Will establish in almost any soil provided there is sufficient moisture. Prefers sunny, open positions but will accept some light shade. From Asia and Eurasia. To 2.1 m (7 ft.). Z6.

var. *variegata*. More commonly seen in gardens than the species, with bright creamy white-striped leaves that can be pink-tinged in cooler conditions. Flowers rarely and is less vigorous than the green form, but still very much a spreader. Ideal for planting banks and for the water's edge. To 60 cm (2 ft.).

Hakonechloa

HAKONE GRASS

Containing only one species, this refined, beautiful, and versatile warm-season deciduous grass comes from relatively moist woodland conditions in the mountains of Japan. Long cultivated in gardens, over time there have been many selections, frequently variegated. While these all have some merit, not all are now easily identifiable.

Hakonechloa macra

HAKONE GRASS

Spreads so slowly in most climates that it can practically be regarded as clump-forming. Very long-lived, tough, and durable, it will gradually make dense weed-proof cover in a variety of garden conditions from full sun to reasonably deep shade. Under garden conditions generally unfussy about soil, though slower in heavy clays, and disliking of winter wet soils in cooler climates. Will cope happily with generally dry soils, though may require some occasional irrigation during prolonged dry periods. Often used around and under trees, where its elegant and elongated leaves create a refined and even-textured outline that requires very little after care. Grown for its foliage effect; flowers are dainty and light, and can go almost unnoticed among the leaves. Has given rise to numerous selections over time, many of which are now infrequently seen. To 60 cm (2 ft.). Z3–6.

Hakonechloa macra 'Albovariegata'

'**Albovariegata**'. Irregular bright white-, cream-, and light green-striped leaves make for a striking, slowly increasing mound of pointed foliage that is happy in sun or part shade, where its refined colouration can lighten an otherwise dull corner. Possibly more heat-tolerant than the golden-variegated forms. To 50 cm (20 in.).

Hakonechloa macra 'All Gold'

'**All Gold**'. An elegant selection with bright yellow-gold leaves that lack any trace of green. Slowly spreading mounds are happiest in some shade and may scorch in hot sunshine. To 45 cm (18 in.).

'**Aureola**'. Forms strong, slowly spreading mounds of gold-and-green-striped foliage that takes on an almost chartreuse-green colouration in shade, and turns a much brighter brassy yellow in sun. Probably the most commonly seen cultivar, with multiple garden uses from durable and attractive cover around tree bases to refined ground cover in open sun. Like all hakone grasses, excellent in pots and containers, where the foliage's cascading effect can be appreciated. To 50 cm (20 in.).

Hakonechloa macra 'Aureola'

Hakonechloa macra 'Stripe It Rich'

Hakonechloa macra 'Mulled Wine'

Hakonechloa macra 'SunFlare'

'Beni-kaze'. A compact, slow-growing form with leaves that can turn many shades of red with autumn's cooler temperatures. To 30 cm (1 ft.).

'Mulled Wine'. A compact, very slow-growing selection from 'Aureola' with very similar golden-striped leaves. Can develop a striking burgundy-red colouration, especially on new foliage, growing more pronounced as the season progresses. To 45 cm (1½ ft.).

'Nicolas'. Slightly more compact than the species, with an attractive wine red colouration on bright green leaves intensifying as the foliage ages. To 45 cm (1½ ft.).

'Samurai'. A taller selection offering creamy white and green striped leaves that are especially effective early in the season. Variegation can fade as summer progresses. To 60 cm (2 ft.).

'Stripe It Rich'. Selected from 'All Gold', this form has a white central stripe on otherwise lightly golden foliage. To 45 cm (1½ ft.).

'SunFlare'. A selection from 'All Gold' having light chartreuse green to yellow leaves that become a stronger gold with more sun. Will have splashes of red tinted foliage with sufficient light. To 45 cm (18 in.).

Helictotrichon
OAT GRASS

Clump-forming and semi-evergreen, this group of cool-season grasses comprises more than one hundred perennial species, most commonly represented in gardens by the blue oat.

Helictotrichon sempervirens
BLUE OAT GRASS

Comes from often dry, rocky mountain areas where it forms attractive silky-looking mounds of metallic blue spiky-ended leaves. Happiest in dry, open, sunny positions but will accept some shade in higher-sunlight areas. Gently pendulous flower stems occasionally produced in summer. In some climates it may suffer from rust, in which case affected foliage can be cut back to encourage fresh growth. From Eurasia. To 90 cm (3 ft.). Z4.

  'Pendulum'. A seldom-seen selection with more strongly pendulous flowers. To 75 cm (2½ ft.).

  'Saphirsprudel'. With bright silvery blue leaves and a greater resistance to rust.

Holcus
VELVET GRASS

This small group of perennial clump-forming or spreading cool-season deciduous grasses has widely naturalized. Found in open grasslands or by open woodland edge. From temperate Africa, North America, and Eurasia. Z5–6.

Holcus lanatus
VELVET GRASS, YORKSHIRE FOG

At its peak during the early summer, this clump-former's leaves are soft, velvety, and often coloured a distinctive grey-green. Upright stems hold soft-textured flowers in myriad shades of pink through white. Best in open sunny spots but may tolerate some light shade. From Asia, Eurasia, and North America. To 90 cm (3 ft.). Z5.

Helictotrichon sempervirens

Helictotrichon sempervirens 'Saphirsprudel'

Holcus lanatus

Imperata cylindrica 'Rubra'

Hordeum
BARLEY

This group of annual and perennial cool-season deciduous grasses includes the common barley, *Hordeum vulgare*. All species share the signature squirrel tail-like barley flowers that have given rise to so many descriptive common names. Widely distributed in temperate regions.

Hordeum jubatum
FOXTAIL BARLEY

Widely naturalized and common in gardens in many parts the world. Clumps of slight foliage produce highly distinctive reddish-pink angular flowers, strongly resembling cultivated barley, at their brightest when first open. Happy in dry soils in sun. Can produce flowers over a long period, especially if cut back at any point during the growing season. Relatively short-lived, plants come easily from seed. From North America. To 75 cm (2½ ft.). Z5.

Imperata
SATIN TAIL, BLOOD GRASS

These strongly spreading perennial warm-season deciduous grasses can be invasive weeds in warmer climates. Widely distributed in temperate and tropical regions.

Imperata brevifolia
SATIN TAIL

Found only in moist meadows and named for its attractive, fluffy, satiny white flowerheads produced from gradually spreading mounds of bright green foliage. Prefers moist soils in sun. From the southern U.S. To 1.2 m (4 ft.). Z7.

Imperata cylindrica

An exceptionally variable species that appears to contain both aggressive and unaggressive strains, thought to originate from tropical and temperate areas respectively. Banned in many warmer areas, where its spreading tendencies and ability to seed identify it as a noxious weed. From China, the Korean Peninsula, and Japan. To 90 cm (3 ft.). Z6.

'Rubra' ('Red Baron'). Selected for its stunning deep red colouration that starts mostly at the leaf tips and works its way down the leaf as the season ages. Although a good garden plant, slowly spreading and non-flowering in temperate areas, there is still a risk of the parent species' invasiveness showing through in warmer climates. Can be very slow to establish, especially on some colder, heavier soils. Often grown in containers, where it makes a strong impact. Best colour in sun. To 40 cm (16 in.).

Jarava
Syn. *Stipa*

FEATHER GRASS, NEEDLE GRASS

Mostly perennial, these cool-season clump-forming evergreen grasses are related to *Nassella*, and are now included in the larger genus of *Stipa* by most to botanical authorities.

For *Jarava ichu* see *Stipa ichu*

Juncus

RUSH

This huge group comprises more than two hundred species of mostly perennial evergreen grass-like rushes, distinguishable by their unique narrow, rounded, strongly vertical stems that lack leaves but carry generally insignificant flowerheads either on top or on one side of the stems. All are spreading, preferring moisture in a variety of situations from damp meadows to nearly open water, though they can adapt to much drier conditions in gardens. The more aggressive types cover extremely large areas under suitable wetland conditions, where their densely packed stems and roots act as both valuable habitat and natural filtration system. Rushes remain evergreen in mild climates and become semi-evergreen in cold areas. Widely distributed in temperate regions.

Juncus acutus subsp. *leopoldii*
Syn. *Juncus acutus* subsp. *sphaerocarpus*

SPINY RUSH

Stiff, spiny stems strongly radiate from a central clump to create a distinctive rounded sphere of green. Very drought-tolerant once established but prefers water and open, sunny conditions. The common name comes from the sharply tipped leaves, with which it is best to avoid close contact. From North America, South America, and Africa. To 1.2 m (4 ft.). Z8.

Juncus effusus

COMMON RUSH, SOFT RUSH

Probably the most commonly seen rush in gardens, with light to dark green, comparatively smooth lax stems (hence its common name of soft rush). Found growing in a wide range of places, from bogs to woods and pastures, though generally preferring some degree of moisture. Individually spreading clumps can make large, dense stands. Happiest and most extensive in sunny, open conditions but also tolerates some shade and dryness, at least on a seasonal basis. Highly variable, it seeds easily and has given rise to many cultivated selections. Widely distributed worldwide. To 1.2 m (4 ft.). Z3.

'Carman's Japanese'. Extremely attractive and refined, with gently curving rounded stems of shiny green, topped with profuse light green clusters of flowers whose combined weight often enhances the weeping effect. Effective in pots. To 45 cm (1½ ft.).

Juncus effusus 'Carman's Japanese'

'Quartz Creek'. A long-established Native Sons selection from the west coast of the United States. This cultivar slowly forms dense colonies of brighter green leaves and darker bases. Best in sun but will accept some light shade. To 90 cm (3 ft.).

var. *spiralis*. The corkscrew rush, well named for its mass of tangled and twisted mid-green stems producing clumps that are often noticeably wider than high. To 45 cm (1½ ft.).

Juncus ensifolius
SWORD LEAF RUSH

Forms tight clumps of flat light green leaves, with ornamental dark reddish-brown to purple-black rounded flowers in summer. Prefers sun and moist or marginal conditions, and is especially useful on the side of garden ponds. From North America and Japan. To 40 cm (16 in.). Z5.

Juncus inflexus
HARD RUSH

Resembles the soft rush in many respects but has much stiffer and often shorter upright stems, varying in colour from grey-green to distinct glaucous blue. Noticeably more drought-tolerant than the soft rush, but happy in wet, boggy, open conditions where spreading clumps can form large masses. The pith found in the hollow stems was used as wick for oil lamps and even candles. Comes easily from seed. Widely distributed. To 90 cm (3 ft.).

Juncus effusus 'Quartz Creek'

Juncus inflexus

'Lovesick Blues'. Distinctive, with comparatively lax stems that form pendulous rounded mounds of blue-grey. To 40 cm (16 in.).

Juncus patens
CALIFORNIA GRAY RUSH

Though preferring moist habitats in sun, this attractive grey-leaved upright rush can tolerate extended periods of drought and warm summer temperatures once established. Forming dense clumps over time, especially with plentiful moisture, this attractive plant is often represented by one of several excellent cultivars. From the U.S. West Coast. To 60 cm (2 ft.). Z7.

'Carman's Gray'. An especially grey-stemmed selection found by Ed Carman in California.

'Elk Blue'. Forms compact clumps with an attractive blue-grey colouration that is most distinct in full sun.

Juncus patens 'Carman's Gray'

Juncus patens 'Elk Blue'

Koeleria
HAIR GRASS

Found in open, often dry habitats, these annual and perennial cool-season grasses are mostly clump forming. Though wider-leaved, in some ways they resemble the popular mounding fescues, sharing their myriad shades of grey-green foliage. Can be short-lived in gardens, but usually set seed easily. Widely distributed in temperate regions.

Koeleria glauca
Syn. *Poa glauca*
BLUE HAIR GRASS

Grey-blue leaves on tidy rounded mounds make this species useful for dry, open, sunny sites, though in warmer areas spring flowering is often followed by summer closedown. Foliage will remain in better condition in cooler climates, and can be cut back to stimulate a fresh crop. Often used in drifts or even meadows, individual plants can be short-lived but are easily replaced by self-seeders under the right conditions. From Asia and Eurasia. To 60 cm (2 ft.). Z6.

Koeleria macrantha
Syn. *Koeleria cristata*
CRESTED HAIR GRASS

Bright green clump-forming foliage supports strongly upright stems and light-coloured flowers that have a distinctive presence in prairies and open grasslands. Prefers sunny, well-drained soils. Useful for 'no mow' or low-maintenance lawns. From North America and Eurasia. To 60 cm (2 ft.). Z6.

Koeleria pyramidata
PYRAMIDAL HAIR GRASS

Forms bluish-green clumps of slowly spreading flattened foliage with tall upright flower spikes that quickly fade to an attractive strawy beige, effective over a long period. Prefers sunny, open positions. From north temperate North America, Asia, and Eurasia. To 90 cm (3 ft.). Z6.

Koeleria pyramidata

Leymus
LYME GRASS, WILD RYE

These cool-season perennials are often found in the testing conditions of coastal areas, in shifting soils and sands where their rapidly moving root systems are an essential stabilizing influence, and their tough glaucous-to-blue foliage is a further adaptation to such coastal conditions as sea spray and salt-laden winds. Some species are valued in gardens for their blue leaves while others make excellent meadow grasses. Widely distributed in north temperate regions. Several previously regarded as members of the *Elymus* family such as *Elymus cinereus*, *E. condensatus*, *E. mollis*, and *E. racemosus* have now been reclassified under *Leymus*.

Leymus arenarius
Syn. *Leymus arenarius* 'Glaucus'
EUROPEAN DUNE GRASS, LYME GRASS

Long grown in gardens for its glaucous blue-green leaves and tall wheat-like flowers of a similar colouration. A major constituent of coastal sand dunes, where its rapidly moving root system allows it to thrive in the constantly shifting ground, which it eventually helps to stabilize in concert with other beach grasses such as marram, *Ammophila arenaria*. Tough and durable, it is often used in public plantings under difficult conditions such as traffic islands and parking areas. Prefers sun and well-drained poor soils. From northern and western Europe, and the U.K. To 1.2 m (4 ft.). Z6.

Leymus cinereus
Syn. *Elymus cinereus*
GREY WILD RYE

With grey-green foliage on erect stems and a less spreading habit than *Leymus arenarius*. Often found at higher elevations through its range, preferring meadows, open woodland, and even streamsides. Best in sun and relatively cool summer temperatures, making a good substitute for giant wild rye in colder areas. From North America. To 2.4 m (8 ft.). Z5.

Leymus condensatus

Leymus arenarius

Leymus condensatus 'Canyon Prince'

Leymus mollis

Leymus condensatus
Syn. *Elymus condensatus*
GIANT WILD RYE

Large, slowly spreading clumps of wide, glaucous green to grey leaves support soaring, stiffly upright flower stems. Prefers sloping dry sunny areas and open woodland. Self-seeds when happy. From North America. To 2.7 m (9 ft.). Z7.

'Canyon Prince'. Introduced by the Santa Barbara Botanic Garden, this relatively compact selection makes a first-class garden plant with tall upright flower spikes arising from bright silvery grey foliage that intensifies almost to blue in full sun conditions. Happy in most soils except boggy. To 1.5 m (5 ft.).

Leymus mollis
Syn. *Elymus mollis*
AMERICAN DUNE GRASS

Native to both coasts of North America, this tough, durable, and superbly adapted beach grass is an essential stabilizer of sand dunes. A questing root system produces flat, bladed grey-green leaves that can cope with similar tough conditions in gardens. From coastal North America. To 1.2 m (4 ft.). Z3.

Leymus racemosus
Syn. *Elymus glaucus, Elymus racemosus*
GIANT BLUE RYE

Similar in many respects to *Leymus arenarius* and often confused with it in gardens. Can exhibit particularly blue foliage on gradually spreading mounds. Best in full sun and not-too-wet soils. From Eurasia. To 1.2 m (4 ft.). Z5.

Leymus triticoides
CREEPING WILD RYE

Occurring in sometimes moist meadow conditions, this strongly spreading species is

Leymus racemosus

characterized by generally green foliage and is often used as a base for garden meadows, bank stabilization, or in revegetation schemes where its tolerance of alkaline and saline conditions is especially valuable. Can retain green foliage through the warmer summer periods. From North America. To 90 cm (3 ft.). Z4.

'**Lagunita**'. A John Greenlee introduction that is more compact, shy flowering, and having largely evergreen foliage that sees it well used for meadow applications. To 40 cm (16 in.).

'**Oceano**'. A good form that offers vigorous rust-free foliage which can take on a grey cast under drought stress and is tolerant of coastal conditions. Named by Dave Fross. To 90 cm (3 ft.).

Leymus triticoides 'Lagunita'

Luzula
WOOD RUSH

These evergreen grass-like wood rushes are actually related to the true rushes, *Juncus* species, but bear little actual resemblance. With broad, flattened leaves, they produce dense rosettes of slowly spreading foliage that can make large, dense patches over time. Widely distributed in cool and temperate regions in the Northern Hemisphere.

Luzula acuminata
HAIRY WOOD RUSH

Slowly spreading basal rosettes of deep green foliage that cope with the tough conditions of woodland and shady places make this quietly attractive species widespread throughout its range. In late spring, relatively insignificant flower spikes appear about fresh green leaves. Useful for shady woodland plantings in association with spring bulbs. From North America. To 40 cm (16 in.). Z4.

Luzula nivea
SNOWY WOOD RUSH

Slowly increasing mounds of frequently toothed-edged dark green leaves are covered in tiny white hairs, creating a light grey to white 'snowy' appearance. Tolerates a variety of soils from very damp to often dry. Happiest in part shade rather than full sun. Covered with spikes of tiny white- to cream-coloured flowers in late spring. From Eurasia. To 60 cm (2 ft.). Z6.

   'Snowflake'. A Knoll Gardens selection chosen for its sparkling bright white flowers.

Luzula pilosa
HAIRY WOOD RUSH

Quietly attractive European native of woods, hedgerows, and shady places forming mounds of unassuming evergreen foliage. Under garden conditions will cope with varying levels of sun and shade and various levels of moisture. Has given rise to several selections. From Eurasia and U.K. To 25 cm (10 in.).

   'Igel'. Tight, compact mounds of sometimes reddish-orange-tinted foliage make this a distinctive selection. To 25 cm (10 in.).

Luzula sylvatica
GREATER WOOD RUSH

Widespread and common throughout its wide range, this tough and adaptable species is found in a variety of habitats including woodlands, moorlands, and most damp places. Happy in different degrees of shade but will tolerate some sun. The largest wood rush, with wide leaves on rosettes that can blanket significant areas with dense weed-proof cover. The flowers, produced in spring, are relatively insignificant as with most wood rushes. Comes easily from seed and has given rise to several different cultivars. From Eurasia and the U.K. To 45 cm (18 in.). Z4.

   'Aurea'. One of the brightest and most effective forms through winter and especially in spring, when the rosettes of wide leaves are at their brightest golden yellow. Best sited in light shade, as the delicate leaves can burn in strong sunlight. To 35 cm (18 in.).

   'Bromel' A selection forming good mats of comparatively large wide leaves. To 35 cm (14 in.).

   'Hohe Tatra'. The true form has the widest leaves of any of the wood sedges but is often confused with 'Aurea' in gardens. To 35 cm (14 in.).

   'Marginata'. An old and excellent cultivar with leaves narrowly margined in creamy white. To 45 cm (18 in.).

Luzula sylvatica 'Marginata'

'Mariusz'. Wide leaves of a fresh green gradually form mats of quietly attractive evergreen foliage in quite tough situations. To 35 cm (14 in.).

'Solar Flair' A stabilized seed strain offering clumps of striking golden yellow foliage that is especially bright in late winter to spring. To 40 cm (18 in.).

Melica
MELIC

A large group of invaluable (if sometimes unassuming) clump-forming deciduous grasses for both shady woodland and sunny, open sites. Being cool-season growers, this group is especially valuable during early spring, with many shutting down or becoming summer dormant with increasing dryness.

Melica altissima
SIBERIAN MELIC

An upright leafy species often represented by the white form 'Alba' or the purple form 'Atropurpurea'. Both come reasonably true from seed and are used in mostly sunny, open areas, though they will tolerate some light shade in reasonable soils. At best in the early part of the year; cutting down after the first flush of flower has finished can stimulate a second flowering. Can self-seed. From Central and Eastern Europe. To 1.2 m (4 ft.). Z5.

Melica californica
CALIFORNIAN MELIC

Native to a variety of conditions and soils, from sunny slopes to almost-damp woodlands. Bright green clumps of foliage produce narrow spikes of initially white flowers that fade and remain intact as the grass enters summer dormancy in drier areas. From California. To 90 cm (3 ft.). Z8.

Melica ciliata
HAIRY MELIC

Gently arching stems produce spikes of attractive creamy white flowers produced from basal clumps of green foliage during early summer. Prefers open sunny conditions but will take some light shade. Can self-seed. Average to dry soils. From Eurasia and North Africa. To 60 cm (2 ft.). Z6.

Melica imperfecta
COAST MELIC, FOOTHILL MELIC

This adaptable species is found in woodlands, dry hillsides, and even coastal dunes where its delicate upright appearance is often melded in a wider matrix of native grasses such as *Nassella*, *Koeleria*, and *Poa*. Understated, and perhaps underestimated, it plays an important role in meadows and woodland gardens. Equally attractive in summer dormancy. Will seed easily when happy. From southern California. To 90 cm (3 ft.). Z8.

Melica uniflora
WOOD MELIC

Usually represented in gardens by one of the following forms, the species has dainty bright green leaves on gradually spreading rootstock with small, sparse purplish-brown flowers. From Eurasia and North Africa. To 60 cm (2 ft.). Z5.

Melica ciliata

Melica imperfecta

Melica uniflora f. *albida*

Melica uniflora 'Variegata'

f. *albida*. With dainty grain-like white flowers that contrast effectively with fresh green foliage. Useful in gardens during the earlier part of the season in shady areas and quiet corners. To 45 cm (18 in.).

'Variegata'. Prettily green-and-white-striped foliage. A little more compact than the species. To 45 cm (18 in.).

Melinis
Syn. Rhynchelytrum
PINK CRYSTALS, RUBY GRASS

Usually evergreen and aptly named for their pretty pink flowers, these warm-season grasses contain some species, such as *Melinis repens*, that are considered noxious weeds in warm climates where they have become naturalized. Requiring full sun, they are very drought tolerant and well adapted to dry environments.

Melinis nerviglumis
PINK CRYSTALS, RUBY GRASS

The common name of pink crystals accurately describes the appearance of this attractive species' bright pink flowers, produced from tidy mounds of grey-green foliage provided the plant is given sufficient protection and a head start in colder areas. Drought-tolerant and will seed in warm climates. To 60 cm (2 ft.). From southern Africa. Z9.

Milium effusum 'Aureum'

Milium effusum 'Yaffle'

Milium
WOOD MILLET

Common in mostly open woodland but occasionally found in sunnier areas, these cool-season deciduous grasses are usually represented in gardens by *Milium effusum*.

Milium effusum
WOOD MILLET

At best in spring with adequate shade and moisture, the clump-forming wood millets can go dormant during the drier summer months but will remain active with enough moisture. Once the initial flush of spring growth is over, cutting back old foliage can stimulate a second period of activity. Will seed when happy and frequently seen in gardens as one of the following forms. From much of the temperate Northern Hemisphere. Z5.

   'Aureum'. Of uncertain garden origin, Bowles' golden grass is perhaps the best-known form, with delicate clumps of foliage, stems, and flowers all coloured a uniform, clear golden yellow which may appear pale green in areas of deeper shade. Will seed around lightly if conditions are to its liking. To 60 cm (2 ft.).

   'Yaffle'. A more recent selection with mid-green leaves having a distinctively narrow golden yellow central line. In spring, golden yellow flowers are held high above the foliage. To 60 cm (2 ft).

Miscanthus
EULALIA GRASS, JAPANESE SILVER GRASS, SUSUKI ZOKU

Miscanthus has long held a deep fascination for gardeners. Many of the oldest cultivars were selected in Japan where these warm-season deciduous grasses are traditionally regarded as a symbol of autumn. In the West, long before grasses became more widely known and accepted, *Miscanthus* forms such as 'Zebrinus' were used by keen Victorian gardeners in formal annual bedding displays. Today, although their use has been rightly tempered in areas such as the southeastern United States, where conditions can allow copious seeding, they remain valuable garden plants in cooler climates where seeding does not present the same issue.

   Offering an impressive range of size, flower, and leaf colour, they are tough, generally long-lived plants needing little after care in return for a very long season of interest. Although generally preferring open sunny positions, some, such as the variegated forms, can grow reasonably well in partial shade. Soils can vary from fairly dry to quite damp if accompanied by commensurate high-sunlight hours.

   Depending on their height, *Miscanthus* can be effectively used as screening, as informal hedges, and especially in larger plantings where their bulk and flower power combine well with so many other plants, including large perennials.

Miscanthus floridulus
GIANT MISCANTHUS

Seemingly rare in gardens, this clump-forming species can reach 2.4 m (8 ft.). Frequently plants which are labelled as this species appear to be *Miscanthus* ×*giganteus*. True *Miscanthus floridulus* is distinguishable from others by its coarse wide foliage and narrow flower. From southern Japan, the Pacific Islands, and Taiwan, China. Z7.

Miscanthus ×*giganteus*
GIANT MISCANTHUS

A most useful hybrid between *Miscanthus sacchariflorus* and *M. sinensis*, with some of the best attributes of both. Bright, slightly pendulous foliage of clear green hangs as a fountain from sturdy tall stems making this plant one of the most distinctive of all among the species. More or less clump-forming, it is often used as an

Miscanthus ×*giganteus*

Miscanthus nepalensis

Miscanthus oligostachyus 'Nanus Variegatus'

informal screen or shelter planting, or in association with other bold plants as part of a border. Several clones from this group are being evaluated for production of bioenergy. Flowers only after extended summer periods. From Japan. To 3 m plus (10 ft.). Z4.

Miscanthus nepalensis
HIMALAYAN FAIRY GRASS

Distinctive for its compact mounds of foliage and gold, braid-like, non-fading flowers produced on dainty stems held high above the basal leaves. Average life span possibly three to five years. Requires sheltered well-drained positions in cooler areas. Comes easily from seed. From Nepal. To 1.5 m (5 ft.). Z8–9 (and possibly colder).

Miscanthus oligostachyus
KARI YASU MODOKI

Though compact in habit and with relatively small flowers, it can be very effective en masse. Will tolerate some shade and can offer yellow-beige fall colour. Several variegated forms have been selected in Japan, with 'Nanus Variegatus' most often encountered in Western gardens. Seldom self-sows. From Japan. To 1.2 m (4 ft.). Z4.

Miscanthus 'Purpurascens'
Syn. Miscanthus sinensis var. purpurascens
AUTUMN FLAME MISCANTHUS

Of uncertain parentage and history; possibly a hybrid with Miscanthus oligostachyus. Its short stature, cold hardiness, bright fall colour, and reluctance to set fertile seed make it a valuable garden plant. In areas with shorter summers such as the United Kingdom, it seldom flowers and is known only for its flame-coloured autumnal leaves. From Japan. To 1.5 m (5 ft.). Z4.

Miscanthus sacchariflorus
SILVER BANNER GRASS

Very similar in garden terms to Miscanthus ×giganteus, and being one parent of the hybrid, often mistaken for it. This species differs in its inclination to spread its roots more freely and in its ability to set viable seed from early flowering

Miscanthus 'Purpurascens'

Miscanthus sacchariflorus

in warm areas. In cooler climates, the running habit is slowed and it frequently fails to flower as the growing season is too short. From Japan, the Korean Peninsula, and China. To 3 m (10 ft.) plus. Z4.

Miscanthus sinensis
EULALIA, SILVER GRASS, SUSUKI

The most widely grown *Miscanthus* species from which a significant number of garden cultivars continue to arise. Pretty much all are clump forming, offering an impressive range of height, flower, and leaf colour. All have a generally rounded outline, usually taller than wide, with flower produced en masse, level with or above the foliage. Viable seed is freely produced to the extent that reseeding can become a significant issue in sensitive areas. Breeding programs such as at the North Carolina State University and the University of Georgia aim to produce triploid low-fertility plants, which are showing some promising results within the wider landscape.

From China, the Korean Peninsula, and Japan. Variable to 2.4 m (8 ft.). Z5–6.

'Abundance'. A lovely selection, making dense mounds of attractive narrow leaves covered in masses of delicate buff-white flowers. From the Yakushima Dwarf group of seedlings, 'Abundance' is a cultivar name given by Knoll Gardens intended to identify this specific form. To 1.5 m (5 ft.).

'Andante'. A striking Kurt Bluemel selection from the United States, possibly with *Miscanthus transmorrisonensis* as one parent. Beautiful pink inflorescences held clear above mounds of green foliage. To 2.1 m (7 ft.).

'Bandwidth'. A low-fertility selection from North Carolina State University breeding program with bright yellow crossbanding on relatively narrow foliage. Compact and a generally upright nature. To 90 cm (3 ft.).

'China'. A form offering narrow dark green foliage, tall long-stemmed red flower plumes, and vibrant autumn colour. Often confused with 'Ferner Osten', from which it differs only in flower detail. To 1.8 m (6 ft.).

'Cindy'. A Knoll Gardens selection with many dainty, semi-pendulous, soft pink-to-red flowers held clear above the rounded compact foliage. To 1.5 m (5 ft.).

'Dixieland'. Slightly more compact than 'Variegatus', with rather wonderful narrow fresh

Miscanthus sinensis 'Dronning Ingrid'

green and white variegated foliage. Will tolerate some light shade. To 1.8 m (6 ft.).

'Dronning Ingrid'. With distinctive dark red upright flowers and foliage that is frequently purple-tinted, often before turning vibrant autumnal colours. To 1.8 m (6 ft.).

'Elfin'. Mounds of attractive narrow leaves covered in masses of light pinky white flowers and distinctive red stems. From the group of Yakushima Dwarf seedlings, 'Elfin' is a cultivar name given by Knoll Gardens intended to identify this specific form. To 1.5 m (5 ft.).

'Emmanuel Lepage'. Highly likeable, with an attractive loose habit and deep pinky red flowers held clear above the foliage from high summer onwards. To 2.1 m (7 ft.).

Miscanthus sinensis 'Emmanuel Lepage'

Miscanthus sinensis 'Ferner Osten'

Miscanthus sinensis 'Fire Dragon'

Miscanthus sinensis 'Flamingo'

'Ferner Osten'. A superb selection and one of the best for general garden use, forming mounds of narrow foliage turning bright copper and red in autumn. Spectacularly dark red flower plumes. To 1.8 m (6 ft.).

'Fire Dragon'. A selection from Klaus Menzel of generally upright habit and soft cream to tan flowers that are supported by strong autumnal foliage colours in many shades of burgundy and maroon to red. To 2.1 m (7 ft.).

'Flamingo'. A long-established first-class cultivar, with many strikingly elegant, slightly pendant dark pinkish flower plumes in late summer and good autumn colour. To 2.1 m (7 ft.).

'Gold Bar'. An interesting addition to the zebra grass family, its yellow banding appearing almost simultaneously with the spring foliage on compact plants. To 90 cm (3 ft.).

'Goliath'. As its name suggests, one of the tallest-flowering selections, with an excellent habit and lots of pinky red flowers on stems that tower above most other plants. To 2.7 m (9 ft.).

'Gracillimus'. An old, established cultivar grown principally for its fine-textured foliage that forms gracefully rounded mounds bleaching to pale straw colour for a winter feature. Reddish flowers produced in long summers. To 2.1 m (7 ft.).

Miscanthus sinensis 'Gold Bar'

Miscanthus sinensis 'Goliath'

Miscanthus sinensis 'Gracillimus'

Miscanthus sinensis 'Graziella'

Miscanthus sinensis 'Kleine Fontäne'

Miscanthus sinensis 'Hermann Müssel'

'Graziella'. Attractive silver flowers open in late summer high above the narrow green foliage, which can turn a vivid rich copper-red and orange autumn colour. To 1.8 m (6 ft.).

'Hermann Müssel'. An Ernst Pagels introduction having strongly upright stems topped with pinky brown flowers that are held some distance above the foliage, giving a distinctive appearance. To 2.1 m (7 ft.).

'Kaskade'. Grown for its slightly pendant, large, loosely opened pink-tinted inflorescences with a narrowly upright habit. To 2.1 m (7 ft.).

'Kleine Fontäne'. A long-established selection, forming mounds of narrow green foliage and many soft pink flowers in summer which later gradually fade beige. To 1.8 m (6 ft.).

'Kleine Silberspinne'. Elegant needle-like green foliage forms distinct compact rounded mounds with masses of silky red silver flowers from late summer onwards. To 1.5 m (5 ft.).

'Little Miss'. A compact selection from Klaus Menzel making mounds of green foliage that turn many shades of red and purple as the season progresses. To 90 cm (3 ft.).

'Malepartus'. An older selection and still the standard by which others are judged today. Striking upright columns of broad foliage and flowerheads of the darkest purple-red, fading silver as they age. Foliage turns clear orange and yellow autumnal tones. To 2.1 m (7 ft.).

Miscanthus sinensis 'Kleine Silberspinne'

Miscanthus sinensis 'Little Miss'

Miscanthus sinensis 'Malepartus'

Miscanthus sinensis 'Memory'

Miscanthus sinensis 'Morning Light'

'Memory'. A selection to honour the famous grass nurseryman Ernst Pagels, with an upright habit and light silvery pink flowers held high above the foliage. Both beautiful and memorable. To 2.1 m (7 ft.).

'Morning Light'. Perfectly named, with upright stems and gracefully arching fine-textured cream and green foliage combining to create a distinctive lightness. Topped with perfectly matched pinkish flowers in good years. To 1.8 m (6 ft.).

'My Fair Maiden'. A low-fertility selection from the North Carolina State University's breeding program. Dramatic clumps of wide arching foliage that are topped by many upright light-coloured flowers in summer. To 2.4 m (8 ft.).

'Nishidake'. Large clumps of relatively wide green leaves and tall heads of light flowers that are held well clear of the autumnal-colouring foliage make this a very worthwhile selection. To 2.4 m (8 ft.).

'Pink Cloud'. Delicate and airy silky pink flowers are enthusiastically produced from relatively compact mounds of green foliage during summer. To 1.2 m (4 ft.).

'Professor Richard Hansen'. A distinctive Pagels selection with broad green leaves topped by tall upright stems with flowers that are red at first before turning beige-white, and which are held high above the foliage. To 2.4 m (8 ft.).

Miscanthus sinensis 'Nishidake'

Miscanthus sinensis 'My Fair Maiden'

Miscanthus sinensis 'Professor Richard Hansen'

Miscanthus sinensis 'Red Spear'

Miscanthus sinensis 'Red Zenith'

Miscanthus sinensis 'Roland'

Miscanthus sinensis 'Rotsilber'

'Red Cloud'. A lovely selection of compact habit and masses of freely produced bright red flowers during summer. To 1.2 m (4 ft.).

'Red Spear'. Tall, strongly upright stems produce flower buds reminiscent of spear heads until they burst into bright red inflorescences that still face skywards. A Knoll Gardens selection. To 2.1 m (7 ft.).

'Red Zenith'. An upright habit with mounds of vigorous foliage noticeably tapered at the base and supporting freely produced bright pinky red flowers during summer. To 2.1 m (7 ft.).

'Roland'. An elegant cultivar and one of the tallest, with beautiful pink-tinted inflorescences held on tall stems from midsummer onwards. To 2.7 m (9 ft.).

'Rosi'. A lovely selection from Marchants, with rosy red flowers that turn a clear silvery white with age. Generally upright habit and good autumnal foliage. To 2.1 m (7 ft.).

'Rotsilber'. Mounds of bright green leaves and many striking deep pink-red-turning-silver flower plumes from summer onwards. Orange-red autumn colour. To 1.8 m (6 ft.).

'Scout'. Released by the University of Georgia as a low-fertility form of *M*. 'Gracillimus' and having similar, gracefully rounded mounds of fine-textured foliage. To 2.1 m (7 ft.).

'Silberfeder'. An older, long-established form having tall upright stems of deep green foliage with distinct silver midrib, and large silver-pink flower plumes in late summer. To 2.1 m (7 ft.).

'Silver Charm'. A rather elegant selection from Poland that produces masses of light and airy silvery white flowers. To 1.5 m (5 ft.).

'Silver Cloud'. Delicately variegated leaves and a compact habit distinguish this selection that also offers burgundy-red flowers produced relatively early in the season. To 90 cm (3 ft.).

'Starlight'. Compact mounds of silvered green foliage topped by masses of beige flowers. A superb compact *Miscanthus*, 'Starlight' is a cultivar name given by Knoll Gardens intended to identify this specific form arising from the Yakushima Dwarf group of seedlings. To 1.2 m (4 ft.).

Miscanthus sinensis 'Silver Charm'

Miscanthus sinensis 'Silver Cloud'

Miscanthus sinensis 'Starlight'

'Strictus'. Erect clumps of spiky green foliage with striking yellow cross banding are topped with pinky red flowers in late summer. Possibly more upright and a little shorter than 'Zebrinus'. To 2.1 m (7 ft.).

'Sunlit Satin'. A light and airy effect is created by mounds of centrally white-striped narrow leaves and delicate, soft satin pink flowers during summer. To 1.5 m (5 ft.).

'Undine'. Mounds of narrow green leaves with beautiful, deep pinky purple flowers turn magnificently light and fluffy late in the season. To 2.1 m (7 ft.).

'Variegatus'. Very distinctive, with strongly green-and-white-striped leaves on upright stems. One of the brightest 'whites' that will tolerate some light shade. To 2.1 m (7 ft.).

Miscanthus sinensis 'Strictus'

Miscanthus sinensis 'Undine'

Miscanthus sinensis 'Variegatus'

Miscanthus sinensis Yakushima Dwarf group

Miscanthus sinensis 'Zebrinus'

Yakushima Dwarf. Known by a variety of similar names, this is not a clonal cultivar but a name given to a group of similar, originally seed-raised plants from the Japanese island of Yakushima, and are characterized by their compact rounded habit and free-flowering nature. While most forms are broadly similar, they do vary in detail, so several of these differing forms have been given specific cultivar names in order to avoid continued confusion. These include 'Abundance', 'Elfin', and 'Starlight'.

'Zebrinus'. One of the oldest zebra grasses having tall bright green stems with striking yellow cross-banded foliage, and occasionally producing copper-tinted flowers. To 2.1 m (7 ft.).

Miscanthus sinensis 'Zwergelefant'

Miscanthus transmorrisonensis 'Sunset'

Miscanthus sinensis var. *condensatus* 'Cabaret'

Miscanthus sinensis var. *condensatus* 'Cosmopolitan'

Miscanthus transmorrisonensis

'Zwergelefant'. Amazing crinkled pinkish flowers emerge from the upright stems, initially reminiscent of an elephant's trunk. Strong mounds of rather coarse foliage. To 2.1 m (7 ft.).

Miscanthus sinensis var. *condensatus*
Syn. *Miscanthus condensatus*
HACHIJO SUSUKI

A variety principally distinguished by stems that are covered in a whitish bloom. Has given rise to several excellent variegated cultivars. Produces reddish flowers late in season most years. From Japan, China, the Korean Peninsula, and the Pacific Islands. To 2.1 m (7 ft.). Z5.

'Cabaret'. Distinctive wide ribbon-like foliage with a reverse variegation of creamy white centres and darker green margins forming sturdy upright clumps. Pinky red flowers are produced in warm summers. May tolerate some light shade.

'Cosmopolitan'. Impressive upright clumps of wide ribbon-like foliage with deep green centres and creamy white margins. Occasional red flowers emerge in late summer. Best in open areas but may tolerate some light shade.

Miscanthus transmorrisonensis
EVERGREEN EULALIA GRASS

An attractive species producing flowers on tall, willowy stems that are held some distance above the foliage on the best forms. Often regarded as evergreen, though only in comparatively mild climates. From Taiwan, China. To 2.1 m (7 ft.). Z6–7.

'Sunset'. Recently selected for its tall stems that hold the large pink flowers high above the foliage to give a light and airy appearance in spite of its height. Foliage turns a deepening mix of oranges and reds as fall draws to a close. From Knoll Gardens. To 2.1 m (7 ft.).

Molinia

MOOR GRASS, PURPLE MOOR GRASS

Widespread and common throughout most of their Eurasian range, these cool-season deciduous grasses can be found in a variety of habitats, from boggy moors to relatively dry heathlands, and bring the same tough and adaptable qualities to the garden. Reliably clump-forming and cold-hardy, *Molinia* is characterized by the generally upright, sometimes gently pendulous, linear outline of the flower stems. Preferring sunny, open positions, they may tolerate some light shade.

Molinia caerulea subsp. *arundinacea*
Syn. *Molinia altissima*, *Molinia arundinacea*, *Molinia litoralis*

TALL PURPLE MOOR GRASS

The taller of the two subspecies, tall purple moor grass is among the most graceful of grasses when in flower. Relatively large mounds of bright green foliage support airy stems that reach upwards, mostly in an ever-widening arc. Tall moor grass is perhaps best given some individual space to take advantage of its refined shape. Of peak interest in autumn, the stems will usually collapse under their own weight before the end of the winter. Can seed easily. From Eurasia. To 2.4 m (8 ft.). Z4–5.

'Bergfreund'. A recent selection, reminiscent of the long-established 'Transparent', with tidy mounds of foliage and slightly shorter, open and airy inflorescences, all turning orange and yellow in autumn. To 1.8 m (6 ft.).

'Breeze'. This beautiful tall purple moor grass from Knoll Gardens has light, airy panicles of flower held clear above basal mounds of green foliage on gracefully arching stems. Stunning autumn colours. To 2.1 m (7 ft.).

'Cordoba'. Unusual, with strong, graceful, gently curving flower stems and good honey-gold colour. Named by Ernst Pagels to commemorate the city he so admired. To 2.1 m (7 ft.).

'Karl Foerster'. Long-established form with gently pendulous, initially green and purple flower spikes that mature to golden brown before turning a superb butter yellow colour in autumn. To 2.1 m (7 ft.).

'Skyracer'. Selected by American nurseryman Kurt Bluemel. Strongly upright and particularly tall, turning the usual warm autumnal colours. To 2.4 m (8 ft.).

'Transparent'. A long-established cultivar, aptly named for its airy, see-through inflorescences. To 1.8 m (6 ft.).

Molinia caerulea subsp. *arundinacea* 'Transparent'

Molinia caerulea subsp. *arundinacea* 'Windsaule'

Molinia caerulea subsp. *caerulea*

Molinia caerulea subsp. *arundinacea* 'Zuneigung'

'**Windsaule**'. Strongly upright, with flower panicles a little more slender than some. Excellent as a specimen plant. To 2.4 m (8 ft.).

'**Windspiel**'. Tall clumps wave airily in the slightest breeze, high above mounds of graceful foliage that turns a stunning honey colour in autumn. To 2.1 m (7 ft.).

'**Zuneigung**'. Distinctive wide-spreading slender stems and heavy arching panicles of flower swaying in the slightest breeze. To 1.8 m (6 ft.).

Molinia caerulea subsp. *caerulea*

PURPLE MOOR GRASS

Commonly referred to as simply *Molinia caerulea*, plants belonging to this group have flower stems up to around 1.2 m (4 ft.) tall. There are a number of good cultivars, nearly all of which follow the same broad outline, producing a tidy clump of thin bright green leaves from which arise the narrow, dainty stems topped with masses of tiny, initially purple flowers. Airy to the point of invisibility at first, their sculptural qualities improve as the flowers age and the season progresses. From Eurasia. Z4–5.

'**Dark Defender**' A selection with generally upright stems and flowers, and dark purplish-black pollen that helps create a dark flower effect. To 1 m (3¼ ft.).

'**Dauerstrahl**'. Superb selection with initially dark purplish flowers held in an upright and open habit. Refined autumnal colour. To 1.2 m (4 ft.).

'**Edith Dudszus**'. Selected for its distinctive purplish-brown to almost black flower stems and dense flower spikes. Good autumnal colour. To 1.2 m (4 ft.).

Molinia caerulea subsp. *caerulea* 'Dauerstrahl'

'Heidebraut'. An infrequently seen, relatively upright form with flower stems that gradually arch outwards as they gain in height. To 1.2 m (4 ft.).

'Heidezwerg'. Compact selection with bright green foliage and generally upright stems topped with many initially dark purple flowers. Orange and yellow autumn colours. To 80 cm (2½ ft.).

'Moorflamme'. Compact mounds of green foliage and upright arching dark flower stems turn a wonderful orange in winter. To 90 cm (3 ft.).

'Moorhexe'. Forms compact clumps of green leaves and strongly vertical architectural flower spikes. To 90 cm (3 ft.).

'Overdam'. A most lovely selection forming strong mounds of green foliage from which come masses of fairly upright stems, topped with initially darkish purple flowers, which turn warm shades of orange and yellow in autumn. To 1 m (3 ft.).

'Poul Petersen'. Possibly the most compact selection, forming strong clumps of reasonably upright stems and masses of initially dark purple flowers. To 80 cm (2½ ft.).

'Strahlenquelle'. Not often encountered, the true form of this unusual cultivar is widely arching and needs space to display its spreading flower stems. To 90 cm (3 ft.).

'Torch'. Strongly upright selection making distinctive columns of stems and flowers, and attractive autumnal colours. To 1 m (3 ft.).

'Variegata'. Low mounds of bright, well-marked green and cream leaves, and topped with many arching buff plumes in autumn. To 90 cm (3 ft.).

Molinia caerulea subsp. *caerulea* 'Heidezwerg'

Molinia caerulea subsp. *caerulea* 'Heidebraut'

Molinia caerulea subsp. *caerulea* 'Overdam'

Molinia caerulea subsp. *caerulea* 'Moorflamme'

Molinia caerulea subsp. *caerulea* 'Torch'

Molinia caerulea subsp. *caerulea* 'Poul Petersen'

Molinia caerulea subsp. *caerulea* 'Variegata'

Muhlenbergia capillaris

Muhlenbergia

MUHLY GRASS

This group of warm-season, mostly clump-forming grasses are durable, airy, and atmospheric. Thriving in drought-prone sun-baked conditions in their native habitats, they are especially useful for gardens in warm and arid climates but can survive in much cooler areas provided soils are well drained.

Muhlenbergia capillaris
PINK MUHLY

Spectacular when in flower: masses of vibrant pink, cloud-like flowers obscure the basal mounds of relatively drab foliage, making the whole plant visible from some distance. Several forms have been named including 'Regal Mist' and 'Pink Cloud'. Requires warm climate with long sunlight hours to flower successfully. From Mexico, the southeastern U.S., and the West Indies. Z6–7. To 90 cm (3 ft.). Z6.

'White Cloud'. A white-flowered form creating a similar cloud-like shape as the pink original. Z6–7. To 90 cm (3 ft.).

Muhlenbergia dubia
PINE MUHLY

Fine textured clumps of greyish green leaves support narrow, upright flower stems, initially bluish-grey, that radiate out to create

Muhlenbergia dubia

Muhlenbergia dumosa

Muhlenbergia lindheimeri 'Autumn Glow'

a distinctive rounded outline. Very drought tolerant. From Texas and New Mexico. To 90 cm (3 ft.). Z7.

Muhlenbergia dumosa
BAMBOO MUHLY

Different from most other family members; grown principally for its gracefully curving bamboo-like stems that support billowing masses of cloud-like tiny green foliage dotted with occasional pale yellow flowers. Evergreen in warmer areas with enough moisture, it will drop its leaves in severe drought or during the winter period in cooler climates. From the southern U.S. and Mexico. To 1.2 m (4 ft.). Z8.

Muhlenbergia lindheimeri
LINDHEIMER'S MUHLY

With basal clumps of attractive semi-evergreen blue-grey leaves that tolerate hot, dry conditions, and even a little shade in high-sunlight areas. Tall, upright stems of lighter grey pink-tinted flower spikes are especially effective later in the season, when they create a strong vertical accent. From Texas and Mexico. To 1.5 m (5 ft.). Z6–7.

'Autumn Glow'. An especially good coloured form that was selected by Mountain States Nursery. To 1.5 m (5 ft.).

Muhlenbergia pubescens
SOFT MUHLY, BLUE MUHLY

Mounds of comparatively soft blue-grey evergreen foliage makes this a very distinctive species. Happy in hot, dry climates in sun or even a small amount of shade. Flowers initially purplish. May dislike being cut back. From Mexico. To 90 cm (3 ft.). Z8.

Muhlenbergia reverchonii
SEEP MUHLY

Clump-forming basal foliage produces masses of tiny pink flowers that billow out in cloud-like profusion during late summer. Resembles the pink muhly in habit and flower. A seed-raised form named 'Undaunted' is described as having more cold tolerance. From Oklahoma and Texas. To 80 cm (2½ ft.). Z6.

Muhlenbergia rigens
DEER GRASS

Established clumps have a memorable, architectural, almost pincushion-like effect wherever it can be grown successfully. At home in warm, drought-prone areas, but also able to perform well in much cooler climates provided it has a sunny, well-drained position. Whether massed or as individuals, enough space should be left around each plant for the development of its stunning outline. From the southern U.S. and Mexico. To 1.5 m (5 ft.). Z6–7.

Muhlenbergia rigida
PURPLE MUHLY

Clump-forming green foliage supports upright to gently arching initially purplish flowers that fade to the usual tan and beige tones. Winter dormant. From the southwestern U.S., such as Arizona and Texas, and South America. To 90 cm (3 ft.). Z7.

'Nashville'. A selection with especially vibrant and graceful purple flowers. To 90 cm (3 ft.).

Nassella
NEEDLE GRASS

These mostly perennial clump-forming cool-season grasses come from open, sunny areas in North and South America. Their collective common name refers to the distinctive needle-like flowers that are a delicately beautiful, and which can set prolific seed. Many species were previously included in the genus *Stipa*.

Nassella cernua
Syn. *Stipa cernua*
NODDING NEEDLE GRASS

Found in open grassland, chaparral, and open woodland. Clump-forming with narrow green leaves in spring, followed by distinctly nodding reddish-purple needle-like flowers that gradually dry, the whole plant becoming summer-dormant and then reawakening with the arrival of autumn rains. Seeds easily and is a popular choice for erosion control and in public plantings. Dislikes summer water while in dormancy. From California. To 90 cm (3 ft.). Z8.

Nassella pulchra

Nassella lepida
Syn. *Stipa lepida*
FOOTHILL NEEDLE GRASS

Very similar to *Nassella cernua* but with narrower leaves, flowers with a less pronounced nodding habit and a greater tolerance for some shade. From California. To 90 cm (3 ft.). Z8.

Nassella pulchra
Syn. *Stipa pulchra*
PURPLE NEEDLE GRASS

Found in dry grasslands and scrub, this delicately beautiful grass has especially long purple needle-like flowers in spring that quickly dry silver beige when fading into summer dormancy. Dispossessed of much of its original range by introduced exotics, it is now the official state grass of California, where it is still widespread in sunny well-drained areas. From California. To 90 cm (3 ft.). Z8.

Nassella tenuissima
Syn. *Stipa tenuissima*
MEXICAN FEATHER GRASS

Clump-forming and easy-growing, with bright mid-green, narrow, hair-like foliage topped by initially light green flowers that quickly fade beige, produced so profusely that they weigh the whole plant down. Will accept regular trimming when in active growth. Short-lived, but sets seed easily and can be divided with equal facility to maintain vigour. Drought-tolerant and happy in full sun, but dislikes wet soils. From the southern U.S. through South America. To 60 cm (2 ft.). Z7.

Nassella trichotoma
Syn. *Stipa trichotoma*
SERRATED TUSSOCK GRASS

Forms neat mounds of fine hair-like foliage covered with hazy, delicately structured flowers. Requires full sun and well-drained soils. Popular in colder climates, its ability to set seed in warmer climates has relegated this grass to a noxious weed in parts of the United States and Australia. From South America. To 45 cm (1½ ft.). Z8.

Ophiopogon
LILY GRASS, MONDO GRASS

Although botanically unrelated to the grass family, these grass-like evergreens from Asia share a characteristic linearity, offering narrow strap-like leaves that are produced on slowly spreading mounds of evergreen foliage. There are numerous broadly similar species and long cultivated forms that can make identification problematic. Reminiscent of *Liriope* with the same deep green strap-like foliage, though lacking the upright spikes of flower. Generally useful in gardens for tough dry shady conditions.

Ophiopogon japonicus
MONDO GRASS

Creates slowly spreading mounds of tough dark green leaves. Has given rise to a number of

Nassella tenuissima

Ophiopogon japonicus 'Minor'

Ophiopogon planiscapus

Ophiopogon planiscapus 'Blackbeard'

Ophiopogon planiscapus 'Kokuryu'

cultivated forms, including those with silver- or golden-striped variegated leaves, and is commonly seen in the following distinctive form. From Asia, especially Japan. Z6.

'**Minor**'. A miniature version of the species, with much-smaller evergreen leaves forming tight, very slow-growing clumps. Used as ground cover and as a lawn replacement in shady places, though it will only tolerate minimal foot traffic. To 10 cm (4 in.).

Ophiopogon planiscapus
MONDO GRASS

Tough, durable, slowly creeping, and perfect for covering dry, shady areas under trees. Slow to establish, it gradually forms low, dense weed-proof mats of dark green leaves dotted with occasional white flowers and purple-black fruits. Seldom needs any attention once established. From Asia. To 25 cm (6 in.). Z6.

'**Black Beard**' A selection similar to but with slightly longer leaves than 'Kokuryu' ('Nigrescens'). Forms gradually spreading clumps of highly unusual strap-shaped black leaves all year, with occasional shiny blue-black berries in autumn. Sun or part shade. To 25 cm (10 in.).

'**Kokuryu**' ('Nigrescens'). Grown for its dramatic black leaves, pinkish-white flowers, and black fruits. Similarly tough and adaptable to a wide range of conditions, it produces weed-proof mounds of strap-like foliage over time. Most effective as ground cover in sun or part shade; the black colouration can revert to shades of green in deep shade. To 25 cm (10 in.).

Panicum

MILLET, PANIC GRASS

Found primarily in tropical areas, this large group of annual and perennial warm-season deciduous grasses also extends into some temperate areas. *Panicum virgatum* is a major constituent of North American prairie and a valuable garden plant that has given rise to many selections. Some annual species, such as *Panicum milaceum*, are popular with gardeners and flower-arrangers for their freely produced, large, and airy flowers; while *Panicum capillare* is a constituent of some bird food mixtures, and is occasionally found in gardens as a result.

Panicum amarum
COAST SWITCH GRASS

A distinctive coastal species, tolerating a wide range of soils and habitats throughout its limited range from dunes to swamp margins. Typically more arching than the better-known *Panicum virgatum*, with upright stems and leaves that gradually splay outwards as flowers develop and age. Leaves vary from green to blue, and the root system can vary between strongly spreading to clumping. All require sun and not-too-fertile soils for best colour and performance. From the North American coast to Mexico. To 1.5 m (5 ft.). Z5.

'Dewey Blue'. A beautiful form with exceptionally silvery blue-grey stems and leaves, selected from wild seed collected by Rick Darke and Dale Hendricks.

'Sea Mist'. A selection from Knoll Gardens forming clumps of fairly upright blue-grey to sea green foliage, and topped with light-coloured spikes of arching flowers in later summer. Orange and yellow autumnal leaf colour. Best in sunny, open positions with a soil that is not winter wet.

Panicum bulbosum
TEXAS GRASS

Forms clumps of light grey-green foliage that comes from swollen bases, and produces upright stems of reddish flowers drying to a warm beige. Provides yellow autumn colour. Seeds under suitable conditions, preferring a sunny, open position and not-too-wet soil. From the southern U.S., Mexico, and western South America. To 90 cm (3 ft.). Z6–9.

Panicum virgatum
PANIC GRASS, SWITCH GRASS

A major constituent of the once-widespread tall-grass prairie, these tough and adaptable grasses can be used on a wide variety of soil types from wet to dry, though most prefer a sunny, open situation. Beautiful in detail and en masse, they will display variation in their native habitat but are largely upright-stemmed and clump-forming. Held on dainty panicles, flowers tend to be tiny and often initially purplish, and produced profusely enough to create a hazy cloud of flower that can virtually obscure the foliage. As with many good garden grasses, heavy rain or snow may bend the taller stems, though most will return to their customary upright stance with the return of better weather. Has given rise to a significant number of selections that vary in foliage effect, height, and habit; with red-tinted late summer to fall leaf colour often an important attribute. Widely distributed in North America. To 2.4 m (8 ft.). Z4.

'Blue Tower'. A really tall and stately selection from Greg Speichert, with leaves a distinct glaucous blue. To 2.4 m (8 ft.).

'Buffalo Green'. A compact free-flowering selection from Jan Spruyt that retains its upright nature and green foliage into the autumn. To 90 cm (3 ft.).

Panicum virgatum 'Buffalo Green'

Panicum amarum

Panicum amarum 'Dewey Blue'

Panicum amarum 'Sea Mist'

Panicum bulbosum

Panicum virgatum

Panicum virgatum 'Blue Tower'

'Cape Breeze'. Selected by Paul Miskovsky and introduced by North Creek Nurseries for its upright habit, compact size, and early-flowering nature. Salt tolerant, the rust-free foliage remains green well into autumn and is topped by masses of tiny light pink flowers. Believed to be a hybrid with *Panicum virgatum* as one parent. To 75 cm (2½ ft.).

'Cheyenne Sky'. An impressive compact selection from Gary Trucks. Offering later summer foliage in many shades of a deep wine red, which in turn is topped by masses of tiny airy flowers. To 80 cm (2½ ft.).

'Cloud Nine'. Impressively tall and airy, with glaucous blue-green foliage, an upright habit, and attractive golden autumn colour. To 2.4 m (8 ft.).

'Dallas Blues'. Among the bluest selections, with blue stems, wide leaves, and showy flower panicles on solid upright mounds. To 1.8 m (6 ft.).

'Hänse Herms'. Green leaves take on red tones in high summer before turning burgundy

Panicum virgatum 'Cape Breeze'

Panicum virgatum 'Cloud Nine'

Panicum virgatum 'Hänse Herms'

Panicum virgatum 'Dallas Blues'

Panicum virgatum 'Heavy Metal'

Panicum virgatum 'Heiliger Hain'

Panicum virgatum 'Kupferhirse'

in autumn. A more relaxed, less strongly upright selection. To 1.2 m (4 ft.).

'Heavy Metal'. With very distinctive clumps of upright grey-green foliage, large panicles of tiny purplish spikelets in summer, and reddish-purple-tinted autumn colour. An eye-catching selection from Kurt Bluemel. To 1.5 m (5 ft.).

'Heiliger Hain'. Upright habit with soft pinky beige flowers and bluish-green foliage that turns a very deep burgundy red in autumn. To 1.2 m (4 ft.).

'Kupferhirse'. Mounds of green foliage, topped with warm coppery brown panicles from late summer. Good yellow-orange autumn foliage. To 1.2 m (4 ft.).

'Merlot'. A recent Knoll Gardens selection that produces masses of airy pinky red flowers in summer supported by generally upright green foliage that will develop many shades of wine red and purple during later summer. To 1.2 m (4 ft.).

Panicum virgatum 'Northwind'

Panicum virgatum 'Prairie Fire'

Panicum virgatum 'Oxblood Autumn'

Panicum virgatum 'Red Cloud'

Panicum virgatum 'Prairie Dog'

'Northwind'. Most impressive selection having a very distinctive narrow vertical habit and wide blue-grey foliage that turns warms shades of yellow in autumn. To 1.8 m (6 ft.).

'Oxblood Autumn'. Clumps of green foliage that turn deepening shades of dark red as summer progresses, and reddish-purple panicles of flower in late summer. To 1.2 m (4 ft.).

'Prairie Dog'. Selected for a more reserved habit with clean blue foliage on upright growth. Flowers freely produced during summer. Introduced by Intrinsic Perennial Gardens. To 1.5 m (5 ft.).

'Prairie Fire'. Selected by Gary Trucks for its upright bluish-green foliage that begins to turn many shades of deep red relatively early in the season. To 1.2 m (4 ft.).

'Prairie Sky'. Introduced by Roger Gettig, with striking blue stems and foliage topped with delicate, airy flowerheads. Stems are mostly upright in poor, well-drained soils. To 1.2 m (4 ft.).

'Purple Breeze'. A European selection with an upright habit and grey-green foliage that gradually turns increasingly deep shades of dark purplish-red from summer onwards. To 90 cm (3 ft.).

'Red Cloud'. A lovely form, grown specially for its large panicles of conspicuous red spikelets and subtle fall colour. To 1.5 m (5 ft.).

'Shenandoah'. Very lovely selection by Hans Simon from seedlings of 'Hanse Herms' with foliage that has dark red tones turning a gorgeous wine colour by late summer. To 1.2 m (4 ft.).

'Straight Cloud'. Effective combination of an upright habit with bluish-green foliage topped with masses of airy purplish spikelets in high summer. To 1.5 m (5 ft.).

'Thundercloud'. Impressive selection from Gary Trucks with a strongly upright habit, greenish grey to steely blue foliage, and topped with masses of tiny flowers produced in later summer. To 2.1 m (7 ft.).

'Warrior'. Clumps of green foliage with flowing habit and topped with masses of purple flowers in summer. Fall foliage can offer purple, orange, yellow, and finally beige. To 1.5 m (5 ft.).

Panicum virgatum 'Shenandoah'

Panicum virgatum 'Thundercloud'

Panicum virgatum 'Purple Breeze'

Panicum virgatum 'Straight Cloud'

Panicum virgatum 'Warrior'

Pennisetum
FOUNTAIN GRASS

A most showy group grown primarily for their cylindrical, elongated bottlebrush-like flowers, which appear to cascade like fountains from rounded mounds of usually green foliage. Being warm-season, they are fast growing and enthusiastically produce long-lasting flowers over an extended period. *Pennisetum* has recently been transferred by some authorities to *Cenchrus*; however, the long-established name of *Pennisetum* has been retained here for clarity.

Fountain grasses are mostly perennial and largely clumping, though several have a spreading habit. Many will set seed easily, causing some to be considered serious weeds in sensitive warmer areas. Coming from warm to tropical climates, many will not survive temperate winters, and those that do require full sun and well-drained soils to perform well, though some light shade may be tolerated by hardier forms in areas of high sunlight. Some tropical species can be grown as summer annuals, including the dark-leaved and dark poker-like-flowered *Pennisetum glaucum* 'Purple Majesty'. Widely distributed in warm temperate to tropical areas.

Pennisetum ×*advena*
Syn. *Pennisetum setaceum*
PURPLE FOUNTAIN GRASS

Listed for some time as *Pennisetum setaceum*, these plants now have their own name, though it is likely that *P. setaceum* may be one parent. Evergreen and quick growing. Hardy in warm climates, they should be treated as tender perennials in colder areas. Most are effectively sterile, so need to be increased by division from overwintered plants. Some forms such as 'Cherry Sparkler' and 'Fireworks' have vivid variegated foliage. From Africa. Z9.

'Eaton Canyon'. A compact form with less vigour and purple leaf colour than its popular counterpart 'Rubrum'. To 75 cm (2½ ft.).

'Rubrum' ('Cupreum', 'Purpureum'). Absolutely stunning in colour, shape, and form, this virtually unique grass has deep red to burgundy stems, foliage, and exquisite red, very tactile arching flowers that gradually fade to beige with age. To 1.2 m (4 ft.).

Pennisetum ×*advena* 'Rubrum'

Pennisetum alopecuroides 'Black Beauty'

Pennisetum alopecuroides
Syn. *Pennisetum compressum, Pennisetum japonicum,*
FOUNTAIN GRASS, FOXTAIL GRASS

This popular fountain grass has given rise to a whole series of cultivars with the same generally rounded mounds of green foliage topped with a wealth of large, fluffy bottlebrush-like flowers mostly held on slightly arching stems. Leaves often colour golden yellow to mark the arrival of autumn. Relatively hardy in colder areas if given good drainage and a sunny, open position. The species does not always flower reliably in such areas, though the cultivars do not appear to have the same shortcoming. In warmer to dry climates, fountain grasses may need more moisture and tolerate some light shade, though they are always happy in full sun. Seed will set freely in warmer areas, where it can become invasive. Breeding programs such as that undertaken by the University of Georgia in the United States have resulted in a range of near-sterile forms to help combat the seeding issue. From Asia. To 1.2 m (4 ft.). Z6–7.

Pennisetum alopecuroides 'Burgundy Bunny'

'Black Beauty'. Nice selection offering large, freely produced dark-toned cylindrical flowers during summer. To 1 m (3 ft. 2 in.).

'Burgundy Bunny'. Arising as a sport from 'Little Bunny' and having the same compact nature, but with red-tinted foliage during summer that intensifies in colour as fall approaches. To 40 cm (16 in.).

'Cassian'. Produces dusky light brown flowers from midsummer onwards and turns rich orange-yellow in autumn. Named by Kurt Bluemel for well-known horticulturist Cassian Schmidt. To 1 m (3 ft. 2 in.).

'Caudatum'. Beautiful, with many large near-white fluffy flowers set above deep green foliage during summer. To 1.2 m (4 ft.).

'Cayenne'. A low-fertility form from the University of Georgia, producing robust mounds of bright green leaves topped by masses of relatively tall bottlebrush-like flowers in summer. To 1.2 m (4 ft.).

'Dark Desire'. Selected by Knoll Gardens for its very large, dark purplish, almost smoky black bottlebrushes freely produced from rounded mounds of bright green foliage. To 1m (3 ft. 2 in.).

'Etouffee'. Produced as part of the University of Georgia's low-fertility breeding program, this lovely form offers masses of large, lighter-coloured bottlebrush-like flowers in summer. To 1.1m (3ft 6").

'Ginger Love'. This selection from Intrinsic Perennial Gardens produces strong mounds of green leaves followed by large red bottlebrush-like flowers in summer. To 1 m (3 ft.).

'Hameln'. A long-established compact form making distinctive rounded mounds of dark green foliage and topped with many off-white bottlebrush-like flowers from high summer. One of the most reliable for cooler climates. To 90 cm (3 ft.).

'Herbstzauber'. A very attractive free-flowering selection with large fluffy greenish-white flowers from high summer onwards, and bright green foliage. To 1.2 m (4 ft.).

'Hush Puppy'. Produced as part of the University of Georgia's low-fertility breeding program, this form appears completely sterile and produces many lighter-coloured flowers on relatively compact plants. To 90 cm (3 ft.).

'Jambalaya'. From the University of Georgia's low-fertility breeding program, this form offers masses of large bottlebrush-like flowers from robust mounds of green foliage in summer. To 1 m (3 ft. 2 in.).

'Little Bunny'. A miniature selection from 'Hameln', with small mounds of foliage and flower, more shyly produced in cooler climates. To 40 cm (16 in.).

Pennisetum alopecuroides 'Little Bunny'

'Love and Rockets'. Introduced by Intrinsic Perennial Gardens as a compact, darker-flowered selection having similar characteristics to the ever-popular 'Hameln'. Mounds of deep green foliage topped with wine red flowers that fade with age. To 75 cm (2½ ft.).

'Moudry'. A compact form with relatively wide, glossy, neat basal mounds of foliage topped by fluffy deep-purple-to-black flowers held only just above leaf height. Later-flowering, to the point of non-flowering, in shorter summer areas. To 75 cm (2½ ft.).

'Piglet'. A free-flowering compact selection from Intrinsic Perennial Gardens forming rounded mounds of green foliage that are topped with many bottlebrush-like flowers in summer. Similar though more compact than the long-established 'Hameln'. To 45 cm (18 in.).

'Praline'. The most compact form resulting from the University of Georgia's low-fertility breeding program, offering relatively petite mounds of foliage and small but freely produced flowers. To 70 cm (2 ft. 3 in.).

'Pure Energy' An unusual selection, having comparatively wide golden yellow foliage, that is happy in sun. Peak foliage colour just as the flowers begin in summer. Introduced by Intrinsic Perennial Gardens. To 90 cm (3 ft.).

'Red Head'. An excellent cultivar from Intrinsic Perennial Gardens chosen for its early-flowering ability and relatively large individual flowers, which open distinctly red before fading through purple shades to beige. To 1 m (3 ft. 2 in.).

'Viridescens' (var. *viridescens*). Considered a botanical variety by some, strongly mound-forming with wide glossy green leaves and a shy flowering habit, at least in cooler areas. To 75 cm (2½ ft.).

'Weserbergland'. Lovely, with mounds of narrow green foliage and many creamy white flowers in late summer. To 90 cm (3 ft.).

'Yellow Ribbons'. An interesting selection from Intrinsic Perennial Gardens offering relatively narrow golden yellow foliage that will mellow to a chartreuse yellow by fall. Light tan-coloured flowers are produced during summer. To 75 cm (2 ft. 6 in.).

Pennisetum alopecuroides 'Love and Rockets'

Pennisetum alopecuroides 'Moudry'

Pennisetum alopecuroides 'Pure Energy'

Pennisetum alopecuroides 'Viridescens'

Pennisetum alopecuroides 'Piglet'

Pennisetum alopecuroides 'Red Head'

Penisetum 'Fairy Tails'
(top) Penisetum macrostachyum 'Burgundy Giant' (middle)

Pennisetum 'Fairy Tails'
'FAIRY TAILS' FOUNTAIN GRASS

A seedling selection from John Greenlee of uncertain parentage, and one of the most striking and distinctive of fountain grasses, with light green mounds of leaves and masses of relatively upright to arching dainty flowers, pinky white before quickly fading to tan, produced in profusion and over a long period. Its upright habit makes an excellent informal screen. Regarded as sterile. To 1.2 m (4 ft.). Z7–8.

Pennisetum macrostachyum
LARGE LEAVED FOUNTAIN GRASS

A tropical broad-leaved species whose upright habit and bold foliage make a striking combination. For warm areas or as a summer display plant. From the South Pacific. To 1.8 m (6 ft.). Z10.

'Burgundy Giant'. A most impressive form with sumptuous burgundy foliage and graceful, soft pinky red flowers fading to white with age. Named by Rick Darke.

Pennisetum macrourum

Pennisetum macrourum
FOUNTAIN GRASS, FOXTAIL GRASS

Forms gradually spreading individual mounds of tough grey-green foliage with many distinct arching stems topped with narrowly cylindrical buff-white flowerheads in summer. Very distinctive in full flower, though can be comparatively late to flower in cooler areas. From Africa. To 1.8 m (6 ft.). Z7.

'Short Stuff'. Selected as a seedling by Knoll Gardens, this form is rather more compact and earlier to flower than the type, with freely produced flowers held just clear of the foliage. To 90 cm (3 ft.).

Pennisetum massaicum
FOUNTAIN GRASS, FOXTAIL GRASS

Coming from open savannah, this species is remarkably cold tolerant given its native range. Always prefers sun and well-drained conditions, but appears able to grow in heavier soils. Usually represented by the following cultivar which comes fairly true from seed. From Africa. Z8.

Pennisetum massaicum 'Red Buttons'

Pennisetum macrourum 'Short Stuff'

Pennisetum orientale

Pennisetum orientale 'Karley Rose'

Pennisetum orientale 'Shogun'

Pennisetum setaceum

'Red Buttons'. Bold, bright green mounds of gradually increasing foliage provide the base for enthusiastically produced, relatively short rounded flowers that are initially bright red before fading to tan and brown. Much earlier-flowering than most other fountain grasses. To 1 m (3 ft. 2 in.).

Pennisetum orientale
ORIENTAL FOUNTAIN GRASS

Less robust in growth and cold-hardiness than *Pennisetum alopecuroides*. Clumps of relatively narrow bright green to grey foliage produce masses of striking pink, fading white flowers from summer onwards. From Africa, Asia, and India. To 70 cm (2 ft. 4 in.). Z6.

'Karley Rose'. Forms mounds of shiny arching leaves and very deep rose-pink flowers held on rather tall upright stems. Good in large drifts and masses, and against more solid companions. To 1.2 m (4 ft.).

'Shogun'. Has more upright, soft blush-pink flowers, freely produced from high summer onwards, and distinct glaucous blue foliage. To 1.2 m (4 ft.).

'Tall Tails'. With light green mounds of foliage and many tall flowerheads with long, semi-pendulous white foxtail-like flowers. Can self-sow in warmer areas and is shorter-lived in colder districts. To 1.5 m (5 ft.).

Pennisetum setaceum
Syn. *Pennisetum ruppelii*
TENDER FOUNTAIN GRASS

When grown as an annual in colder areas, it makes an attractive summer display in gardens. However, its ability to reseed prolifically in warmer climates has led to invasiveness, and it is considered a serious weed in sensitive areas.

Will go summer-dormant in dry climates. From Africa, and Asia. To 1.2 m (4 ft.). Z9.

Pennisetum spathiolatum
SLENDER VELDT GRASS

An airy haze is created by the freely produced narrowly elongated flowers on top of wiry stems that appear over a long summer period. Clumps of neat foliage remain evergreen in warm climates. Uncertain origin. To 1.2 m (4 ft.). Z7.

Pennisetum villosum
FEATHERTOP

Gradually spreading mounds of relatively plain foliage are covered with large, fluffy caterpillar-like white flowers. Tender in colder areas, where it can be grown as an annual. From Africa. To 80 cm (2 ft. 8 in.). Z8.

Pennisetum villosum

Pennisetum spathiolatum

Phalaris arundinacea 'Arctic Sun'

Phalaris
CANARY GRASS

This group of widespread annual and perennial cool-season semi-evergreen grasses includes *Phalaris canariensis*, an annual often found in bird seed mixes.

Phalaris arundinacea
REED CANARY GRASS

A strongly spreading species found in moist areas and marshes, where it is extremely vigorous and can cover very large areas, but avoiding open water. Excellent for restoration and conservation work where it is native. Mostly represented by variegated selections in gardens. From North America and Eurasia. To 1.5 m (5 ft.). Z4.

   'Arctic Sun'. Strongly marked creamy yellow to golden variegated foliage. More compact and less inclined to move around than the species. Prefers average to damp soils in sun or light shade. To 75 cm (2½ ft.).

   'Picta'. Possibly the oldest known selection, often seen as large established patches in gardens. Bright white-and-green-striped leaves are sometimes suffused pink in cooler periods. To 1.2 m (4 ft.).

Phalaris arundinacea 'Picta'

Phragmites australis

Phragmites
REED

Consisting of one species, this warm-season deciduous grass is widespread over most continents, where it occurs in moist areas. Highly variable over its range. European genotypes introduced to North America have been found to be of significantly less value for biodiversity, and have become a serious problem in some areas.

Phragmites australis
COMMON REED

Has a vigorous questing rootstock that allows it to colonize a variety of wet and marshy areas, gradually spreading to encompass vast tracts of land. Tough leaves are distinctively tapered in many shades of glaucous green. Of enormous benefit to biodiversity where it is native, it is much used for restoration and conservation projects. Prefers generally open areas of fresh or brackish water, and not too tolerant of salt. To 4 m (13 ft.). Z4.

'Variegatus'. Attractive with bright yellow-and-green-striped foliage, considerable vigour and spreading ability. Happy in sun or light shade. To 2.7 m (9 ft.).

Phragmites australis 'Variegatus'

Pleuraphis rigida

Poa labillardierei

Pleuraphis

GALLETA

A small group of warm-season drought-tolerant grasses native to part of western North America.

Pleuraphis rigida

BIG GALLETA

Very tolerant of dry landscapes and forming slowly spreading recumbent mounds that are topped with freely produced dainty flowers. Spring green foliage turns to dry beige as conditions dry. To 90 cm (3 ft.). Z8.

Poa

BLUE GRASS

Poa is a huge group of more than five hundred annual and perennial cool-season semi-evergreen grasses. Many are used as turfgrass and in lawns; fine-textured, they resemble their

Rhynchospora latifolia

close relatives, the fescues. Widespread in cool temperate regions.

Poa labillardierei
AUSTRALIAN BLUE GRASS

Hazy mounds of steely blue narrow foliage and a succession of silvery blue stems and flowers are produced during early summer. Happiest in sun or very light shade. Prefers dry soils in colder areas, and more moisture in warmer climates. From Australia. To 1.2 m (4 ft.). Z8.

Rhynchospora
WHITE-TOP SEDGE, STAR SEDGE

These mostly perennial evergreen grass-like sedges prefer moist soils with some degree of sun. Their distinctive flowers are, in fact, extended bracts. Widespread in warm temperate regions.

Rhynchospora latifolia
Syn. *Dichromena latifolia*
STAR SEDGE

Native to pond edges, swamps, and savannahs, with conspicuously elongated white bracts held on thin green stems. Happy in a variety of damp areas. Increases by a slowly running rootstock. From the southeastern U.S. To 75 cm (2½ ft.). Z8.

Saccharum
SUGAR CANE

This group of several dozen warm-season deciduous grass species is best known for the commercial production of sugar cane from *Saccharum officinarum*, which can be a highly ornamental plant in its own right. Sugar canes have some broad similarities to *Miscanthus*, with which they can be confused in gardens, especially when not in flower, as they form similar large mounds of wide green leaves—though these are topped with plumes that give them a superficial resemblance to pampas. Previously a separate genus, *Erianthus* is now included under *Saccharum*. Sugar canes prefer open, moist situations to fuel their fast rate of growth, though they seem happy enough adapting to drier areas in gardens. Widely distributed in temperate to tropical areas.

Saccharum arundinaceum
HARDY SUGAR CANE

Fast-growing, the best forms having rather attractive, wide, almost-glaucous sea green foliage that can make very large mounds. Stiff upright plumes, produced in late summer, are initially a deep pinky red before fading to silver grey. Happiest in full sun in a range of soils. From Asia. To 4 m (14 ft.). Z7.

Saccharum officinarum
SUGAR CANE

Well-known for its provision of cane sugar. Can attain massive proportions of up to 6 m (20 ft.) high in tropical areas, where it is valued for its ornamental qualities. In less ideal localities where it is less vigorous, it is often used as a tender or seasonal subject. Forms with purple-tinted foliage are especially favoured in gardens. Prefers sunny, open positions with sufficient moisture, but is at least seasonally drought tolerant. From Asia. To 2.4 m (8 ft.). Z10.

'Pele's Smoke'. A beautiful form with dramatically marked dark purplish black stems and lighter reddish-purple-tinted foliage. Very ornamental, with less vigour than the green forms. Always best in sun and reasonable soils. To 2.1 m (7 ft.).

Saccharum ravennae
Syn. *Erianthus ravennae*
RAVENNA GRASS

Clump-forming, with large mounds of grey-green leaves which support masses of tightly packed, tall, sometimes-arching upright stems and pampas-like flower plumes of a delicate silvery pink, fading to silver grey. Requires a long season to bloom well, so is best in full sun in a variety of soils. From Africa, Asia, and Europe. To 3 m (10 ft.). Z6.

Saccharum officinarum 'Pele's Smoke'

Saccharum ravennae

Schizachyrium
BLUESTEM, BEARDGRASS

Among this large group of widely distributed annual and perennial warm-season deciduous grasses, only one species is readily cultivated in gardens. Originally *Schizachyrium scoparium* was classified under the genus *Andropogon*, from which it differs due to the structure of its flowers. Widely distributed in temperate to tropical areas.

Schizachyrium scoparium
Syn. *Andropogon scoparium*
LITTLE BLUESTEM

Beautiful, tough, and adaptable, little bluestem is a major constituent of the American tallgrass prairie. Usually clumping, with basal mounds of fine-textured leaves and characteristically upright to strongly vertical stems. Flowers offer a striking palette of red, orange, copper, and rust in autumn. Foliage and stems are often glaucous to silvery blue, and several selections have been made for this quality. Best in open sun, and does well in a range of soils, from moist to fairly dry. Poor rather than fertile soils will produce the most upright growth. From North America. To 1.2 m (4 ft.). Z3–8.

'Blue Heaven'. A robust selection from the University of Minnesota with tall light blue-grey foliage that offers many shades of pink and burgundy as fall approaches. Best in sun and well-drained or poor soils. To 1.5 m (5 ft.).

'Jazz'. A great compact selection from Intrinsic Perennial Gardens that comes from 'The Blues', with similar blue foliage but rather shorter. Retains its upright habit and offers purple-tinted fall colourations. To 75cm (2 ft. 6 in.).

'Prairie Blues'. A seed-raised strain with a generally upright habit, and stems and leaves of an overall grey-green appearance, turning warm orange and brown in autumn. Needs full sun and well-drained poor soil for best growth. To 90 cm (3 ft.).

'Smoke Signal'. With a reliably upright habit, this selection forms mounds of glaucous blue-green foliage that develops increasing

Schizachyrium scoparium

Schizachyrium scoparium 'Prairie Blues'

Schizachyrium scoparium 'Standing Ovation'

shades of scarlet, red, and purple in fall. To 1.2 m (4 ft.).

'Standing Ovation'. Chosen for its strongly upright habit even in relatively rich soils. This selection from North Creek Nurseries offers bluish-green leaves and stems that gradually transition into myriad shades of red, yellow, and orange during fall. To 90 cm (3 ft.).

'The Blues'. A selection from Kurt Bluemel with striking glaucous blue foliage that is accented by red-tinted flower stems. Offers purple, blue, and orange shades in fall. To 90 cm (3 ft.).

Sesleria
MOOR GRASS

A group of foliage-based, cool-season clump-forming grasses that have proved of great value in a variety of garden applications from meadows to green roofs. Coming from generally dry and rocky places in Europe, Asia, and North

Schizachyrium scoparium 'The Blues'

Sesleria autumnalis

Sesleria argentea

Sesleria autumnalis 'Campo Verde'

Sesleria caerulea

Africa, they tolerate a range of soil types, though not generally happy in wet soils. Semi-evergreen to evergreen in warmer climates. Some seedling variation. Best in sun, they will tolerate a level of shade, especially in higher sunlight areas.

Sesleria autumnalis
AUTUMN MOOR GRASS

Attractive and durable mounds of yellowish, almost chartreuse foliage mark this apart from most other species. Freely produced creamy white flowers later in the season contribute an additional light touch. Happy in full sun or light shade in a variety of soils. From southern Europe. To 60 cm (2 ft.). Z4.

'Campo Verde'. A selection from Dave Fross of Native Sons, having darker green foliage, a more lax growth habit, and a noticeably more spreading nature than the species. Flowers produced during later season. Drought tolerant and happy in sun or a reasonable level of shade in higher sunlight areas. To 60 cm (2 ft.).

Sesleria argentea
MOOR GRASS

Mounds of light green to pale yellow foliage are topped by freely produced creamy white flowers on dainty stems. Similar in some respects to *Sesleria autumnalis*. Happy in full sun or light shade in a variety of soils. To 60 cm (2 ft.). Z4.

Sesleria caerulea
Syn. *Sesleria albicans*
BLUE MOOR GRASS

Relatively slow-growing mound-forming species, with foliage a light glaucous blue on the upper surface and darker green below. Leaves are held so that both colours are visible at the same time. Dark at first, pale spikes of flowers are produced on short stems early in the season. Drought-tolerant in sun or light shade. From Europe and the U.K. To 20 cm (8 in.). Z4.

'Campo Azul'. An impressive selection from Dave Fross of Native Sons, featuring slowly spreading mounds of distinctive blue-accented foliage topped with many airy white flowers. Drought tolerant and best in sun or light shade. To 60 cm (2 ft.).

Sesleria 'Greenlee Hybrid'

Sesleria heufleriana

Sesleria nitida

Sesleria 'Greenlee Hybrid'
'GREENLEE HYBRID' MOOR GRASS

A distinctive selection named after John Greenlee, with clumps of bright green relatively compact foliage, and topped with many initially light-coloured narrow flowers held just above the leaves. Offers improved tolerance to high inland temperatures. Happy in sun or partial shade. To 50 cm (20 in.). Z4.

Sesleria heufleriana
BLUE-GREEN MOOR GRASS

Similar in some respects to blue moor grass, but with flowers a little taller and leaves slightly more grey green. Possibly happiest in warm climates in sun or light shade. From Europe. To 40 cm (16 in.). Z4.

Sesleria nitida
GREY MOOR GRASS

A valuable early-flowering species forming mounds of spiky blue-grey leaves topped by attractive light flowerheads held clear above the foliage in late spring. Prefers a sunny, open spot and is reasonably drought tolerant. From Europe. To 60 cm (2 ft.). Z4.

Sesleria 'Spring Dream'
MOOR GRASS

A possible hybrid between *Sesleria caerulea* and *S. nitida*. This compact and durable selection from Knoll Gardens has bluish-green slow-growing foliage and attractive dainty flowers, initially dark in colour, in early spring. Prefers sunny, open positions, but will take some light shade. To 30 cm (1 ft.).

Sesleria 'Spring Dream'

Sesleria 'Summer Skies'

Sesleria 'Summer Skies'
BLUE MOOR GRASS

A selection with relatively stiff leaves of a soft blue-grey and a gradually spreading habit. The many light and airy white flowers are produced during summer. Best in sunny, open positions. From Knoll Gardens. To 60 cm (2 ft.).

Sorghastrum
PRAIRIE GRASS

Though only one species is commonly cultivated, this group includes both annual and perennial species of warm-season grasses. From Africa and North America. Z3–6.

Sorghastrum nutans

Sorghastrum nutans
Syn. *Sorghastrum avenaceum*
YELLOW PRAIRIE GRASS

Once extremely common in the tallgrass prairie, this beautiful, adaptable, primarily clump-forming grass contributes strongly upright flower stems arising from mounds of often-glaucous blue leaves that can colour during the fall. Will self-sow. Best in full sun and adaptable to a range of soil types. From North America, including Mexico. To 2.4 m (8 ft.). Z3.

'Golden Sunset'. An excellent green-leaved selection from the University of Minnesota that retains its distinctively upright habit and produces masses of golden yellow flower plumes comparatively early in the year. To 1.8 m (6 ft.).

'Indian Steel'. An excellent seed-raised strain with (as its name suggests) steel grey foliage and an upright habit. To 1.5 m (5 ft.).

'Sioux Blue'. An impressive selection from Rick Darke with very blue-grey leaves and stems, and an upright nature. To 1.5 m (5 ft.).

Sorghastrum nutans 'Sioux Blue'

Sorghastrum nutans 'Indian Steel'

Spartina pectinata

Spartina pectinata 'Aureomarginata'

Spartina

CORD GRASS

These primarily coastal, perennial, warm-season evergreen grasses prefer wet soils and brackish to saltwater environments, and are of major importance to coastal ecologies where they are used in restoration and habitat provision. Vigorous, spreading root systems can preclude their use in all but the largest of gardens.

Spartina pectinata

PRAIRIE CORD GRASS

Found from freshwater habitats to wet prairie lands throughout much of North America, prairie cord grass will grow happily in most soils, even tolerating seasonal droughts, which makes it amenable to garden situations. Strongly spreading, it can form dense patches of strong bright green foliage and relatively lightweight panicles of flower. Best in open, sunny conditions with some moisture. To 2.1 m (7 ft.). Z3.

'Aureomarginata' ('Variegata'). Bold, bright yellow-and-green-striped foliage on slightly less vigorous plants make this a good selection for gardens. To 2.1 m (7 ft.).

Spodiopogon

GREYBEARD GRASS

Among this small group of perennial warm-season deciduous species at home in open grassland, only one species is cultivated to any extent.

Spodiopogon sibiricus

SIBERIAN GREYBEARD GRASS

A distinctive grass with a neatly rounded form. Thin, green flat leaves, held nearly horizontal, turn a wonderful deep red in most autumns. Erect terminal panicles emerge in late summer. Happy in sun or light shade where not too dry. From China, Japan, and Siberia. To 1.2 m (4 ft.). Z3.

Spodiopogon sibiricus

Sporobolus
DROPSEED

This very large group of annual and perennial warm-season deciduous grasses is largely represented in gardens by the temperate North American species that are found in mostly open grasslands. From tropical to temperate areas.

Sporobolus airoides
ALKALI SACATON, ALKALI DROPSEED

Produces clumps of grey-green foliage and masses of effervescent arching flowerheads, opening pink before fading to silver in late summer. Can colour an attractive yellow-orange in autumn. Well-adapted to alkaline soils as well as drought and heat. Always prefers sunny, open positions. From the southern and western U.S. To 1.2 m (4 ft.). Z4.

Sporobolus heterolepis
PRAIRIE DROPSEED

Relatively slow-growing, this is one of the most elegant of prairie grasses, forming finely textured dense flowing mounds that turn deep orange to copper in winter. Delicate flower panicles sit high above the foliage on slender stalks, with fresh flowers having a slight fragrance redolent of coriander. Long lived and highly

Sporobolus airoides

Sporobolus heterolepis

drought tolerant. Prefers full sun but tolerates light shade in a variety of different soils. From North America. To 90 cm (3 ft.). Z3.

'**Tara**'. A compact selection from Roy Diblik with slightly stiffer foliage and good orange-red autumn colour. To 60 cm (2 ft.).

'**Wisconsin**'. Selected by Hans Simon for reliable flowering under cooler European conditions.

Sporobolus wrightii
GIANT SACATON

The largest of all dropseeds, with grey-green clumps of arching foliage topped by sculptural flower spikes that offer dramatic impact over a long period. Amazingly drought-tolerant and even shows some resistance to salt in coastal situations. Always best in sun. From the southern U.S. to Mexico. To 2.4 m (8 ft.). Z5.

Sporobolus wrightii

Stipa barbata

Stipa gigantea

The Splitting of *Stipa*

Recent taxonomic research has led to several grasses previously well-known as *Stipa* being reclassified under other genera. Although perhaps irritating to gardeners uninterested in the background science, the name changes have been observed here purely for expediency, as the new names are already in general circulation.

- *Stipa arundinacea*: see *Anemanthele lessoniana* (page 163)
- *Stipa calamagrostis*: see *Achnatherum calamagrostis* (page 155)
- *Stipa tenuissima*: see *Nassella tenuissima* (page 266)

Stipa
FEATHER GRASS, NEEDLE GRASS

This large and varied group of mostly clump-forming cool-season evergreen grasses, originating in Africa and Eurasia, have long been used extensively in gardens.

Stipa barbata
FEATHER GRASS

From tidy clumps of rather uninteresting green foliage appear magnificent, slender, arching silvery flowerheads with a flowing motion even in the slightest of breezes. Requires a sunny well-drained spot. Can be difficult to establish. From southern Europe and northern Africa. To 75 cm (2½ ft.). Z7.

Stipa gigantea
GIANT OAT GRASS, SPANISH OAT GRASS

Tall, elegant heads of light golden-brown, oat-like flowers are produced each spring from bulky basal clumps of tough narrow evergreen leaves. Requires full sun and a reasonably well-drained

Stipa gigantea 'Gold Fontaene'

soil. Dislikes being shaded or overgrown. Seedling variation can result in a range of heights from a relatively compact 1.2 m (4 ft.) upwards. From southern Europe and northern Africa. To 2.1 m (7 ft.). Z5.

'Gold Fontaene'. An impressive selection by German nurseryman Ernst Pagels. Huge clumps of narrow foliage and many stiff spikes of oat-like golden brown flowers held high above the foliage make this the largest form of Spanish oat grass. To 2.4 m (8 ft.).

'Goldilocks'. A relatively compact selection combining tough green foliage with large golden oat-like heads of flower that are held on comparatively short upright stems. Needs a sunny, well-drained spot. From Knoll Gardens. To 1.8 m (6 ft.).

'Pixie'. A variable dwarf selection with less vigour than the species but retaining much of the original's grace. Most compact when grown in containers. To 1.5 m (5 ft.).

Stipa ichu
Syn. *Jarava ichu*
PERUVIAN FEATHER GRASS
Clumps of soft, light green hair-like foliage bear a strong likeness to that of the quick-growing former *Stipa*, *Nassella tenuissima*. Spectacular long, narrow, fluffy white flowers that wave dramatically in the slightest wind are produced during the summer months. Drought tolerant and requiring well-drained soils in plenty of sun. From South America. To 90 cm (3 ft.). Z8.

Stipa pennata
EUROPEAN FEATHER GRASS
Flowerheads bearing long, feathery tails are held well above tight clumps of slightly arching leaves. Can be difficult to establish and must have a sunny, well-drained spot. Often confused with *Stipa barbata*. From Europe, Africa, and Asia. To 75 cm (2½ ft.). Z6.

Stipa pulcherrima
EUROPEAN FEATHER GRASS
Similar to *Stipa barbata* and *S. pennata*, and equally graceful, with even longer flowering tails produced from mounds of ordinary green leaves. Needs full sun. From Europe, Africa, and Asia. To 75 cm (2½ ft.). Z6.

Tridens
TRIDENS
This small group of warm-season deciduous perennial grasses originates in areas ranging from woodland edge to open meadow in the eastern United States through Mexico.

Stipa gigantea 'Pixie'

Stipa gigantea 'Goldilocks'

Stipa ichu

Tridens flavus
PURPLETOP

Upright and clump-forming, providing distinct hues of purple in meadows, woodland edges, and open grasslands during summer, when the graceful flowers are freshly opened. Prefers sun but will tolerate some light shade in a variety of soils, ideally with some moisture. From the eastern U.S. through Mexico. To 1.2 m (4 ft.). Z6.

Typha
BULRUSH, CATTAIL, REEDMACE

The deciduous, grass-like cattails are present in most areas in any suitable moist to wet ground but especially common along drainage ditches, streamsides, and riverbanks. Tolerating saline and partially polluted waters, they are essential to wetland ecology, providing habitat for wildlife and acting as a natural filtering system. Widely distributed in temperate and tropical areas.

Typha angustifolia
LESSER BULRUSH, NARROW-LEAVED CATTAIL

A more slender version of the common bulrush that tends to prefer shallower water. Distinctive spikes of rounded brown flowerheads, separated into male and female parts by a small gap on the flower stem. Has a spreading habit and will colonize large areas under suitable conditions. Needs sun. From North and South America and Eurasia. To 1.8 m (6 ft.). Z3.

Typha latifolia
COMMON BULRUSH, COMMON CATTAIL, GREAT REEDMACE

Widely distributed and can be found in any suitably wet area. Forms vigorous spreading clumps of tall upright foliage and rounded cylindrical brown flowerheads that are not separated like those of the narrow-leaved cattail. Will cover large areas, though always prefers sunny, open positions. Widely distributed in the Northern Hemisphere, South America, and Africa. To 2.7 m (9 ft.). Z3.

'Variegata'. A striking variegated form, with attractive bright creamy white-and-green-variegated foliage and typical bulrush flowers. Ideal in containers but less cold-hardy than the species. To 1.5 m (5 ft.).

Typha minima
MINIATURE CATTAIL

A distinctive miniature form smaller than other cattails in all its parts, with the same running habit, bright green leaves, and narrowly pointed male and oval female flowers separated by a section of bare stem. Will tolerate the water's edge or very moist soils in sun or lightest shade. Perfect for small watery areas. From Eurasia. To 75 cm (2½ ft.). Z5.

Uncinia
HOOK SEDGE

The grass-like hook sedges produce seeds that hook themselves onto passing animals, including gardeners, for distribution. Although this group of mostly clump-forming perennial evergreens is relatively large, only a few are used in gardens. From Australasia and South America. Z8.

Uncinia rubra
HOOK SEDGE

Unassuming tussocks of deep reddish-brown evergreen foliage produce tiny insignificant flowers that eventually turn into hooked seeds. Often confused with two similar species, *Uncinia egmontiana* and *U. unciniata*, from which it differs due to its more compact nature and narrower, more uniform, darker purplish to bronze-red foliage. Prefers sun for best colour. From New Zealand. To 30 cm (1 ft.). Z8.

'Everflame'. A selection that is very similar to the species in habit but offers delicately pink and reddish-brown striped leaves.

Typha minima

Uncinia rubra

Uncinia rubra 'Everflame'

Where to See Grasses

This list represents only a tiny fraction of the many gardens and designed spaces that have used grasses successfully. As grasses increase in popularity, more and more public spaces, parks, shopping centres, and commercial operations will also have successful schemes from which to gain inspiration.

Canada

VanDusen Botanical Garden, 5251 Oak Street, Vancouver, BC V6M 4H1. vandusengarden.org

United States

The Battery Promenade and the Gardens of Remembrance, State Street and Battery Place, New York, NY 10004. www.thebattery.org

California Botanic Garden, 1500 North College Avenue, Claremont, CA 91711. www.calbg.org

Chanticleer Garden, 786 Church Road, Wayne, PA 19087. www.chanticleergarden.org

Chicago Botanic Garden, 1000 Lake Cook Road, Glencoe, IL 60022. www.chicago-botanic.org

Denver Botanic Gardens, 1007 York Street, Denver, CO 80206. www.botanicgardens.org

Great Plains Ecotourism Coalition. www.visittheprairie.com/visit/seas-of-grass/

The High Line, New York, NY. www.thehighline.org

The Huntington Library, Art Museum, and Botanical Gardens, 1151 Oxford Road, San Marino, CA 91108. www.huntington.org

Lady Bird Johnson Wildflower Center, 4801 La Crosse Avenue, Austin, TX 78739. www.wildflower.org

Longwood Gardens, 1001 Longwood Road, Kennett Square, PA 19348. www.longwoodgardens.org

Lurie Garden, Millennium Park, 201 E. Randolph Street, Chicago, IL. www.luriegarden.org

Minnesota Landscape Arboretum, 3675 Arboretum Dr., Chaska, MN 55318. arb.umn.edu

Mt. Cuba Center, 3120 Barley Mill Road, Hockessin, DE 19707. www.mtcubacenter.org

Regional Parks Botanic Garden, Tilden Park, Wildcat Canyon Road and South Park Drive, Berkeley, CA 94708. www.nativeplants.org

San Diego Zoo's Wild Animal Park, 15500 San Pasqual Valley Road, Escondido, CA 92027. sdzsafaripark.org

San Francisco Botanical Garden at Strybing Arboretum, 9th Avenue and Lincoln Way, San Francisco, California 94122. www.sfbotanicalgarden.org

Santa Barbara Botanic Garden, 1212 Mission Canyon Road, Santa Barbara, California 93105. www.sbbg.org

The Scott Arboretum of Swarthmore College, 500 College Avenue, Swarthmore, PA 19081. www.scottarboretum.org

Springs Preserve, 333 S. Valley View Boulevard, Las Vegas, NV 89107. www.springspreserve.org

Tongva Park, 1615 Ocean Avenue, Santa Monica, CA 90401. www.santamonica.gov/places/parks/tongva-park

United Kingdom

Beth Chatto Gardens, Elmstead Market, Colchester, CO7 7DB. www.bethchatto.co.uk

The Bressingham Gardens, Bressingham, Diss, Norfolk, IP22 2AB. www.thebressinghamgardens.com

Cambo Gardens & The Stables, Cambo Estate, Kingsbarn, St Andrews, Fife, KY16 8QD. www.cambogardens.org.uk

Dove Cottage Nursery & Garden, Shibden Hall Rd, Halifax, HX3 9XA. www.dovecottagenursery.co.uk

Hauser & Wirth, Durslade Farm, Dropping Lane, Bruton, Somerset, BA10 0NL. www.hauserwirth.com/locations/10068-hauser-wirth-somerset/

Knoll Gardens, Hampreston, Wimborne, Dorset, BH21 7ND. www.knollgardens.co.uk

National Botanic Garden of Wales, Middleton Hall, Llanarthne, Carmarthenshire, SA32 8HN. www.botanicgarden.wales

Pensthorpe Natural Park, Fakenham Road, Fakenham, Norfolk, NR21 0LN. www.pensthorpe.com

The Royal Botanic Gardens Kew, Richmond, Surrey, TW9 3AE. www.kew.org

The Royal Horticultural Society Garden Bridgewater, Occupation Rd, Worsley, Manchester, M28 2LJ. www.rhs.org.uk/gardens/bridgewater

The Royal Horticultural Society Garden Harlow Carr, Crag Lane, Harrogate, North Yorkshire, HG3 1QB. www.rhs.org.uk/gardens/harlow-carr

The Royal Horticultural Society Garden Hyde Hall, Buckhatch Lane, Rettendon, Chelmsford, Essex CM3 8ET. www.rhs.org.uk/gardens/hyde-hall

The Royal Horticultural Society Garden Rosemoor, Great Torrington, Devon, EX38 8PH. www.rhs.org.uk/gardens/rosemoor

The Royal Horticultural Society Garden Wisley, Wisley, Woking, Surrey, GU23 6QB. www.rhs.org.uk/gardens/wisley

Scampston, Malton, North Yorkshire, YO17 8NG. www.scampston.co.uk

Sir Harold Hillier Gardens, Jermyns Lane, Ampfield, Romsey, Hampshire, SO51 0QA. www.hants.gov.uk/thingstodo/hilliergardens

Sussex Prairie Garden, Morlands Farm, Wheatsheaf Road, Near Henfield, West Sussex, BN5 9AT. www.sussexprairies.co.uk

Trentham, Stone Road, Trentham, Stoke on Trent, ST4 8JG. www.trentham.co.uk

Wildside, Wildside Nursery, Green Lane, Buckland Monachorum, Devon, PL20 7NP. www.wileyatwildside.com

Europe

Karl-Foerster-Garten, Am Raubfang 7, 14469 Potsdam, Germany. www.denkmalschutz.de/denkmal/wohnhaus-und-garten-karl-foerster.html

Hermannshof, Babostrasse 5, D-69469 Weinheim/Bergstrasse, Germany. www.sichtungsgarten-hermannshof.de

Le Jardin Plume, 76116 Auzouville sur Ry, France. www.lejardinplume.com

Priona Gardens, Schuineslootweg 13, 7777 RE Schuinesloot, Netherlands. www.henkgerritsenfoundation.nl

Lianne's Siergrassen, Jan Gosseswijk 31, 9367 TE De Wilp, Netherlands. www.siergras.nl/en/prairiegarden

Westpark, Westendstrasse, Munich, Germany

Where to Buy Grasses

Grasses can be found in so many good horticultural outlets that this suggested list can only represent a tiny fraction of the specialist nurseries and more generalist garden centres that offer them for sale.

Canada

Norview Gardens (wholesale), 2628 Windham Road 19, Norwich, ON N0J 1P0, Canada. norviewgardens.ca

United States

Digging Dog Nursery, 31101 Middle Ridge Road, Albion, CA 95410. www.diggingdog.com

Earthly Pursuits Inc, 2901 Kuntz Road, Windsor Mill, MD 21244. www.earthlypursuits.net

Emerald Coast Growers (wholesale), 7410 Klondike Road, Pensacola, FL 32526, ecgrowers.com

Greenlee & Associates, 284 Visitacion Avenue, Brisbane, CA 94005. www.greenleeandassociates.com

Green Meadow Growers (wholesale), 31957 Aquaduct Road, Bonsall, CA 92003. www.greenmeadowgrowers.com

High Country Gardens, 2902 Rufina Street, Santa Fe, NM 87507. www.highcountrygardens.com

Hoffman Nursery (wholesale), 5520 Bahama Road, Rougemont, NC 27572. www.hoffmannursery.com

Intrinsic Perennial Gardens (wholesale), 10702 Seaman Road, Hebron, IL 60034-9535. www.intrinsicperennialgardens.com

Jelitto Perennial Seeds, North American Office, 125 Chenoweth Lane, Suite 301, Louisville, KY 40207. www.jelitto.com

Kurt Bluemel (wholesale), 2740 Greene Lane, Baldwin, MD 21013. www.kurtbluemel.com

Larner Seeds, 230 Grove Road, Bolinas, CA 94924. www.larnerseeds.com

Mostly Native Nursery, 54 B Street, Unit D, Point Reyes Station, CA 94956. www.mostlynatives.com

Mountain States Wholesale Nursery, 13803 W. Northern Avenue, Glendale, AZ 85307. www.mswn.com

Native Sons (wholesale), 379 W. El Campo Road, Arroyo Grande, CA 93420. www.nativeson.com

New Moon Nursery (wholesale), 910 Kings Highway, Woodstown, NJ 08098. www.newmoonnursery.com

North Creek Nurseries (wholesale), 388 North Creek Road, Landenberg, PA 19350. www.northcreeknurseries.com

Northwind Perennial Farm, 7047 Hospital Road, Burlington, WI 53105. northwindperennialfarm.com

Ornamental Grasses of Puget Sound, 2009 South Bay Road NE, Olympia, WA 98505, ornamental-grasses.com

Plant Delights Nursery, 9241 Sauls Road, Raleigh, NC 27603. www.plantdelights.com

Plants of the Southwest, 3095 Agua Fria Road, Sante Fe, NM 87507. www.plantsofthesouthwest.com

Pinelands Nursery (wholesale), 323 Island Road, Columbus, NJ 08022. www.pinelandsnursery.com

Prairie Moon Nursery, 32115 Prairie Lane, Winona, MN 55987. www.prairiemoon.com

Prairie Nursery, P.O. Box 306, Westfield, WI 53964. www.prairienursery.com

Stock Seed Farms, 28008 Mill Road, Murdock, NB 68407. www.stockseed.com

The Perennial Farm (wholesale), 12017 Glen Arm Road, Glen Arm, MD 21057. www.perennialfarm.com

Walla Walla Nursery, 4176 Stateline Road, Walla Walla, WA 99362. www.wallawallanursery.com

Western Native Seed, P.O. Box 188, Coaldale, CO 81222. www.westernnativeseed.com

Wildtype, Native Plants and Seeds, 900 N. Every Road, Mason, MI 48854. www.wildtypeplants.com

Wind River Seed, 3075 Lane 51½, Manderson, WY 82432. www.windriverseed.com

United Kingdom

The Alpine and Grass Nursery, Northgate, Pinchbeck, Spalding, Lincolnshire, PE11 3TB. www.specialistgrower.co.uk

Arvensis Perennials, Lower Wraxhall, Bradford on Avon, BA15 2RU (wholesale). www.arvensisperennials.co.uk

Ashcroft's 63a Hesketh Lane, Tarleton, Lancashire, PR4 6AQ. www.ashcroftsperennials.co.uk

Ashwood Nurseries, Ashwood Lower Lane, Kingswinford, DY6 0AE. www.ashwoodnurseries.com

Avondale Nurseries, Mill Hill, Baginton, Coventry, CV8 3AG. www.avondalenursery.co.uk

Beth Chatto Gardens, Elmstead Market, Colchester, CO7 7DB. www.bethchatto.co.uk

Binny Plants, Binny Estate, Ecclesmachan Road, Uphall, Scotland, EH52 6NL. www.binnyplants.com

Dove Cottage Nursery & Garden, Shibden Hall Road, Halifax, HX3 9XA. www.dovecottagenursery.co.uk

Knoll Gardens, Hampreston, Wimborne, Dorset, BH21 7ND. www.knollgardens.co.uk

Macplants, Berrybank Nursery, 5 Boggs Holdings, Pencaitland, EH34 5BA. www.macplants.co.uk

Marchants Hardy Plants, 2 Marchants Cottages, Mill Lane, Laughton, East Sussex, BN8 6AJ. www.marchantshardyplants.co.uk

Meadowgate Nursery, Street End Lane, Sidlesham West Sussex PO20 7RG. www.meadowgatenursery.co.uk

The Plantsman's Preference, Hopton Road, Garboldisham, Diss, Norfolk, IP22 2QN. www.plantpref.co.uk

The Royal Horticultural Society Garden Bridgewater, Occupation Rd, Worsley, Manchester, M28 2LJ. www.rhs.org.uk/gardens/bridgewater

The Royal Horticultural Society Garden Harlow Carr, Crag Lane, Harrogate, North Yorkshire, HG3 1QB. www.rhs.org.uk/gardens/harlow-carr

The Royal Horticultural Society Garden Hyde Hall, Buckhatch Lane, Rettendon, Chelmsford, Essex CM3 8ET. www.rhs.org.uk/gardens/hyde-hall

The Royal Horticultural Society Garden Rosemoor, Great Torrington, Devon, EX38 8PH. www.rhs.org.uk/gardens/rosemoor

The Royal Horticultural Society Garden Wisley, Wisley, Woking, Surrey, GU23 6QB. www.rhs.org.uk/gardens/wisley

Scampston, Malton, North Yorkshire, YO17 8NG. www.scampston.co.uk

Europe

Bambous de Planbuisson, Rue Montaigne, 24480 Le Buisson de Cadouin, France. www.planbuisson.com

Coen Jansen Vaste Planten, Ankummer Es 13-A, 7722 RD Dalfsen, Netherlands. www.coenjansenvasteplanten.nl

De Hessenhof, Hessenweg 41, 6718 TC Ede, Netherlands. www.hessenhof.nl

Jacob's Nursery, 5e Dalweg 4, 9699 T S Vriescheloo, Netherlands

Jan Spruyt-Van der Jeugd BV, Mostenveld 30, B-9255 Buggenhout, Belgium. www.perennials.be

Le Jardin Plume, 76116 Auzouville sur Ry, France. www.lejardinplume.com

Lianne's Siergrassen, Jan Gosseswijk 31, 9367 TE De Wilp, Netherlands. www.siergras.nl/en/prairiegarden

Les Pépinière Lepage, Chemin du Portu, 49130 Les Ponts-de-Ce France. www.lepage-vivaces.com

Overdam Nursery, Agiltevej 11, DK-2970 Hørsholm, Denmark. www.overdam.dk

Priola, Priola Farm via delle Acquette, 4 – 31100 Treviso Italy, vivaipriola.it

Stauden Peters (wholesale), Drullerweg 1, 47559 Kranenburg, Germany. www.stauden-peters.de

Szkółka Słowińscy, Ląd 48, 62-405 Lądek, Poland. www.szkolkaslowinscy.pl

Zillmer Young Plants (wholesale), Hammer Kirchwg 55, 31600 Uchte, Germany. www.perennial-youngplants.com

Resources

United States

The Calflora Database is a nonprofit organization providing information about California plant biodiversity for use in education, research, and conservation. www.calflora.org

The California Invasive Plant Council site contains much information about invasive plants in California's precious natural areas. www.cal-ipc.org

The California Native Grasslands Association's mission is to promote, preserve, and restore the diversity of California's native grasses and grassland ecosystems through education, advocacy, research, and stewardship. www.cnga.org

The California Native Plant Society works to protect California's native plant heritage and preserve it for future generations. www.cnps.org

The California Society for Ecological Restoration is a nonprofit membership-based organization dedicated to bringing about the recovery of damaged California ecosystems. www.sercal.org

The Center for Biological Diversity is dedicated to protecting biodiversity, working to secure a future for all species, great and small, hovering on the brink of extinction. www.biologicaldiversity.org

The Lady Bird Johnson Wildflower Center is the official botanic garden of Texas, and uses native plants to restore and create sustainable, beautiful landscapes. www.wildflower.org

NatureServe is an authoritative source for biodiversity data throughout North America. www.natureserve.org

PlantRight lists invasive plants, and suggests non-invasive plants for use in different areas of California. www.plantright.org

The United States Department of Agriculture Plants Database provides standardized information about the vascular plants, mosses, liverworts, hornworts, and lichens of the U.S. and its territories. Here you will find native plants listed state by state. plants.usda.gov

United Kingdom

The Botanical Society of Britain & Ireland is the leading scientific society in Britain and Ireland for the study of plant distribution and taxonomy. bsbi.org.uk

Plant Life is a British conservation charity working nationally and internationally to save threatened wild flowers, plants, and fungi. www.plantlife.org.uk

Buglife is Europe's only organization devoted to the conservation of all invertebrates. Their site has lots of useful information on this essential group. www.buglife.org.uk

Kew GrassBase is a comprehensive reference for researching grasses. www.kew.org/data/grassbase/index.html

Kews Gardens' impressive Plants of the World Online lists over one million plant entries, including grasses. powo.science.kew.org

The National Biodiversity Network gathers and records information on biodiversity. nbn.org.uk

The NBN Atlas is an online tool that educates and informs people about the natural world. nbnatlas.org

Europe

The Eurasian Dry Grassland Group is a network of researchers and conservationists interested in Palaearctic natural and semi-natural grasslands. edgg.org

References

Bornstein, Carol, Fross, David and O'Brien, Bart. *California Native Plants for the Garden*. Los Olivos, California: Cachuma Press, 2005.

Chatto Beth. *The Damp Garden (New Edition)*. London: Orion, 1998.

Chatto, Beth. *The Dry Garden (New Edition)*. London: Orion, 1998.

Chatto, Beth. *The Beth Chatto Handbook: A Descriptive List of Unusual Plants*. Essex, U.K.: Beth Chatto Gardens, 2015.

Cope, Tom and Gray, Alan. *Grasses of the British Isles*. London: Botanical Society of the British Isles, 2009.

Darke, Rick. *The American Woodland Garden*. Portland, Oregon and London: Timber Press, 2007.

Darke, Rick. *The Encyclopedia of Grasses for Livable Landscapes*. Portland, Oregon and London: Timber Press, 2007.

Darke, Rick and Tallamy, Doug. *The Living Landscape*. Portland, Oregon and London: Timber Press, 2014.

Diblik, Roy. *The Know Maintenance Perennial Garden*. Portland, Oregon and London: Timber Press, 2014.

Dunnett Nigel and Clayden, Andy. *Rain Gardens*. Portland, Oregon and London: Timber Press, 2007.

Dunnett, Nigel and Kingsbury, Noël. *Planting Green Roofs and Living Walls: Revised and Updated Edition*. Portland, Oregon and London: Timber Press, 2008.

Gerritsen, Henk. *Essay on Gardening*. Netherlands: Architectura & Natura Press. 2014.

Greenlee, John. *Meadows by Design: Creating a Natural Alternative to the Traditional Lawn*. Portland, Oregon and London: Timber Press, 2009.

Grounds, Roger. *Grasses: Choosing and Using These Ornamental Plants in the Garden*. London: Quadrille Publishing Ltd., 2005.

Simpson, David, Foley, Michael, Jermy, Anthony Clive and Oswald, PH. *Sedges of the British Isles*. United Kingdom: Botanical Society of the British Isles, 2007.

King, Michael and Oudolf, Piet. *Gardening with Grasses*. London: Frances Lincoln, 1998.

Korn, Peter. *Peter Korn's Garden: Giving Plants What They Want*. Sweden: Peter Korn, 2013.

Liptan, Thomas W., and Santen, Jr., J. David. *Sustainable Stormwater Management*. Portland, Oregon and London: Timber Press, 2017.

Lloyd, Christopher. *Meadows*. London: Cassell Illustrated, 2006.

Mabey, Richard. *Flora Britannica: The Definitive New Guide to Britain's Wild Flowers, Plants and Trees*. London: Sinclair-Stevenson, 1996.

Oehme, Wolfgang and Van Sweden, James. *Bold Romantic Gardens*. Hong Kong: Spacemaker Press, 1998.

Oudolf, Piet and Gerritsen, Henk. *Planting the Natural Garden*. Portland, Oregon and London: Timber Press, 2003.

Oudolf, Piet and Kingsbury, Noël. *Designing with Plants*. London: Conran Octopus Ltd., 1999.

Oudolf, Piet and Kingsbury Noël. *Planting, A New Perspective*. Portland, Oregon and London: Timber Press, 2013.

Phillips, Roger and Rix, Martyn. *Perennials: Volume 1, Early Perennials*. London: Pan Books, 1993.

Phillips, Roger and Rix, Martyn. *Perennials: Volume 2, Late Perennials*. London: Pan Books, 1993.

Polunin, Oleg and Wright, Robin Southey. *A Concise Guide to the Flowers of Britain and Europe*. Oxford and New York: Oxford University Press, 1988.

Robinson, William. *The Wild Garden*. United Kington: Sagapress, 1895.

Rounsaville, Todd J., Touchell, Darren H., and Ranney, Thomas G. 2011. Fertility and Reproductive Pathways in Diploid and Triploid *Miscanthus sinensis*. Hortscience 46(10): 1353-1357.

Schilthuizen, Menno, *Darwin Comes to Town: How the Urban Jungle Drives Evolution*. New York: Picador, 2018.

Snodgrass, Edmund C. and Snodgrass, Lucie L. *Green Roof Plants*. Portland, Oregon and London: Timber Press, 2006.

Tallamy, Douglas W. *Bringing Nature Home*. Portland, Oregon and London: Timber Press, 2007.

Weaner, Larry and Christopher, Thomas. *Garden Revolution: How Our Landscapes Can Be a Source of Environmental Change*. Portland, Oregon and London: Timber Press, 2016.

Wiley, Keith. *On the Wild Side: Experiments in New Naturalism*. Portland, Oregon and London: Timber Press, 2004.

Photography Credits

All photos are by the author except for the following:

Alexandre Bailhache, page 30
Rick Darke, page 269 (top right)
Devon Pond Plants, page 305 (top right)
Genesis Plant Marketing, page 250 (second from top)
John Greenlee, page 231 (bottom)
Wayne Hanna Pictures, page 276 (left, second from bottom; bottom right)
Hoffman Nursery, Inc., pages 161 (left), 179 (left)
Ross Humphrey, page 11
Intrinsic Perennial Gardens, pages 160, 161 (top right), 169 (bottom), 215 (top left), 272 (bottom left), 276 (bottom left), 278 (left), 279 (top left and top right)
Longwood Gardens, page 27
Melissa Gorman, page 291
Klaus Menzel, page 244 (bottom left)
North Carolina State University, pages 242 (top right), 249 (bottom left)
North Creek Nurseries, page 270 (top left)
Plantipp, pages 215 (bottom left), 251 (top right), 268
Edmund. C. Snodgrass, page 129 (bottom)
Amanda Walker, page 110

Index

A

Achillea, 71
    'Terracotta', 70
Achnatherum, 85, 152, 155
Achnatherum calamagrostis, 155, 300
    'Lemperg', 155
Acorus, 96, 133, 140, 152, 155–156
Acorus calamus, 155
Acorus gramineus, 95, 155–156
    'Golden Edge', 133, 156
    'Ogon', 95, 105, 156
    'Variegatus', 95, 156
African lovegrass, 211
Agapanthus 'Northern Star', 70
Agropyron magellanicum, 209
Agrostis, 152, 156
Agrostis capillaris, 156, 157
Agrostis nebulosa, 156
alkali dropseed, 298
alkali sacaton, 84, 298
Allium 'Millenium', 70
Alopecurus, 152, 157
Alopecurus pratensis 'Aureovariegatus', 157
Amaryllis belladonna, 70
American beach grass, 158
American dune grass, 230
American manna grass, 219
Ammophila, 76, 120, 150, 152, 157–158
Ammophila arenaria, 108, 158
Ammophila breviligulata, 158, 159
    'Cape', 158
    'Hatteras', 158
Ampeledesmos, 152, 159
Ampelodesmos, 85
Ampelodesmos mauritanicus, 83, 159
Amsonia, 71
    'Blue Ice', 70
Andropogon, 136, 152, 160–163
Andropogon gerardii, 160
    'Blackhawks', 160
    'Dancing Wind', 160
    'Holy Smoke', 160
    'Lord Snowden's Big Blue', 160–161
    'New Wave', 161
    'Red October', 161
Andropogon glomeratus, 161
    var. *scabriglumis*, 161
Andropogon scoparium, 289
Andropogon ternarius, 161, 162
    'Black Mountain', 162
Andropogon virginicus, 162–163
    var. *abbreviatus*, 161
    var. *glaucus*, 163
Anemanthele, 96, 106, 152, 163
Anemanthele lessoniana, 45, 94, 151, 163, 300
Anemone, 72
Anemone nemerosa 'Alba', 73
animals, 147
Apaganthus, 71
aphids, 147
Appalachian sedge, 179
Apple Campus, Cupertino, 112, 119, 130
Aquilegia vulgaris, 72, 73
Aristida, 54, 76, 85, 152, 163
Aristida purpurea, 39, 123, 147, 163
Arrhenatherum, 152
Arundo, 21, 101, 104, 151, 152, 165–166
Arundo donax, 21, 164, 165
    'Golden Chain', 165
    'Macrophylla', 165
    'Variegata', 165
    'Versicolor', 165
Arundo formosana, 166
    'Green Fountain', 166
    'Oriental Gold', 166
Aster, 31
Aster pyrenaeus 'Lutetia', 68, 70
Atlas fescue, 216
Australian blue grass, 287
Austrostipa, 152
autumn flame miscanthus, 241
autumn moor grass, 291
autumn sedge, 181

B

backlight, 40
Ballerini, Fred, 123
bamboo, 165
bamboo muhly, 263
barley, 224
beach grass, 76, 108, 157–158
beardgrass, 160, 166–168, 289
bent grass, 156
Beth Chatto Gardens, Essex, 82–83, 98, 99
big bluestem, 160
big galleta, 286
biodiversity, 13, 27, 60
black mondo grass, 86–87
black sedge, 187
blood grass, 224
blue fescue, 214
blue grama, 169

blue grass, 286
blue-green moor grass, 293
blue hair grass, 228
blue moor grass, 291, 294
blue muhly, 264
blue oat grass, 223
bluestem, 289
blue wheatgrass, 209
blurring, 13–14
Boer lovegrass, 210
Bothriochloa, 40, 76, 80, 85, 152, 166
Bothriochloa barbinodis, 40, 166
Bothriochloa bladhii, 81, 166, 167
Bothriochloa caucasica, 166
Bothriochloa ischaemum, 168
bottlebrush grass, 209
Bouteloua, 85, 119, 127, 136, 152, 168–169
Bouteloua curtipendula, 168, 169
Bouteloua dactyloides, 169
Bouteloua gracilis, 39–40, 116, 169
  'Blonde Ambition', 169
  'Honeycomb', 169
bracken, 57
Briza, 119, 127, 153, 170
Briza maxima, 170
Briza media, 49, 170–171
  'Golden Bee', 170, 171
  'Limouzi', 170
  'Russells', 170
broadleaved cotton grass, 213
broadleaved sedge, 194–195
Bromus, 153
broomsedge, 162–163
brown sedge, 179–180, 183
Buchloe dactyloides, 169
buffalo grass, 169

bulbs, 31, 34, 35, 46, 47, 60, 70, 73, 92, 116
bulrush, 304
bunchgrass, 166
Burle Marx, Roberto, 28
burrowers, 147
bushy beardgrass, 161

C

Calamagrostis, 21, 54, 84, 85, 91, 96, 120, 133, 136, 151, 153, 172–176
Calamagrostis ´acutiflora
  'Avalanche', 172
  'Eldorado', 172–173
  'Karl Foerster', 45, 47, 52, 63, 64, 172, 174, 175
  'Overdam', 174, 175
  'Stricta', 174
  'Waldenbuch', 64, 174, 175
Calamagrostis arundinacea var. *brachytricha*, 175
Calamagrostis brachytricha, 39, 40, 85–86, 175
Calamagrostis emodensis, 176
Calamagrostis epigejos, 98, 172, 176
Calamagrostis foliosa, 176
Calamagrostis 'Little Nootka', 176
Calamagrostis nutkaensis, 176, 177
  'The King', 176, 177
Calamagrostis varia, 176, 177
  'Knightshayes', 182
California Academy of Sciences, 126
California fescue, 214
California gray rush, 227
California meadow sedge, 193
Californian melic, 234
Camassia, 31
Canada wild rye, 209
canary grass, 284

Carex, 23, 68, 86, 89–90, 91, 96, 100, 101, 106, 117, 119, 120, 127, 129, 133, 140, 147, 153, 178–200
  'Silver Sceptre', 72, 73, 197
Carex alba, 178
Carex albicans, 179
Carex amphibola, 179
Carex appalachica, 179
Carex arenaria, 118, 119, 179
Carex berggrenii, 179
Carex brunnea, 179–180
  'Jenneke', 179
  'Variegata', 180
Carex buchananii, 180
  'Red Rooster', 180
  'Viridis', 180
Carex cherokeensis, 180
Carex comans, 180, 183
  'Bronze', 180
  'Frosted Curls', 180
  'Milk Chocolate', 180
Carex conica, 180
  'Marginata', 180
  'Snowline', 180
  'Variegata', 180
Carex dipsacea, 181
  'Dark Horse', 181
Carex divulsa, 44, 90, 97, 130, 182
Carex elata, 182
  'Aurea', 40, 98, 99, 182
  'Knightshayes', 183
Carex flacca, 153, 183, 193
  'Blue Zinger', 183
Carex flaccosperma, 89
Carex flagellifera, 183
Carex flava, 183
Carex fortunei, 184
Carex grayii, 184

Carex laxiculmis, 89, 184
   'Bunny Blue', 184
Carex morrowii, 184
   'Everglow', 184
   'Fisher's Form', 184, 185
   'Ice Dance', 92–94, 185
   'Silk Tassel', 185
   'Vanilla Ice', 94, 185
Carex muskingumensis, 89, 90, 187
   'Little Midge', 186–187
   'Oehme', 187
   'Silberstreif', 187
Carex nigra, 187
   'Online', 187
Carex obnupta, 188, 189
   'Golden Day', 188, 189
Carex oshimensis, 45, 90, 189
   'Evercream', 90, 189
   'Everest', 90, 189
   'Everglow', 90, 104
   'Evergold', 90, 140, 153, 189
   'Everillo', 90, 104, 190–191
   'Everlime', 90, 104, 133, 191
   'Feather Falls', 191
   'Gold Strike', 183
   'Old Gold', 189
   'Variegata', 189
Carex panicea, 192, 193
Carex paniculata, 99, 192, 193
Carex pansa, 192, 193
Carex pellita, 192, 193
Carex pendula, 153, 192, 193
   'Moonraker', 193
Carex pensylvanica, 89, 90, 115, 194
   'Straw Hat', 194
Carex phyllocephala, 194
   'Sparkler', 194, 195

Carex plantaginea, 194–195
Carex praegracilis, 112, 117, 118, 120, 121, 193, 195
Carex remota, 73, 196
Carex riparia, 100, 196
   'Variegata', 196
Carex secta, 98, 99, 151, 196, 197
Carex siderosticha
   'Banana Boat', 197
   'Variegata', 197
Carex spissa, 198
Carex stricta, 98, 99, 100, 199
Carex tenuiculmis, 198, 199
   'Cappuccino', 198
Carex testacea, 44–45, 104, 183, 199
Carex texensis, 200
Carex trifida, 200
   'Rekohu Sunrise', 200
carnation grass, 183
carnation sedge, 193
cats, 147
cattail, 304–305
chalky bluestem, 163
Chasmanthium, 91, 96, 153, 200
Chasmanthium latifolium, 85–86, 86, 200
Chasmanthium laxum, 200
Chatto, Beth, 82
'Chelsea chop', 138–140
Chelsea Flower Show, 140
Cherokee sedge, 180
Chicago Botanic Gardens, 31, 100
Chinese feather reed grass, 176
Chinese palm sedge, 194
Chionochloa, 153, 200–201
Chionochloa conspicua, 200
Chionochloa flavicans, 200–201
Chionochloa rubra, 201
chipped bark, 57

climatic conditions, 10–11, 151, 152
cloud grass, 156
clumpers, 150
coast melic, 234
coast switch grass, 268
colour, 40–42
common barley, 224
common bulrush, 304–305
common cattail, 304–305
common club rush, 101
common cotton grass, 213
common reed, 96, 108, 110, 285
common rush, 225–226
community, 13–14, 17–23, 26
compost, 57
coneflower, 27, 68
conifers, 31
containers, 102–106
continuity, 40–42
cool-season grasses, 151
Cortaderia, 28, 150, 153, 201–204
Cortaderia argentea, 202–204
Cortaderia richardii, 202
Cortaderia selloana, 202–204
   'Albolineata', 202
   'Aureolineata', 203
   'Evita', 202
   'Gold Band', 203
   'Monstrosa', 203
   'Patagonia', 203
   'Point du Raz', 203
   'Pumila', 203
   'Rendatleri', 203
   'Silver Feather', 204
   'Silver Stripe', 202
   'Splendid Star', 204
   'Sunningdale Silver', 58, 63, 204
   'Tiny Pampa', 203

Cortaderia toetoe, 204
cotton grass, 98, 213
cotton sedge, 213
creeping wild rye, 230–231
crested hair grass, 228
cyclamen, 73
Cyperus, 101

D

daffodils, 31, 60, 70
daisy, 62
Death Valley, 76, 78
deciduous grasses, 21, 23, 35, 40, 104, 134, 136–140, 143, 146
deer, 147
deer grass, 50, 82, 265
delphiniums, 9
Deschampsia, 91, 96, 98, 101, 119, 127, 129, 133, 153, 205–208
　'Goldtau', 40, 68
Deschampsia cespitosa, 16, 97
　'Bronzeschleier', 205
　'Goldgehange', 205
　'Goldtau', 205
　subsp. *holciformis*, 206
　subsp. *holciformis* 'Marin', 206
　subsp. *holciformis* Shell Beach', 206
　'Mill End', 205
　'Schottland', 205
　'Tardiflora', 205
　'Tautrager', 206
　var. *vivipara*, 206
　var. *vivipara* 'Fairy's Joke', 206
　'Waldschatt', 206
Deschampsia flexuosa, 207
Desert Botanical Garden, Arizona, 78
Desmoschoenus, 153, 208

Desmoschoenus spiralis, 208
Dichromena latifolia, 287
Digitalis purpurea, 73
diseases, 146–147
Distichlis, 153, 208
Distichlis spicata, 123, 208
division, 34, 38, 45, 50, 52, 53, 57
dogs, 147
dropseed, 298–299
drought conditions, 76–77, 85
dry conditions, 76–85, 90, 95, 130, 151
dune grass, 157
Dutch iris, 66, 68, 70–71

E

Echinacea, 21, 31, 35, 71
Echinacea pallida, 68, 69, 70
Elymus, 76, 85, 96, 153, 208–210
Elymus arenarius, 208
Elymus canadensis, 209
Elymus cinereus, 208, 229
Elymus condensatus, 208, 230
　'Canyon Prince', 230
Elymus elymoides, 109, 209
Elymus hystrix, 209
Elymus magellanicus, 209
Elymus mollis, 208, 230
Elymus racemosus, 208, 230
Elymus solandri, 210
Eragrostis, 40, 85, 106, 136, 153
Eragrostis chloromelas, 210, 211
Eragrostis curvula, 210–211
　var. *conferta*, 210
　'Totnes Burgundy', 104, 211
Eragrostis elliottii, 211
　'Tallahassee Sunset', 211
Eragrostis spectabilis, 211
Eragrostis trichodes, 212, 213
　'Bend', 213

Erianthus, 288
Erianthus ravennae, 288
Eriophorum, 101, 133, 153, 213
Eriophorum angustifolium, 98, 212, 213
Eriophorum latifolium, 213
Eriophorum vaginatum, 212, 213
Eriophorum virginicum, 213
erosion control, 120–121
Eucalyptus, 11
eulalia, 238, 241–255
Euonymus, 11, 63
Eupatorium, 21, 35, 63, 99, 100
Eupatorium maculatum 'Atropurpureum', 64
Euphorbia, 63
Euphorbia palustris, 62, 63, 64
European beach grass, 158
European dune grass, 229
European feather grass, 302

F

'Fairy Tails' fountain grass, 280
feather grass, 225, 300–302
feather reed grass, 98, 172–175, 176
feathertop, 283
Ferndown Common, Dorset, 28, 29, 31
fescue, 213–219
Festuca, 40, 76–77, 81, 85, 86, 87, 106, 119, 120, 127, 151, 153, 213–219
　'Hoggar', 216
Festuca amethystina, 214
　'Phils Silver', 214
　'Scott Mountain', 214
　'Serpentine Blue', 214
Festuca glauca, 153, 214–215, 217
　'Boulder Blue', 214, 215

'Cool as Ice', 215
'Elijah Blue', 76, 215
'Golden Toupee', 215
'Intense Blue', 76, 215
'Sunrise', 215
Festuca idahoensis, 216
    'Stony Creek', 216
    'Tomales Bay', 77, 216
Festuca mairei, 33, 153, 216
Festuca ovina, 216, 217
Festuca rubra, 119, 153, 217
    'Blue Haze', 77, 217, 218
    'Jughandle', 219
    'Molate', 219
    'Patrick's Point', 77, 87, 218, 219
Festuca 'Siskiyou Blue', 218, 219
Filipendula, 100
fire, 147
foothill melic, 234
foothill needle grass, 265
fountain grass, 21, 23, 39, 79–80, 274–283
foxgloves, 18, 21
foxtail, 157
foxtail barley, 224
foxtail grass, 275–279, 281
Francoa sonchifolia 'Pink Bouquet', 70
Fritillaria meleagris, 73
Fross, Dave, 39, 50, 74, 87, 94, 118, 119, 124, 231, 291
Fross, Rainie, 39, 50, 74, 87, 94, 118, 119, 124

G

Galanthus
    'Lady Elphinstone', 73
    'Sam Arnott', 73
galleta, 286

garden design
    biodiversity, 13
    blurring, 13–14
    blurring/merging, 13–14
    building blocks, 38–39
    colour, 40–42
    as community, 13–14, 17–23, 26
    continuity, 40–42
    division, 34, 38, 45, 50, 52, 53, 57
    editing, 24, 62
    erosion control, 120–121
    formal gardens, 21–22
    gravel gardens, 81, 82–83
    green roofs, 124–127
    ground cover, 56–57
    habitat restoration, 123–124
    informal designs, 22–23
    inspiration, 29–34
    lawn replacement, 114–119
    light conditions, 39–40
    mass, 45–47
    matrix, 31, 47, 66, 72, 105
    'meadow style' approach, 14, 66
    merging, 13–14, 34, 35, 65
    movement, 49
    'naturalistic' approach, 11, 27–28, 31–34, 60–73
    plant choice, 23
    rain gardens, 97, 128–134
    repetition, 54
    rhythm, 17–23
    screening, 53
    seasonality, 17–23, 38, 40–42, 62
    shape, 42–45
    sound, 49
    subdivisions, 34
    texture, 42–45
    transparency, 50
    year-round garden, 24–26

garden tools, 137
Geranium, 21
geraniums, 18
giant blue rye, 230
giant miscanthus, 239–241
giant oat grass, 300–302
giant reed, 165
giant sacaton, 299
giant wild rye, 230
glaucous sedge, 183
Glyceria, 97, 98, 101, 153, 219
Glyceria grandis, 219
Glyceria maxima, 219
    var. *variegata*, 219
golden meadow foxtail, 157
goldenrod, 27
golden sand sedge, 208
golf courses, 12, 123, 124
gophers, 147
Gothenburg Botanical Garden, 119
grama grass, 168–169
gravel gardens, 81, 82–83
grazers, 147
greater pond sedge, 196
greater tussock sedge, 193
greater woodrush, 232–233
great reedmace, 304–305
green desert, 22
Greenlee, John, 23, 47, 91, 211, 231, 280, 293
'Greenlee Hybrid' moor grass, 91, 292, 293
green roofs, 124–127
greybeard grass, 297
grey moor grass, 293
grey sedge, 179, 182
grey wild rye, 229
ground cover, 56–57

growing conditions
    arid and dry conditions, 78–80
    drought conditions, 76–85
    dry conditions, 76–85
    gravel gardens, 82–83
    pots and containers, 102–106
    shade conditions, 85–96, 151
    sun-baked and dry conditions, 80–81
    sun-baked conditions, 76–85
    wet conditions, 96–101, 151
Gunnera, 99

H

habitat restoration, 114, 123–124, 143
hachijo susuki, 255
hair grass, 16, 205–208, 228
hairy melic, 234
hairy sedge, 180
hairy woodrush, 232
Hakonechloa, 23, 54, 96, 106, 153, 220–222
Hakonechloa macra, 42, 85, 86, 94, 102, 221–222
    'Albovariegata', 221
    'All Gold', 221, 222
    'Aureola', 86, 94, 102, 221
    'Beni-kaze', 222
    'Mulled Wine', 222
    'Nicolas', 222
    'Samurai', 94, 222
    'Stripe It Rich', 222
    'SunFlare', 222
Hakone grass, 94, 220–222
Hardiness Zones, 154
hard rush, 226–227
hardscape, 22, 77, 105
hardy sugar cane, 288

hare's tail, 213
Hauser and Wirth, Somerset, 34
Helenium, 31
Helictotrichon, 40, 54, 76, 85, 86, 153, 223
Helictotrichon sempervirens, 87, 223
    'Pendulum', 223
    'Saphirsprudel', 223
Hermannshoff Gardens, Weinheim, 60
Hesperantha coccinea 'Major', 70
Hesperantha 'Major', 68
Himalayan fairy grass, 241
Hime-kan-suge, 180
Holcus, 153, 223
Holcus lanatus, 223
hook sedge, 305
Hordeum, 153, 224
Hordeum jubatum, 224
Hordeum vulgare, 224
Hosta, 76
Huntington Library, Art Museum, and Botanical Gardens, 33, 44, 52, 78, 79

I

ice plant, 123
Idaho fescue, 216
Imperata, 106, 153, 224–225
Imperata brevifolia, 224
Imperata cylindrica, 224–225
    'Red Baron', 225
    'Rubra', 102, 225
insects, 147
Iris, 99
    'Lion King', 70
    'Rosario', 70
    'Sapphire Beauty', 70
Ixia hybrids, 70

J

Japanese silver grass, 238
Jarava, 153, 225
Jarava ichu, 302
Jarava ichu, 81
Juncus, 68, 97, 98, 100, 101, 129, 130, 133, 140, 153, 225–227
Juncus acutus
    subsp. *leopoldii*, 225
    subsp. *sphaerocarpus*, 225
Juncus effusus, 225–226
    'Carman's Japanese', 225
    'Quartz Creek', 226
    var. *spiralis*, 226
Juncus ensifolius, 226
Juncus inflexus, 16, 226–227
    'Lovesick Blues', 227
Juncus patens, 227
    'Carman's Gray', 227
    'Elk Blue', 227

K

kan suge, 184
kari yasu modoki, 241
Knautia, 71
Knautia macedonica, 70
Kniphofia caulescens 'John May', 70
Knoll Gardens, Dorset
    containers, 102, 106
    Decennium border, 60–64, 65, 66, 148
    Dry Meadow, 65–71, 130–133
    garden design, 52
    grassland, 31
    Gravel Garden, 81
    ground cover, 57
    lawn replacement, 119
    light conditions, 40

maintenance, 11, 89, 140
Mill End borders, 18-22
native plants, 107
'naturalistic' approach, 11, 31-34, 60-73
Rain Garden, 65-66, 68, 69, 130-133
repetition, 54
rhythm, 18-22
screening, 53
seasonality, 18-22, 24-26, 40-42
shade conditions, 89, 91
Shady Meadow, 71-73
sun-baked and dry conditions, 80-81, 85
transparency, 50
woody plants, 11
Koeleria, 119, 153, 228, 234
Koeleria cristata, 228
Koeleria glauca, 228
Koeleria macrantha, 228
Koeleria pyramidata, 228
Korean feather grass, 85
Korean feather reed grass, 175

L

large leaved fountain grass, 280
lawn replacement, 114-119
lawns, 15, 22, 23, 35
leaf litter, 56-57
leatherleaf sedge, 180
lesser bulrush, 304
'less is more' approach, 28
Leucanthemum vulgare, 62
Leymus, 40, 76, 85, 120, 153, 158, 208, 229-231
Leymus arenarius, 76, 77, 120, 208, 229
    'Glaucus', 229

Leymus cinereus, 208, 229
Leymus condensatus, 208, 230
    'Canyon Prince', 76
Leymus mollis, 208, 230
Leymus racemosus, 208, 230
Leymus triticoides, 230-231
    'Lagunita', 231
    'Oceano', 231
Libertia, 65, 68
Libertia grandiflora, 66, 69, 70, 71
lifespans, 151
light conditions, 39
Ligularia, 76
lily grass, 266-267
Lindheimer's muhly, 263
Liriope, 96
little bluestem, 289-290
Lloyd, Christopher, 28
Longwood Gardens, 27
lovegrass, 210-213
Lurie Garden, Chicago, 28
Luzula, 86, 91, 96, 97, 101, 120, 129, 133, 140, 153, 232-234
Luzula acuminata, 95, 232
Luzula multiflora, 95
Luzula nivea, 68, 94, 232, 233
    'Snowflake', 133, 232, 233
Luzula pilosa, 232, 233
    'Igel', 232, 233
Luzula sylvatica, 95, 232-233
    'Aurea', 95, 232, 233
    'Bromel', 95, 232
    'Hohe Tatra', 232
    'Marginata', 95, 232
    'Mariusz', 234
    'Solar Flair', 95, 133, 234
lyme grass, 77, 120, 229-231
Lythrum, 100

M

mace sedge, 184
maintenance
    containers, 143-144
    deciduous grasses, 136-140
    diseases, 146-147
    evergreen grasses, 140-142
    feeding, 142-143
    ground cover, 56
    Knoll Gardens, Dorset, 11, 89, 140
    low maintenance, 142
    mulching, 142-143
    pests, 146-147
    pots, 143-144
    semi-evergreen grasses, 142
    summer-dormant grasses, 140
Makepeace, Jenny, 50
Makepeace, John, 50
manna grass, 219
manure, 57
marram, 76, 157
mass, 45
matrix, 31, 47, 66, 72, 105
meadows, 8, 16, 22, 27-28, 29, 33, 34, 35, 66, 109, 112
'meadow style' approach, 14, 115-118
mealybug, 147
melic, 92, 234-237
Melica, 76, 91, 92, 96, 153, 234-237
Melica altissima, 234
    'Alba', 234
    'Atropurpurea', 234
Melica californica, 234
Melica ciliata, 234
Melica imperfecta, 234, 235
Melica uniflora
    f. *albida*, 72, 73, 92, 236, 237
    'Variegata', 237

Melinis, 153, 237
Melinis nerviglumis, 237
Melinis repens, 237
Mendocino reed grass, 176
merging, 13–14, 34, 35, 65
Mexican feather grass, 266
Milium, 92, 96, 151, 153, 238
Milium effusum, 238
    'Aureum', 238
    'Yaffle', 238
Millennium Park, Chicago, 28
millet, 92, 268–273
miniature cattail, 305
Miscanthicoccus miscanthi, 147
Miscanthus, 21, 26, 40, 54, 63, 91, 96, 101, 104, 106, 120, 136, 146, 147, 150, 151, 153, 238–255, 287
    'Flamingo', 44
    'Purpurascens', 241
    'Zebrinus', 98, 99, 238
Miscanthus condensatus, 255
Miscanthus floridulus, 239
Miscanthus ´giganteus, 53, 239–241
Miscanthus nepalensis, 81, 240, 241
Miscanthus oligostachyus, 241
    'Nanus Variegatus', 240, 241
Miscanthus sacchariflorus, 150, 239, 241
Miscanthus sinensis, 239, 241–255
    'Abundance', 242, 243, 253
    'Andante', 242, 243
    'Bandwidth', 242, 243
    'China', 243
    'Cindy', 58, 64, 242, 243
    var. *condensatus*, 255
    'Dixieland', 242, 243
    'Dronning Ingrid', 243
    'Elfin', 242, 243, 253
    'Emmanuel Lepage', 243, 244
    'Ferner Osten', 40–42, 64, 244, 245
    'Fire Dragon', 244, 245
    'Flamingo', 42, 58, 64, 244, 245
    'Gold Bar', 245
    'Goliath', 245
    'Gracillimus', 52, 245
    'Graziella', 246, 247
    'Hermann Müssel', 246, 247
    'Kaskade', 247
    'Kleine Fontäne', 246, 247
    'Kleine Silberspinne', 247
    'Little Miss', 247
    'Malepartus', 63, 64, 247
    'Memory', 248, 249
    'Morning Light', 248, 249
    'My Fair Maiden', 249
    'Nishidake', 249
    'Pink Cloud', 249
    'Professor Richard Hansen', 249
    var. *purpurascens*, 241
    'Red Cloud', 250
    'Red Spear', 250
    'Red Zenith', 250
    'Roland', 250
    'Rosi', 250
    'Rotsilber', 250
    'Scout', 250
    'Silberfeder', 250
    'Silver Charm', 250, 251
    'Silver Cloud', 250, 251
    'Starlight', 91, 250, 251, 253
    'Strictus', 252
    'Sunlit Satin', 252
    'Undine', 252
    'Variegatus', 252
    Yakushima Dwarf, 91, 243, 250, 253
    'Zebrinus', 253
    'Zwergelefant', 254, 255
Miscanthus transmorrisonensis, 255
    'Sunset', 254, 255
moles, 147
Molinia, 31, 40, 50, 54, 63, 91, 96, 101, 133, 136, 153, 256–261
    'Edith Dudszus', 18
    'Transparent', 50
Molinia altissima, 256
Molinia arundinacea, 256
Molinia caerulea, 28, 29, 31, 44, 69, 98, 100, 107, 153
    subsp. *arundinacea*, 50, 54, 58, 64, 153, 256–259
    subsp. *arundinacea* 'Bergfreund', 256, 257
    subsp. *arundinacea* 'Breeze', 256
    subsp. *arundinacea* 'Cordoba', 256, 257
    subsp. *arundinacea* 'Karl Foerster', 256, 257
    subsp. *arundinacea* 'Skyracer', 256, 257
    subsp. *arundinacea* 'Transparent', 256, 257
    subsp. *arundinacea* 'Windsaule', 258, 259
    subsp. *arundinacea* 'Windspiel', 259
    subsp. *arundinacea* 'Zuneigung', 258, 259
    subsp. *caerulea*, 258–261
    subsp. *caerulea* 'Dark Defender', 259

subsp. *caerulea* 'Dauerstrahl', 63, 64, 70, 148, 259
subsp. *caerulea* 'Edith Dudszus', 70, 259
subsp. *caerulea* 'Heidebraut', 260
subsp. *caerulea* 'Heidezwerg', 260
subsp. *caerulea* 'Moorflamme', 260, 261
subsp. *caerulea* 'Moorhexe', 260
subsp. *caerulea* 'Overdam', 68, 70, 260, 261
subsp. *caerulea* 'Poul Petersen', 31, 260, 261
subsp. *caerulea* 'Strahlenquelle', 260, 261
subsp. *caerulea* 'Torch', 260
subsp. *caerulea* 'Variegata', 260, 261
Molinia litoralis, 256
Monarda, 31
mondo grass, 86–87, 89, 266–267
monocultures, 12
moor grass, 98, 256–259, 290–294
mop head sedge, 183
mosquito grass, 169
movement, 49
Mt. Tabor School, Portland, 129
Muhlenbergia, 50, 54, 65, 78, 85, 106, 130, 262–265
Muhlenbergia capillaris, 54, 78, 262
Muhlenbergia dubia, 44, 52, 74, 78, 262–263
Muhlenbergia dumosa, 104, 105, 263

Muhlenbergia lindheimeri, 263
'Autumn Glow', 263
Muhlenbergia pubescens, 264
Muhlenbergia reverchonii, 264
'Undaunted', 264
Muhlenbergia rigens, 78
Muhlenbergia rigens, 44, 50, 70, 81, 82, 265
Muhlenbergia rigida, 78, 265
'Nashville', 265
muhly grass, 262–265
mulch, 56

N

Narcissus 'Blushing Lady', 70
narrow-leaved cattail, 304
Nassella, 54, 76, 84, 85, 127, 153, 234, 265–266
Nassella cernua, 84, 265
Nassella lepida, 84, 265
Nassella pulchra, 84, 265
Nassella tenuissima, 49, 83, 151, 265, 300
Nassella trichotoma, 266
native plants, 84, 89, 107–111, 123–124
natural grassland, 27–28, 29–31, 34, 147
Natural History Museum of Los Angeles County, 83, 87
'naturalistic' approach, 11, 27–28, 31–34, 60–73
needle grass, 225, 265, 300–302
Nepeta, 65, 68, 71
Nepeta grandiflora 'Dawn to Dusk', 70
Nepeta racemosa 'Walker's Low', 68, 70

New Zealand blue sedge, 200
New Zealand tussock sedge, 197
nodding needle grass, 265
nutbrown sedge, 179

O

oat grass, 223
Ophiopogon, 86, 96, 127, 140, 153, 266–267
Ophiopogon japonicus, 266–267
'Minor', 153, 267
Ophiopogon planiscapus, 86–87, 89, 267
'Black Beard', 267
'Kokuryu' ('Nigrescens'), 86–87, 267
orange sedge, 199
organic material, 57
oriental fountain grass, 282
Ornithogalum nutans, 73
Ornithogalum umbellatum, 73
Oshima kan suge, 189
Oudolf, Piet, 31, 34, 60

P

Pacific reed grass, 176
paddlers, 97, 98–99, 101
palm sedge, 89, 187
pampas grass, 28, 58, 111, 202–204, 288
panic grass, 268–273
Panicum, 21, 26, 40, 54, 85, 104, 120, 133, 136, 147, 151, 154, 268–273
Panicum amarum, 268, 269
'Dewey Blue', 268, 269
'Sea Mist', 268, 269
Panicum bulbosum, 268, 269

Index 323

Panicum virgatum, 11, 24–26, 38, 49, 100, 268
   'Blue Tower', 268, 269
   'Buffalo Green', 268
   'Cape Breeze', 270
   'Cheyenne Sky', 270
   'Cloud Nine', 270
   'Dallas Blues', 270, 271
   'Hänse Herms', 270–271
   'Heavy Metal', 64, 271
   'Heiliger Hain', 271
   'Kupferhirse', 271
   'Merlot', 271
   'Northwind', 44, 272
   'Oxblood Autumn', 272
   'Prairie Dog', 272
   'Prairie Fire', 272
   'Prairie Sky', 272–273
   'Purple Breeze', 273
   'Red Cloud', 272, 273
   'Shenandoah', 28, 273
   'Straight Cloud', 64, 273
   'Thundercloud', 273
   'Warrior', 273
Papaver orientale 'Beauty of Livermere', 64
paperbark mulberry, 94
pathways, 13, 21, 22, 31, 34, 35, 37, 42, 52, 57, 119, 133
Patrinia, 31
pearl grass, 170
pendulous sedge, 193
Pennisetum, 21, 23, 26, 40, 54, 79–80, 85, 86, 106, 136, 154, 274–283
   'Dark Desire', 39
   'Fairy Tails', 23, 39, 52, 64, 78, 280
   'Red Buttons', 18, 21

Pennisetum ´advena, 274
   'Cherry Sparkler', 274
   'Cupreum', 274
   'Eaton Canyon', 274
   'Fireworks', 274
   'Purpureum', 274
   'Rubrum', 79, 80, 105, 274
Pennisetum alopecuroides, 80, 275–279, 282
   'Black Beauty', 275
   'Burgundy Bunny', 275
   'Cassian', 277
   'Caudatum', 276, 277
   'Cayenne', 277
   'Dark Desire', 80, 276, 277
   'Etouffee', 276, 277
   'Ginger Love', 276, 277
   'Hameln', 64, 80, 276, 277
   'Herbstzauber', 276, 277
   'Hush Puppy', 276, 277
   'Jambalaya', 277
   'Little Bunny', 275, 277
   'Love and Rockets', 278
   'Moudry', 278
   'Piglet', 278, 279
   'Praline', 278
   'Pure Energy', 278, 279
   'Red Head', 80, 278, 279
   var. *viridescens*, 278
   'Viridescens', 278, 279
   'Weserbergland', 278
   'Yellow Ribbons', 278
Pennisetum compressum, 275
Pennisetum japonicum, 275
Pennisetum macrostachyum, 280
   'Burgundy Giant', 280
Pennisetum macrourum, 40, 281
   'Short Stuff', 281

Pennisetum massaicum, 281–282
   'Red Buttons', 281, 282
Pennisetum orientale, 79–80, 282
   'Karley Rose', 282
   'Shogun', 282
   'Tall Tails', 282
Pennisetum ruppelii, 282
Pennisetum setaceum, 79, 110, 111, 274, 282–283
Pennisetum spathiolatum, 283
Pennisetum villosum, 79, 283
Pennsylvania sedge, 194
perennials, 21, 26, 31, 34, 35, 42, 59, 64, 65, 66, 70–71, 73, 100, 116, 120, 136, 138, 150–151
Persicaria, 21, 35
Persicaria amplexicaulis 'Rosea', 63, 64
Peruvian feather grass, 302
pests, 146–147
Phalaris, 101, 120, 154, 284
Phalaris arundinacea, 284
   'Arctic Sun', 284
   'Picta', 284
pheasant grass, 94
pheasant tail, 163
Phlomis russeliana, 63, 64
Phragmites, 100, 101, 120, 154, 285
Phragmites australis, 96, 108, 110, 120, 285
   'Variegatus', 100, 285
pine muhly, 262–263
pink crystals, 237
pink muhly, 78, 262
plant adaptation, 100
plant choice
   environmentally sensitive, 111
   garden design, 23

native plants, 84, 107–111
pots and containers, 102–106
shade conditions, 85–96, 151
sun-baked and dry conditions, 76–85
wet conditions, 102–106, 151
plant division, 145–146
plant height, 50, 66, 151
planting, 144–146
planting densities, 82, 145, 151, 152
planting distances, 152
plant names, 151–152
plant tolerance, 100
Pleuraphis, 286
Pleuraphis rigida, 286
plumed tussock grass, 200
Poa, 54, 68, 71, 76, 80, 81, 85, 127, 154, 234, 286–287
Poa glauca, 228
Poa labillardierei, 40, 65, 66, 68, 69, 70, 77, 286, 287
poppies, 18, 21, 27
pots, 102–106
prairie cord grass, 297
prairie dropseed, 298–299
prairies, 27–28, 29, 35
prairie switch grass, 24–26, 100
preparation, 145
Primula, 72
Primula vulgaris, 73
propagation, 145–146
purple fountain grass, 274
purple lovegrass, 211
purple moor grass, 28, 29, 256–259
purple muhly, 265
purple needle grass, 265
purple three awn, 163
purpletop, 304
pyramidal hair grass, 228

Q
quaking grass, 49, 170

R
rabbits, 147
rain gardens, 97, 128–134
rattle grass, 170
ravenna grass, 288
reclaimed materials, 83
red fescue, 217
red tussock grass, 201
reed, 97, 108, 165, 285
reed canary grass, 284
reed grass, 172–176
reedmace, 304
remote sedge, 196
repetition, 54
restoration, 29, 114, 123–124, 143
rhododendrons, 11
RHS Garden Hyde Hall, Essex, 84
RHS Garden Wisley, 44, 45, 47, 52
Rhynchelytrum, 237
Rhynchospora, 101, 154, 287
Rhynchospora latifolia, 287
rhythm, 17–23
'right plant, right place' approach, 10–11, 108, 111
rodents, 147
rope grass, 159
Royal Botanic Gardens, Kew, 29, 31, 40
ruby grass, 237
Rudbeckia, 31, 35, 63
Rudbeckia laciniata, 64
Rudbeckia maxima, 70
runners, 150
rush, 97, 123, 124, 225–227
rust, 146

S
Saccharum, 154, 287–288
Saccharum arundinaceum, 288
Saccharum officinarum, 287, 288
  'Pele's Smoke', 288
Saccharum ravennae, 288
saltgrass, 123, 208
San Diego sedge, 198
sand lovegrass, 213
sand sedge, 179
Sanguisorba, 31, 71
  'Janet's Jewel', 64
  'Ruby Red', 70
Sanguisorba tenuifolia
  'Purpurea', 64
Santa Barbara Botanic Garden, 116
sap suckers, 147
satin tail, 224
Scampston Hall, Yorkshire, 31
Schizachyrium, 119, 154, 289–290
Schizachyrium scoparium, 289–290
  'Blue Heaven', 289
  'The Blues', 290
  'Jazz', 289
  'Prairie Blues', 289
  'Smoke Signal', 289
  'Standing Ovation', 290
Schizostylis coccinea 'Major', 70
Schoenoplectus, 97, 100, 101, 133
Schoenoplectus lacustris
  subsp. *tabernaemontani*
  'Albescens', 100
Schoenoplectus tabenaemontani, 101
screening, 22, 31, 34, 50, 53
seasonality, 17–23, 38, 40–42, 62
sedge, 12, 44–45, 89, 98, 99, 104, 115, 117, 121, 123, 124, 127, 178–200

Sedum, 35, 46
seeders, 150–151
seep muhly, 264
serrated tussock grass, 266
Sesleria, 76, 77, 85, 86, 87, 91, 96, 119, 127, 154, 290–294
    'Greenlee Hybrid', 91, 292, 293
    'Spring Dream', 77, 293
    'Summer Skies', 294
Sesleria albicans, 291
Sesleria argentea, 291
Sesleria autumnalis, 46, 87, 291
    'Campo Verde', 91, 291
Sesleria caerulea, 70, 77, 91, 291
    'Campo Azul', 77, 291
Sesleria heufleriana, 292, 293
Sesleria nitida, 69, 70, 77, 292, 293
shade
    damp shade, 90, 95, 96
    dry shade, 92–94, 96
    growing conditions, 85–96, 151
    light conditions, 39–40, 85–94
    open shade, 90–91, 96
shape, 42–45
sheep's fescue, 217
Siberian greybeard grass, 297
Siberian melic, 234
side oats grama, 169
silver banner grass, 241
silver beardgrass, 166
silver grass, 241–255
silver maple, 89
'Silver Sceptre' sedge, 197
silver spear grass, 155
sitting areas, 34, 35
slender veldt grass, 283
slender wild oat, 200
slough sedge, 189

snowy woodrush, 94, 232
soft muhly, 264
soft rush, 225–226
Sorghastrum, 119, 154, 294–295
Sorghastrum avenaceum, 295
Sorghastrum nutans, 295
    'Golden Sunset', 295
    'Indian Steel', 295
    'Sioux Blue', 295
sound, 49
spangle grass, 85–86, 200
Spanish oat grass, 82, 300–302
Spartina, 101, 154
Spartina pectinata, 296, 297
    'Aureomarginata', 100, 296, 297
    'Variegata', 297
spiny rush, 225
split bluestem, 162
Spodiopogon, 154, 297
Spodiopogon sibiricus, 297
Sporobolus, 85, 119, 127, 154, 298–299
Sporobolus airoides, 45, 78, 84, 298
Sporobolus heterolepis, 70, 298–299
    'Tara', 299
    'Wisconsin', 299
Sporobolus wrightii, 299
Springs Preserve, Las Vegas, 45, 47
squirrel tail, 209
star sedge, 287
steppes, 27–28
Stipa, 50, 80, 84, 85, 86, 106, 151, 154, 225, 300–302
Stipa arundinacea, 94, 163, 300
Stipa barbata, 300
Stipa calamagrostis, 155, 300
Stipa cernua, 265
Stipa gigantea, 50, 51, 82, 83, 151, 154, 300–302
    'Gold Fontaene', 301

    'Goldilocks', 302, 303
    'Pixie', 302
Stipa ichu, 81, 106, 154, 302, 303
Stipa lepida, 265
Stipa pennata, 302
Stipa pulcherrima, 302
Stipa pulchra, 265
Stipa tenuissima, 49, 266, 300
Stipa trichotoma, 266
straw, 57
stress, 76
subdivisions, 34
successional planting, 42
Succisia, 31
sugar cane, 287–288
sun-baked conditions, 76–77
sunlight, 39–40, 151
surface mulch, 56
susuki, 241–255
susuki zoku, 238
sweet flag, 155–156
swimmers, 97, 100, 101
switch grass, 100, 268–273
sword leaf rush, 226

T

Taiwanese reed grass, 166
Tallamy, Doug, 56, 108
tall purple moor grass, 256–259
tawny cotton grass, 213
tender fountain grass, 282–283
Texas grass, 268
Texas sedge, 200
texture, 42–45
three awn, 163
toetoe, 202, 204
Tongva Park, Santa Monica, 47
totter grass, 170
transparency, 50, 51, 53

tridens, 302–304
Tridens, 154, 302–304
Tridens flavus, 304
Triticum solandri, 210
Tritonia, 71
Tritonia disticha subsp. *rubrolucens*, 70
tufted fescue, 214
tufted hair grass, 16, 205–206
turfgrass, 12, 82, 205
turkey foot, 160
tussock grass, 200–201
tussock sedge, 182, 199
Typha, 100, 133, 154, 304–305
Typha latifolia, 304–305
　'Variegata', 304–305
Typha minima, 305

U

Uncinia, 154, 305
Uncinia rubra, 305
　'Everflame', 305
University Botanic Garden, Cambridge, 45

V

velvet grass, 223
Verbena bonariensis, 41, 64
Veronicastrum virginicum, 63, 64
Viburnum, 31
vine rope, 159
Virginia cotton grass, 213
voles, 147

W

warm-season grasses, 151
Watsonia sp., 70
weeds, 107
western meadow sedge, 117, 195
wet conditions, 95, 96–101, 130, 151
wheatgrass, 208–210
white sedge, 178
whitetinge sedge, 179
white-top sedge, 287
wild oat, 85–86, 200
wild rye, 76, 208–210, 229–231
wind grass, 163
wood anemone, 73
woodland sedge, 184

woodland species, 89
wood melic, 234
wood millet, 238
woodrush, 95, 232–234
woody plants, 11, 31, 34, 35, 38, 42, 65, 91, 92, 119
woolly sedge, 193
'wow factor', 17, 31, 35, 40

X

year-round garden, 24–26
yellow bluestem, 168
yellow prairie grass, 295
yellow sedge, 183

Y

Yorkshire fog, 223

Z

Zion National Park, 8

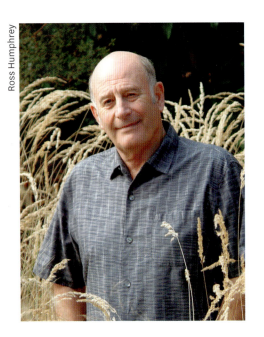

Neil Lucas is a leading ornamental grass specialist and director of Knoll Gardens. Located in Dorset, England, the gardens are renowned for their naturalistic approach. Along with the nursery, he has established a charity, the Knoll Gardens Foundation, which is devoted to a greater understanding of biodiversity and related sustainable garden practices. He is a former member of the RHS Council and the recipient of ten consecutive gold medals for the nurseries' displays at the Chelsea Flower Show.